PENGUIN BOOKS

Generations

Melanie Hart lives and works in London.

James Loader was for many years Head of English at St Olave's Grammar School in Orpington. He is the Editor of *Cold Comfort: Stories of Death and Bereavement* (1996).

Generations

Poems between Fathers, Mothers, Daughters, Sons

Edited by Melanie Hart
and James Loader

PENGUIN BOOKS

To dearest Jessie, Zoë and Matilda
and to our parents

Thanks

We are deeply grateful to the many friends and colleagues who have
encouraged and helped us. In particular our thanks go to Prophecy
Coles, Sharon Cutler, Margaret Gardiner, Mark Glanville, Martha Kapos,
Jonathan Keates, Dennis Kennedy, Tony Lacey, Janet Montefiore,
Michael Parsons, Jennifer Helsham Whistler, Dennis Wiseman and the
staff of the Arts Council Poetry Library.

A special debt of gratitude to Ronald Baker.

PENGUIN BOOKS

Published by the Penguin Group
Penguin Books Ltd, 27 Wrights Lane, London W8 5TZ, England
Penguin Putnam Inc., 375 Hudson Street, New York, New York 10014, USA
Penguin Books Australia Ltd, Ringwood, Victoria, Australia
Penguin Books Canada Ltd, 10 Alcorn Avenue, Toronto, Ontario, Canada M4V 3B2
Penguin Books (NZ) Ltd, 182–190 Wairau Road, Auckland 10, New Zealand

Penguin Books Ltd, Registered Offices: Harmondsworth, Middlesex, England

This collection first published 1998
10 9 8 7 6 5 4 3 2 1

Editorial matter copyright © Melanie Hart and James Loader, 1998
All rights reserved

The Acknowledgements on pages 340–50 constitute an extension of this copyright page

The moral right of the authors has been asserted

Typeset in Monotype Walbaum
Typeset by Rowland Phototypesetting Ltd, Bury St Edmunds, Suffolk
Printed in England by Clays Ltd, St Ives plc

Contents

FATHER TO SON

FATHER TO CHILD

MOTHER TO CHILD

DAUGHTER TO FATHER

DAUGHTER TO MOTHER

DAUGHTER TO PARENTS

SON TO FATHER

SON TO MOTHER

Introduction

The way we understand ourselves has changed enormously in the last hundred years. Human personality is no longer regarded as given, as something in the newborn infant that is entirely predetermined and simply unfolds with maturity. Instead we know it to be the complex and evolving outcome of each individual's interaction with the world. In particular, it is now generally accepted that the formation of personality depends crucially upon the emotional vicissitudes of childhood. This twentieth-century vision of what makes us the people we are has developed alongside a growing, popular inclination to speak more freely than in the past about the actual emotional experiences of both parenthood and childhood. It was this background that provoked the questions lying at the heart of our anthology. If poetry offers the most concentrated delivery of feeling that words can bear, what difference have these changes made to poetry which addresses the relationships that make us human? Can poetry which has this particular focus offer us ways to understand more fully the effect of these enduring, primary attachments?

The first question is more easily approached. Even a cursory glance at the contents list of this book will reveal the preponderance of twentieth-century poetry. This reflects the huge increase in the volume of work which speaks directly of parent or child, the only decrease happily being in the number of sad and simple verses to prematurely dead children. The new openness has released extraordinarily vigorous creative energy, particularly in North America and especially on the part of the child. It is almost like witnessing the birth of a new poetic genre. Some older poetry remains unsurpassed in the expression of feelings which have always been acceptable – love, joy, grief (Mehetabel Wright's angry poem 'To Her Father' is exceptional). But in much recent writing there is greater emotional complexity, strangeness, darkness, which come as something of a relief from the conventions of the past. Real, lived experience is more honestly and intensely conveyed. Ambivalence has become manageable, even expected. On both sides of the parent/child border the range of feeling is wider and there is an enhanced preparedness to take risks, the writer moving into more intimate contact, including physically intimate contact, with the object of poetic focus than has ever been attempted before.

The rapid growth of interest in this subject has meant that, while older poetry more or less selected itself, we have had to make many difficult decisions about which contemporary poems to include. In order to maximize the range of voices within the scope of the book we have restricted ourselves to one poem per poet within any one section. In the case of poets who have devoted a great deal of attention to this area, such as Michael Hofmann, Sharon Olds and George Szirtes, this was very frustrating. Had we space enough, we should also have liked to include work by poets writing *in loco parentis*. Gabriela Mistral's 'Sleep Close to Me', T. S. Eliot's 'Marina', and Charles Lamb's 'Parental Recollections' are major examples of loss on this account.

We have arranged the book in the simplest possible way, with no framework beyond the status of poet and addressee as son, daughter, mother or father. There are various and subtle thematic connections amongst the poems, to do with the quality of primary relationships and the conscious and unconscious meanings invested in them, which we felt any further ordering would obscure rather than clarify. Nor did we want to pre-empt the reader's own discovery of the sorts of experiences, preoccupations and imagery the poems in any one section may be found to share.

Simple as it is, this arrangement proved not to be entirely straightforward. A child has two parents and there is a wide and interesting range of allusion made to the partner both in the poems by a parent and in those addressed by the child only to one. We have, for example, included Maya Angelou's poem 'Amoebaean for Daddy' and Andrew Motion's 'A Dying Race' as poems to the father, although in each case the implied quality of the relationship between *both* parents is a profoundly important component of the work. In striking contrast is the complete isolation from each other of the two overwhelmingly painful parental figures evoked by Sylvia Plath in 'The Colossus' and 'Medusa'. The difficulty she has in proposing the existence of any link between them, let alone a creative one, is poignantly reinvoked in her poem 'For a Fatherless Son', in which she attacks the image of a good father in her child's mind, reducing the relationship to mother and son only.

The arrangement we have chosen also seemed to us to be the most playful. It gives each poem the chance to come as a surprise and allows very different poetic sensibilities to rub shoulders. Periods and cultures are free to jostle each other and it throws up all sorts of odd and fascinating pairings, as well as moving sequences (Hugo, Jonson and Kipling on their daughters, for example, or the poems which open the section Mother to Child with variations upon the themes of pregnancy and birth). We hope this serendipity will illuminate the enormously varied range of behaviour, feeling and voice of which people are capable. Human uniqueness seems to disclose itself most vividly in speaking about these common experiences.

To return to the second of the questions that interested us. Contemporary understanding of human psychological development maintains that there is a direct link between a child's emotional environment and the later adult's capacity to engage lovingly with life. If this is true, evidence for it should surely show up in this sort of poetry. Does it? A simple way to begin to explore this is to look more closely at individual works.

The poems in the astonishingly rich sequence Son to Father vary considerably in the extent of their emotional range and their freedom of access to deep levels of feeling. Kingsley Amis has only limited freedom along both axes, and this is what he writes about. 'In Memoriam', although an affectionate poem, brilliantly conveys the strangled quality of his feelings and concomitantly awkward dealings with his father. The poet reveals his conscious wish to have had a warmer, more expressive relationship, regrets not having taken the lead in this himself as an adult. But at a less conscious level, the inhibited form of the poem, its restricted imagery, the boyish longing for his father's presence as admiring spectator of his son's play, confirm the degree to which the writer actually remained bound to emotional limitations as a result of his father's inhibited capacity for contact.

Compare Robert Pack's 'The Boat'. This is a very different sort of poem. Like many others in the collection (those by Liz Almond, Selima Hill and Wallace Stevens, for example), it imaginatively evokes the internal emotional texture of a relationship without being specifically attached to autobiographical incident. It is an elusive, lyrical poem and one more densely filled with meaning than 'In Memoriam'. While Amis's father is placed on the periphery, Pack touches his in the very first line and they stay in contact throughout. Opening with a playful image of infantile omnipotence (infant patronizing Dad), the poet moves through an encounter with his own real powerlessness, terror at loss and helplessness, to find gratitude for a father's love and protection. The poet attributes to this paternal care his recognition of the separate realities of father and son, and his dawning strength to confront what is truly omnipotent – death. Pack, in other words, knows what it means to be able to find the presence of a father lovingly with him in the tightest of emotional corners. As a consequence he is free to be himself and to enjoy life on his own terms. This is revealed in the richness and physicality of the imagery, the pleasure he gives and takes in his imaginative liveliness, the way control is deeply present and not obtrusive or diminishing. While Amis plays by rules, Pack is confident enough to do so on his own authority. His tribute to the sort of father who can make this development possible is a profoundly touching, beautiful piece of work.

Poetry can be forged from hatred. John Berryman's 'Dream Song 384' is a good example. But the rage and hatred the poet, in the persona of Henry, expresses here for his father is only the surface of the work. The poem's power is fuelled by what gave rise to those feelings, the poet's despair that he cannot free himself from his father's dreadfully disturbing personality and the driving need to make contact with him, even if contact means death. Berryman's deep theme is the permanent injury felt by a child whose father attacks the potential bond between them. The experience leaves him in a world shockingly different from that of either Pack or Amis – a harsh world in which catastrophic incompleteness, anguish at being left out of touch with love, are so intensely felt as to become the poetic subject itself.

But what happens next? Two of these men wrote poems when they became fathers of sons in their turn. In 'A Sympathy, A Welcome' Berryman welcomes his son Paul as Satan might a fallen angel. Exit from the womb means permanent rupture from grace, entry to desolation, to 'this world like a knife'. Paul may 'get to know' his mother (an enigmatic line) and have a laugh or two, but pain and loneliness will be the order of the day. As far as Berryman is concerned, that's just how things are. The emotional world he has constructed from his personal experience, a world without joy, is handed on to Paul to grow up in as if there were no alternative.

Robert Pack also wrote about the birth of his son. 'Welcoming Poem' celebrates the event with such exuberance that all darkness is pushed to the very last line, where it temporarily skulks, eclipsed by joy at new life. We chose to include here instead, however, a poem he wrote when his son was leaving home. In 'Departing Words to a Son', Pack exploits the complex kaleidoscopic possibilities of the pantoum form (see Marilyn Hacker's 'Iva's Pantoum' for another example of its use). Memories of the life they have shared since his son's birth are recalled as fragments in a shifting pattern. In all art, but especially in work such as collected here where life and death are foregrounded, the exigencies of time and the demands we place upon it have a crucial rôle. This poem is Janus-faced. The gift that Pack creates for his son to carry with him into the future expresses his desire to be a part of that future himself, both as poet and as father. The poem could be created, however, only at a time when Pack has accepted the beginnings of his own recession into the past from which his child has emerged. In particular, this loving poem conveys the hope that his son, in his independent life, will possess as profound a sense of security in a father's care as the father of 'The Boat' gave him.

These poems, extreme contrasts, dramatically reveal both the powerful impact that parental personality has on the child and the way in which this reverberates across generations. Any reader who is interested will be able to make other fascinating cross-references and comparisons. This is not the complete picture, however. There are, as well, all the cruelties from which no parent can protect a child – illness, loss, hardship, human barbarity. These are just as much a cause of disturbance and their impact falls most heavily upon the vulnerable, developing psyches of children, as Edith Brück, Karen Gershon and Louis MacNeice, amongst others, testify. Parental anxiety about children as hostages to fortune is constantly surfacing in this collection, and the anguish of parents for whom the natural order is upset, and who survive their children, gives rise to some of the most uncomplicated, heartbreaking poetry ever written, such as Paula Meehan's 'Child Burial', Jon Silkin's 'Death of a Son' and Lewis Glyn Cothi's great fifteenth-century 'Lament for Siôn Y Glyn'.

Above all, the theme of passing on, in the senses of dying and of bequeathing and inheriting, is deeply present here. We now know that what passes on from parent to child in their emotional interaction with one another is fundamental to the identities of each. As poets in this collection confront personal identity and purpose, this particularly twentieth-century enrichment of the metaphor is evoked time and again. It adds to the multifarious ways there are of encountering poems such as these. We can read them as insights into the construction of the unique systems of meaning and value which all human beings unconsciously create from their childhood experience of those closest to them, and imaginatively inhabit in their own lives as adults.

Melanie Hart
James Loader

NOTE: An asterisk after a poet's name indicates a reference to be found in the Biographical Notes on page 335.

Father
to
Daughter

First Lesson

Lie back, daughter, let your head
be tipped back in the cup of my hand.
Gently, and I will hold you. Spread
your arms wide, lie out on the stream
and look high at the gulls. A dead-
man's float is face down. You will dive
and swim soon enough where this tidewater
ebbs to the sea. Daughter, believe
me, when you tire on the long thrash
to your island, lie up, and survive.
As you float now, where I held you
and let go, remember when fear
cramps your heart what I told you:
lie gently and wide to the light-year
stars, lie back, and the sea will hold you.

PHILIP BOOTH *b.* 1925 USA

The Poet's Welcome to his Love-begotten Daughter

Thou's welcome, wean! mishanter[1] fa' me,
If ought of thee, or of thy mammy,
Shall ever daunton me, or awe me,
    My sweet wee lady,
Or if I blush when thou shalt ca' me
    Tit-ta or daddy.

1 *mishanter*: misfortune

Wee image of my bonnie Betty,
I fatherly will kiss and daut[2] thee,
As dear an' near my heart I set thee
    Wi' as guid will,
As a' the priests had seen me get thee
    That's out o' hell.

What tho' they ca' me fornicator,
An' tease my name in kintra[3] clatter:[4]
The mair they talk I'm kent the better,
    E'en let them clash;[5]
An auld wife's tongue's a feckless[6] matter
    To gie ane fash.[7]

Welcome, my bonnie, sweet wee dochter —
Tho' ye come here a wee unsought for,
An' tho' your comin I hae fought for
    Baith kirk an' queir;
Yet, by my faith, ye're no unwrought for!
    That I shall swear!

Sweet fruit o' mony a merry dint,
My funny toil is now a' tint,[8]
Sin' thou came to the warl asklent,[9]
    Which fools may scoff at;
In my last plack[10] thy part's be in't —
    The better half o't.

An' if thou be what I wad hae thee,
An' tak the counsel I shall gie thee,
A lovin' father I'll be to thee,
    If thou be spar'd;
Thro' a' thy childish years I'll ee thee,
    An' think't weel war'd.[11]

2 *daut*: fondle, dote on   3 *kintra*: country   4 *clatter*: idle talk
5 *clash*: gossip   6 *feckless*: ineffectual   7 *fash*: trouble   8 *tint*: lost
9 *asklent*: indirectly   10 *plack*: an old Scotch coin, the third part of
a Scotch penny   11 *war'd*: spent, bestowed

Tho' I should be the waur[12] bested,
Thou's be as braw[13] an' bienly[14] clad,
An' thy young years as nicely bred
  Wi' education,
As ony brat o' wedlock's bed
  In a' thy station.

Gude grant that thou may aye inherit
Thy mother's person, grace, an' merit,
An' thy poor worthless daddy's spirit,
  Without his failins;
Twill please me mair to see and hear o't,
  Than stockit[15] mailins.[16]

ROBERT BURNS 1759–1796 Scotland

12 *waur*: worst 13 *braw*: handsome, gaily dressed 14 *bienly*: richly
15 *stockit*: stocked 16 *mailins*: farms

The Distress'd Father
or, the
Author's Tears
over his
Dear Daughter Rachel

Oh! lead me where my Darling lies,
 Cold as the Marble Stone;
I will recall her with my Cries,
 And wake her with my Moan.

Come from thy Bed of Clay, my dear!
 See! where thy Father stands;
His Soul he sheds out Tear by Tear,
 And wrings his wretched Hands.

But ah! alas! thou canst not rise,
   Alas! thou canst not hear,
Or, at thy tender Father's Cries,
   Thou surely wouldst appear.

   Since then my Love! my Soul's delight!
      Thou canst not come to me,
   Rather than want thy pleasing sight,
      I'll dig my way to thee.

HENRY CAREY *c.* 1687–1743 England

At the Smithville Methodist Church

It was supposed to be Arts & Crafts for a week,
but when she came home
with the 'Jesus Saves' button, we knew what art
was up, what ancient craft.

She liked her little friends. She liked the songs
they sang when they weren't
twisting and folding paper into dolls.
What could be so bad?

Jesus had been a good man, and putting faith
in good men was what
we had to do to stay this side of cynicism,
that other sadness.

O.K., we said. One week. But when she came home
singing 'Jesus loves me,
the Bible tells me so,' it was time to talk.
Could we say Jesus

doesn't love you? Could I tell her the Bible
is a great book certain people use
to make you feel bad? We sent her back
without a word.

It had been so long since we believed, so long
since we needed Jesus
as our nemesis and friend, that we thought he was
sufficiently dead,

that our children would think of him like Lincoln
or Thomas Jefferson.
Soon it became clear to us: you can't teach
disbelief to a child,

only wonderful stories, and we hadn't a story
nearly as good.
On parents' night there were the Arts & Crafts
all spread out

like appetizers. Then we took our seats
in the church
and the children sang a song about the Ark,
and Halleleulah

and one in which they had to jump up and down
for Jesus.
I can't remember ever feeling so uncertain
about what's comic, what's serious.

Evolution is magical but devoid of heroes.
You can't say to your child
'Evolution loves you.' The story stinks
of extinction and nothing

exciting happens for centuries. I didn't have
a wonderful story for my child
and she was beaming. All the way home in the car
she sang the songs,

occasionally standing up for Jesus.
There was nothing to do
but drive, ride it out, sing along
in silence.

STEPHEN DUNN   *b.* 1946   USA

Margaret, Are You Grieving?

From the contours of the envelope
It is a greetings card
For my birthday and by the Canadian
Postage Stamp — the Common Loon —
I can tell it must be
From my daughter in Montreal,
Where she's got a job in the bar
Of the Marguerite Yourcenar Reading Club.

I am cheekbone-smug, beard-proud
That she should remember my birthday,
Much less send me a card.
It's one of those
Tall as a telephone booth
Birthday Cards
With three words
In black capitals:
JESUS LOVES YOU.

Sweet and thoughtful of her.
Inside it continues in italics:
Everyone Else Thinks You're An Asshole.

I remember her when she was two years old
Playing hide-and-seek with me
Behind telegraph poles in the snow,
Lodgepole pines
Adrift in the early morning snow.
How then at dawn she giggled as then at midnight she
    screeched
At the spider in the plug hole of the sink.

No one will ever know what it was like
To spend so much as one night alone
And fugitive, penniless and homeless,
In the snow in downtown Montreal.
No one will ever know what it was like
To have been my daughter
Or what it was like to have been my daughter's father.

Wrist warmers; headphones; earmuffs; study lamps;
Because tomorrow's headlines are today's inscriptions
Does not make them any the less the original
And indecipherable inscriptions that they are:
'Father Hopkins Accused Of Writing Poems To Little Girls';
He sleeps in her boat while she rows him home.
'Jesus Loves You – Everyone Else Thinks You're An Asshole';
He sleeps in her boat while she rows him home.

And she's singing a song because she's that kind of girl
Who in darkness on water sings to her father:
'Donnybrook Garage,' she sings, 'Donnybrook Garage.'
And he's singing a song because he's that kind of man
Who in darkness on water sings to his daughter:
'Anglesea Road,' he sings, 'Anglesea Road.'
He sleeps in her boat while she rows him home.

PAUL DURCAN   *b.* 1944   Ireland

Letter to My Daughter at the End of Her Second Year

Now it is only hours before you wake
to your third year and to the gifts that lie
piled on the coffee-table, yet I keep
the only gift that is mine to make.

But how can I offer, among the paper hats,
among the balloons and coloring books and dolls
gleaming with golden hair and the sweet primaries,
this shabby vision of myself seeking
among these gestures and images, myself?
My gift is wrought, not in the fire of love,
but in the consuming egotism of night
that blots out daughter, lover, wife and friend,
a time to take, my darling, not to give.

So smear this book with the sweetness of your fingers,
and mock with your eyes the brightness of this doll;
come learn our urgent language and put on
mask after mask to match our smiling faces,
seeking what gestures and images may serve
to charm the tall world down from which we smile.

Standing there in the shadow of your gifts,
may you forgive the love that lugged them home,
then turn and take the gift I could not give —
the language of childhood looking for itself
under a mountain of masks and dolls — the poem.

DONALD FINKEL   *b.* 1929   USA

A Hazel Stick for Catherine Ann

The living mother-of-pearl of a salmon
just out of the water

is gone just like that, but your stick
is kept salmon-silver.

Seasoned and bendy,
it convinces the hand

that what you have you hold
to play with and pose with

and lay about with.
But then too it points back to cattle

and spatter and beating
the bars of a gate —

the very stick we might cut
from your family tree.

The living cobalt of an afternoon
dragonfly drew my eye to it first

and the evening I trimmed it for you
you saw your first glow-worm −

all of us stood round in silence, even you
gigantic enough to darken the sky

for a glow-worm.
And when I poked open the grass

a tiny brightening den lit the eye
in the blunt cut end of your stick.

SEAMUS HEANEY   *b.* 1939   Ireland

Getting Drunk with Daughter

Caught without wife and mother, child,
We squat close, scratching gibberish in the sand,
Inspect your castle, peek into the pail
Where shells await your signal to attack
The stick gate, strike down squads of stones,
And storm the tower of the Feather Queen,
When, perchspine arrow in his head,
Lord Cork falls dead, his bride carted away.
And my pailful of ice is melting down
Around what will be two dead soldiers soon.

Odors remind me your cheeks reeked with kisses:
Whiskey, tobacco, dentures − sourdough −
When Father found you on the trail he misses.
Too bad the old man had to see you grow
Into my blonde wag with your woman's wishes,
Playing pretend wife, Daughter . . . even though
He threw himself to rags and knows his bliss is
Walking the sweaty mares he can't let go.

Precocious runt. Noting our shapely neighbor
Is amber from toenails to Brillo hair,
Has rolled, and drops her top and props her cleavage,

You grin above your army. Dear, her spine's
Not likely to compete with you or Bourbon
Since you're your mother's small ape from behind.
Oh, I know you know I know love likes beaches —
For blood outruns the heart, no doubt,
But mine runs to your lordship's mortal splinter.
I've one cork left. So let the spearmen start.

Tomorrow's going to come. We'll be together.
The sun will bake us, and we'll let our bones
Fly with the wastrel gulls, who love this weather,
Enlisting stronger sticks, more stalwart stones.
Your mother's got a feather where she itches.
Your daddy's got a fish bone in his brain.
The world lies down and waits in all its ditches.
But you and I aren't going to let it rain.

ROBERT HUFF   *b.* 1924   USA

Full Moon and Little Frieda

A cool small evening shrunk to a dog bark and the
      clank of a bucket —

And you listening.
A spider's web, tense for the dew's touch.
A pail lifted, still and brimming — mirror
To tempt a first star to a tremor.

Cows are going home in the lane there, looping the
     hedges with their warm wreaths of breath —
A dark river of blood, many boulders,
Balancing unspilled milk.

'Moon!' you cry suddenly, 'Moon! Moon!'
The moon has stepped back like an artist gazing
       amazed at a work
That points at him amazed.

TED HUGHES   *b.* 1930   England

'She formed the habit in her earliest years'

She formed the habit in her earliest years
of coming to my room each morning so
I'd wait for her as you might hope for light.
She'd enter, say hello, take up my pen,
open my books, sit on my bed, disturb
my papers, laugh – then leave abruptly as
a bird that passes. Easier then in mind
I'd take up what she'd interrupted till
among my manuscripts I'd come across
some funny arabesque she'd scribbled or
a few blank pages which she'd crumpled up –
and somehow, though I don't know why, on these
would always come my most successful lines.
She loved our God, loved flowers, stars, green fields –
pure spirit long before she was a woman!
Her eyes mirrored the brightness of her soul.
She'd tend to ask me what I thought of things –
so many radiant winter evenings spent
discussing history or points of language,
four children grouped around my knees, their mother
close by, some friends too chatting near the fire.
I called that life being content with little.

And now she's dead. God help me. How could I
be happy when I knew that she was sad?
I was despondent at the gayest ball
if earlier I'd seen shadows in her eyes.

November 1846, All Souls' Day

VICTOR HUGO* 1802–1885 France
Translated by Harry Guest

On My First Daughter

Here lies to each her parents ruth,
Mary, the daughter of their youth:
Yet, all heavens gifts, being heavens due,
It makes the father, lesse, to rue.
At six moneths end, shee parted hence
With safetie of her innocence;
Whose soule heavens Queene, (whose name shee beares)
In comfort of her mothers teares,
Hath plac'd amongst her virgin-traine:
Where, while that sever'd doth remaine,
This grave partakes the fleshly birth,
Which cover lightly, gentle earth.

BEN JONSON *c.* 1572–1637 England

'Of all the tribe of Tegumai'

Of all the tribe of Tegumai
  Who cut that figure, none remain, –
On Merrow Down the cuckoo cry –
  The silence and the sun remain.

But as the fearful years return
   And hearts unwounded sing again,
Comes Taffy dancing through the fern
   To lead the Surrey spring again.

Her brows are bound with bracken-fronds,
   And golden elf-locks fly above;
Her eyes are bright as diamonds
   And bluer than the skies above.

In moccasins and deer-skin cloak,
   Unfearing, free and fair she flits,
And lights her little damp wood smoke
   To show her Daddy where she flits.

For far — oh, very far behind,
   So far she cannot call to him,
Comes Tegumai alone to find
   The daughter that was all to him.

RUDYARD KIPLING*   1865–1936   England

Song for Naomi

Who is that in the tall grasses singing
By herself, near the water?
I can not see her
But can it be her
Than whom the grasses so tall
Are taller,
My daughter,
My lovely daughter?

Who is that in the tall grasses running
Beside her, near the water?
She can not see there
Time that pursued her

In the deep grasses so fast
And faster
And caught her,
My foolish daughter.

What is the wind in the fair grass saying
Like a verse, near the water?
Saviours that over
All things have power
Make Time himself grow kind
And kinder
That sought her,
My little daughter.

Who is that at the close of the summer
Near the deep lake? Who wrought her
Comely and slender?
Time but attends and befriends her
Than whom the grasses though tall
Are not taller,
My daughter,
My gentle daughter.

IRVING LAYTON   *b.* 1912   Canada

A Celebration

Fires had been kindled on the twenty-third
Along the bog road from the hospital.
People had lit them for the solstice. Now
They seemed a celebration of our child
Who had just been born. It was the Feast of
The Sacred Heart. Midsummer madness, too,
And everything was cured, and had come through.

I drove past, smiling, watching the flames rise
And the sparks settle, and the children run.
I saw this one in Finland, years before,

Only in Finland, never in England,
The same bright, atavistic urge for summer
To burn away in one convulsive blaze
And leave no cinder. This was just the same.

I thought about our child. Her sudden head
Through your strained flesh, and then the slippery limbs,
The twisting marble of the cord, the tripes
And purplish ox-heart she had fattened on
Through nine months of your dreaming heaviness.
Now you were smaller, and our girl was born,
Red as the sun, to celebratory fires.

I drove on to my future. Fatherhood
Like vernix now lay white around my brow,
A caul of love, a laurel wreath of joy.
The years declining offered me their arms
Like glowing embers, and I warmed my age
In growing hope. Here was the fiery heir,
A queen of Ireland in her vitreous cot.

I felt my leg revive. Stepped out at home
Into a morning new as light at Moyne,
Sniffing the air. Here was another day
Wherein you waking would arouse and feed
Her sleeping lips, toy with her pixy ears
And know the mystery of genesis
First hand. Happy, I went indoors to sleep.

GEORGE MACBETH   1932–1992   Scotland

Cinders

After the pantomime, carrying you back to the car
On the coldest night of the year
My coat, black leather, cracking in the wind.

Through the darkness we are guided by a star
It is the one the Good Fairy gave you
You clutch it tightly, your magic wand.

And I clutch you tightly for fear you blow away
For fear you grow up too soon and — suddenly,
I almost slip, so take it steady down the hill.

Hunched against the wind and hobbling
I could be mistaken for your grandfather
And sensing this, I hold you tighter still.

Knowing that I will never see you dressed for the Ball
Be on hand to warn you against Prince Charmings
And the happy ever afters of pantomime.

On reaching the car I put you into the baby seat
And fumble with straps I have yet to master
Thinking, if only there were more time. More time.

You are crying now. Where is your wand?
Oh no. I can't face going back for it
Let some kid find it in tomorrow's snow.

Waiting in the wings, the witching hour.
Already the car is changing. Smells sweet
Of ripening seed. We must go. Must go.

ROGER MCGOUGH   *b.* 1937   England

Song

Never take her away,
The daughter whom you gave me,
The gentle, moist, untroubled
Small daughter whom you gave me;
O let her heavenly babbling
Beset me and enslave me.
Don't take her; let her stay,
Beset my heart, and win me,

That I may put away
The firstborn child within me,
That cold, petrific, dry
Daughter whom death once gave,
Whose life is a long cry
For milk she may not have,
And who, in the night-time, calls me
In the saddest voice that can be
Father, Father, and tells me
Of the love she feels for me.
Don't let her go away,
Her whom you gave – my daughter –
Lest I should come to favor
That wilder one, that other
Who does not leave me ever.

VINICIUS DE MORAES   1913–1980   Brazil
Translated by Richard Wilbur

Elegy for His Daughter Ellen

Too sad is the grief in my heart! down my cheeks run salt streams. I have lost my Ellen of the hue of fair weather, my bright-braided merry daughter.

My darling, bright-shaped, beautiful, my warm-smiling angel; a golden speech was the infant talk of her lips, the girl of the colour of the stars (what profit now to speak?), whose form was delicate, whose voice was soft, with a happy cry to welcome her father, that orphaned man. Orphaned is her father, with a crushing wound in his pierced and broken heart, in inconsolable distress – how well I know, bound down with my yearning for her!

Since I lost my neat slender girl, all the time I mourn her sadly and ponder on her ways. When I think of her, anguish springs up and wretched affliction in my breast, my heart is faint for her and broken because of her; it is a pang to speak of her, my trim daughter, of the dear gentle words she uttered, and of her delicate pale white hands.

Farewell my soul, my joyful gay princess, farewell again, my Nelly, pure of heart, farewell my pretty little merry daughter, my angel, resting in the midst of the graveyard at Walton, until the far assembly of the white Saints and the cry of the clamour of the unfailing Messengers. When the earth shall give up its meek and innocent, when the throngs shall be summoned from the mighty oceans, you shall get, my soul, you too, a fine gold crown and a place in the light of the host of angels.

GORONWY OWEN   1723–1769   Wales
Translated by Kenneth Hurlstone Jackson

Remembering Golden Bells

Ruined and ill, – a man of two score;
   Pretty and guileless, – a girl of three.
Not a boy, – but still better than nothing:
To soothe one's feeling, – from time to time a kiss!
There came a day, – they suddenly took her from me;
Her soul's shadow wandered I know not where.
And when I remember how just at the time she died
She lisped strange sounds, beginning to learn to talk,
Then I know that the ties of flesh and blood
Only bind us to a load of grief and sorrow.
At last, by thinking of the time before she was born,
By thought and reason I drove the pain away.
Since my heart forgot her, many days have passed
And three times winter has changed to spring.
This morning, for a little, the old grief came back,
Because, in the road, I met her foster-nurse.

PO CHU-I   772–846   China
Translated by Arthur Waley

'You grow like a beanstalk'

You grow like a beanstalk
as tall as a tale;
twining your time a garland, the leaves are all
shaped in a single heart, to climb until
you stand as high as your wish and what's over the wall
flowers in your eye, a marvel, to teach the tongue
the scale of tomorrow and elsewhere. The song to be sung.

Once, o legends ago,
in the halfway house
by the fire where bedward candles beg their flame
I read you the tale of the thumb-tall girl who was swept
away on a lily leaf, the toad, the mouse;
you so still on my lap I thought you slept.
But the story darkened. The mole's long galleries came
nowhere to guess or glimmer of ending: grief.
Tears that would not, would not be comforted, no
though the risen bird was king and south was home
would not: away on a woman's tears far past belief
in a happy ever and after I watched you go
Ceres in search of her child a child gone down to the dark.
I heard you a woman cry
and born a maiden you wept for the maidens who die.

Soon I listen
and you, the traveller, make
plans for an early start; your turn to tell
the other side of the story. The path you take
is worn like a wish: beasts are clumsy and kind
the birds are concerned about orphans, nothing has changed, the
    lake
copies its only landscape of turrets and trees, you find
the house they told you was ruined and there at last
the sun is taking the girl in her bridal dress,

the six white horses are waiting, across the park
bells are rising, immaculate doves fly past
over your future and after them into the dark
my fears go up like fireworks, salute and bless
as far as a wish can see or a heart can guess.

SÉAN RAFFERTY   1909–1993   Scotland

Janet Waking

Beautifully Janet slept
Till it was deeply morning. She woke then
And thought about her dainty-feathered hen,
To see how it had kept.

One kiss she gave her mother,
Only a small one gave she to her daddy
Who would have kissed each curl of his shining baby;
No kiss at all for her brother.

'Old Chucky, Old Chucky!' she cried,
Running across the world upon the grass
To Chucky's house, and listening. But alas,
Her Chucky had died.

It was a transmogrifying bee
Came droning down on Chucky's old bald head
And sat and put the poison. It scarcely bled,
But how exceedingly

And purply did the knot
Swell with the venom and communicate
Its rigor! Now the poor comb stood up straight
But Chucky did not.

So there was Janet
Kneeling on the wet grass, crying her brown hen
(Translated far beyond the daughters of men)
To rise and walk upon it.

And weeping fast as she had breath
Janet implored us, 'Wake her from her sleep!'
And would not be instructed in how deep
Was the forgetful kingdom of death.

JOHN CROWE RANSOM   1888–1974   USA

To Ianthe

I love thee, Baby! For thine own sweet sake;
    Those azure eyes, that faintly dimpled cheek,
    Thy tender frame, so eloquently weak,
    Love in the sternest heart of hate might wake;
But more when o'er thy fitful slumber bending
    Thy mother folds thee to her wakeful heart,
    Whilst love and pity, in her glances bending,
    All that thy passive eyes can feel impart:
More, when some feeble lineaments of her,
    Who bore thy weight beneath her spotless bosom,
    As with deep love I read thy face, recur! –
More dear art thou, O fair and fragile blossom;
    Dearest when most thy tender traits express
    The image of thy mother's loveliness.

PERCY BYSSHE SHELLEY*   1792–1822   England

Reconstructions

This fall, we left your Grandma's
And had to leave your plant behind;
You said if no one watered it
And it would die, you didn't mind.
You mean to play the zinnia
In some sorry melodrama.

You offered me, one day, your doll
To sing songs to, bubble and nurse,
And said that was her birthday;
You reappeared then, grabbed her away,
Said just don't mess with her at all;
It was your child, yours.

Amd earlier this summer, how
You would tell the dog he had to 'Stay!'
Then always let him sit
There, ears up, tense, all
Shivering to hear you call;
You turned and walked away.

We are like patients who rehearse
Old unbearable scenes
Day after day after day.
I memorize you, bit by bit,
And must restore you in my verses
To sell to magazines.

We keep what our times allow
And turn our grief into play.
We left you at your mother's; now
We've given the dog away.

W. D. SNODGRASS* b. 1926   USA

To My Daughter

Bright clasp of her whole hand around my finger,
My daughter, as we walk together now.
All my life I'll feel a ring invisibly
Circle this bone with shining: when she is grown
Far from today as her eyes are already.

STEPHEN SPENDER   1909−1995   England

The Painter

for my daughter Rina

I'm her palette of ash and fanned embers:
someone commands her to take up a paintbrush and dip it in.
The colors are faces, swimming. They tremble
with terrified whites of my pupils.
And the blue ruins frozen in my prophetic visions
make the canvas blue until even she becomes
the inheritor of darkness in the halfday of sunny sabras,
as though a sea of candelabras were snuffed out in the window.

I'm her palette of snow, like torn manuscripts;
her paintbrush rambles in my twilight tracings.
A sunbeam hides itself in the woods. In a ravenous mist
a familiar sight is etched among the twigs.
From her model the painter swallows the color of my silence
and prays; she prays in order to rescue him among the twigs.
Then, when the sunbeam is hanging in the woods, burned out,
the daughter distances herself from her father — in order to feel
    closer to him.

And again sparks begin to play in damp crystal
and someone commands her to dip her paintbrush and paint.
A small cloud with green sun-eyes trembles in the room
as though behind the canvas a child fidgets in the raspberry
    bushes.
A single chimney crumbles into shapes like bricks
to feed the artist's paintbrush with the color of clay.
And where is the father? Blue knives rain down:
one of them has already slaughtered his sleep for him.

At night when sun-blue flecks bless the painter,
the canvases swim to the father to awaken him from the truth.
Thus do sails sail at night on the sea without sailors,
drenched only with farewell words and clouds.

The canvases sail through the walls into his mirror
and with its bricks the chimney begins to rebuild itself.
And when he awakens from his truth, like a sleeper from a
     dream —
the grace of the creator is shining in the blue ruins.

1972

ABRAHAM SUTZKEVER*   *b.* 1913, Estonia   Israel
Translated by Ruth R. Wisse

Old Man

Old Man, or Lad's-love, — in the name there's nothing
To one that knows not Lad's-love, or Old Man,
The hoar-green feathery herb, almost a tree,
Growing with rosemary and lavender.
Even to one that knows it well, the names
Half decorate, half perplex, the thing it is:
At least, what that is clings not to the names
In spite of time. And yet I like the names.

The herb itself I like not, but for certain
I love it, as some day the child will love it
Who plucks a feather from the door-side bush
Whenever she goes in or out of the house.
Often she waits there, snipping the tips and shrivelling
The shreds at last on to the path, perhaps
Thinking, perhaps of nothing, till she sniffs
Her fingers and runs off. The bush is still
But half as tall as she, though it is as old;
So well she clips it. Not a word she says;
And I can only wonder how much hereafter
She will remember, with that bitter scent,
Of garden rows, and ancient damson-trees
Topping a hedge, a bent path to a door,
A low thick bush beside the door and me
Forbidding her to pick.

As for myself,
Where first I met the bitter scent is lost.
I, too, often shrivel the grey shreds,
Sniff them and think and sniff again and try
Once more to think what it is I am remembering,
Always in vain. I cannot like the scent,
Yet I would rather give up others more sweet,
With no meaning, than this bitter one.

I have mislaid the key. I sniff the spray,
And think of nothing; I see and I hear nothing;
Yet seem, too, to be listening, lying in wait
For what I should, yet never can, remember:
No garden appears, no path, no hoar-green bush
Of Lad's-love, or Old Man, no child beside,
Neither father nor mother, nor any playmate;
Only an avenue, dark, nameless, without end.

EDWARD THOMAS   1878–1917   England

Looking On

Hearing our voices raised –
Perhaps in anger,
Or in some trivial argument
That is not anger –
She screams until we stop
And smile, and look at her,
Poised on the sheer drop
Which opens under her.

If these, her parents, show
How the gods can fail,
Squabbling on Olympus,
How can she fail
To see that anarchy
Is what one must expect,
That to be happy
One must be circumspect?

But the reverse is true
Also, when we kiss,
Seeing herself excluded
Even from that kiss.
The gods' too gross affairs
Made myths for innocent men,
So the innocent eye stares
At love in its den.

Like a strange motley beast
Out of an old myth,
Anger and love together
Make up her own myth
Of these two who cherish,
Protect, feed, deny,
In whose arms she will flourish
Or else will die.

ANTHONY THWAITE *b.* 1930 England

The Writer

In her room at the prow of the house
Where light breaks, and the windows are tossed with linden,
My daughter is writing a story.

I pause in the stairwell, hearing
From her shut door a commotion of typewriter-keys
Like a chain hauled over a gunwale.

Young as she is, the stuff
Of her life is a great cargo, and some of it heavy:
I wish her a lucky passage.

But now it is she who pauses,
As if to reject my thought and its easy figure.
A stillness greatens, in which

The whole house seems to be thinking,
And then she is at it again with a bunched clamour
Of strokes, and again is silent.

I remember the dazed starling
Which was trapped in that very room, two years ago;
How we stole in, lifted a sash

And retreated, not to affright it;
And how for a helpless hour, through the crack of the door,
We watched the sleek, wild, dark

And iridescent creature
Batter against the brilliance, drop like a glove
To the hard floor, or the desk-top,

And wait then, humped and bloody,
For the wits to try it again; and how our spirits
Rose when, suddenly sure,

It lifted off from a chair-back,
Beating a smooth course for the right window
And clearing the sill of the world.

It is always a matter, my darling,
Of life or death, as I had forgotten. I wish
What I wished you before, but harder.

RICHARD WILBUR   *b.* 1921   USA

Sugar Daddy

You do not look like me. I'm glad
England failed to colonize
Those black orchid eyes
With blue, the colour of sun-blindness.

Your eyes came straight to you
from your mother's Martinique
Great-grandmother. They look at me
Across this wide Atlantic

With an unborn feeling for my weaknesses.
Like loveletters, your little phoney grins
Come always just too late
To reward my passionate clowning.

I am here to be nice, clap hands, reflect
Your tolerance. I know what I'm for.
When you come home fifteen years from now
Saying you've smashed my car,

I'll feel the same. I'm blood brother,
Sugar Daddy, millionaire to you.
I want to buy you things.

I bought a garish humming top
And climbed into your pen like an ape
And pumped it till it screeched for you,
Hungry for thanks. Your lip

Trembled and you cried. You did not need
My sinister grenade, something
Pushed out of focus at you, swaying
Violently. You owned it anyway

And the whole world it came from.
It was then I knew
I could only take things from you from now on.

I was the White Hunter,
Bearing cheap mirrors for the Chief,
You saw the giving-look coagulate in my eyes
And panicked for the trees.

HUGO WILLIAMS *b.* 1942   England

Sonnet

Surprised by joy – impatient as the Wind
I turned to share the transport – Oh! with whom
But thee, deep buried in the silent tomb,
That spot which no vicissitude can find?
Love, faithful love, recalled thee to my mind –
But how could I forget thee? Through what power
Even for the least division of an hour,
Have I been so beguiled as to be blind
To my most grievous loss! – That thought's return
Was the worst pang that sorrow ever bore,
Save one, one only, when I stood forlorn,
Knowing my heart's best treasure was no more;
That neither present time, nor years unborn
Could to my sight that heavenly face restore.

WILLIAM WORDSWORTH*   1770–1850   England

A Prayer for My Daughter

Once more the storm is howling, and half hid
Under this cradle-hood and coverlid
My child sleeps on. There is no obstacle
But Gregory's wood and one bare hill
Whereby the haystack- and roof-levelling wind,
Bred on the Atlantic, can be stayed;
And for an hour I have walked and prayed
Because of the great gloom that is in my mind.

I have walked and prayed for this young child an hour
And heard the sea-wind scream upon the tower,
And under the arches of the bridge, and scream
In the elms above the flooded stream;

Imagining in excited reverie
That the future years had come,
Dancing to a frenzied drum,
Out of the murderous innocence of the sea.

May she be granted beauty and yet not
Beauty to make a stranger's eye distraught,
Or hers before a looking-glass, for such,
Being made beautiful overmuch,
Consider beauty a sufficient end,
Lose natural kindness and maybe
The heart-revealing intimacy
That chooses right, and never find a friend.

Helen being chosen found life flat and dull
And later had much trouble from a fool,
While that great Queen, that rose out of the spray,
Being fatherless could have her way
Yet chose a bandy-legged smith for man.
It's certain that fine women eat
A crazy salad with their meat
Whereby the Horn of Plenty is undone.

In courtesy I'd have her chiefly learned;
Hearts are not had as a gift but hearts are earned
By those that are not entirely beautiful;
Yet many, that have played the fool
For beauty's very self, has charm made wise,
And many a poor man that has roved,
Loved and thought himself beloved,
From a glad kindness cannot take his eyes.

May she become a flourishing hidden tree
That all her thoughts may like the linnet be,
And have no business but dispensing round
Their magnanimities of sound,
Nor but in merriment begin a chase,
Nor but in merriment a quarrel.
O may she live like some green laurel
Rooted in one dear perpetual place.

My mind, because the minds that I have loved,
The sort of beauty that I have approved,
Prosper but little, has dried up of late,
Yet knows that to be choked with hate
May well be of all evil chances chief.
If there's no hatred in a mind
Assault and battery of the wind
Can never tear the linnet from the leaf.

An intellectual hatred is the worst,
So let her think opinions are accurst.
Have I not seen the loveliest woman born
Out of the mouth of Plenty's horn,
Because of her opinionated mind
Barter that horn and every good
By quiet natures understood
For an old bellows full of angry wind?

Considering that, all hatred driven hence,
The soul recovers radical innocence
And learns at last that it is self-delighting,
Self-appeasing, self-affrighting,
And that its own sweet will is Heaven's will;
She can, though every face should scowl
And every windy quarter howl
Or every bellows burst, be happy still.

And may her bridegroom bring her to a house
Where all's accustomed, ceremonious;
For arrogance and hatred are the wares
Peddled in the thoroughfares.
How but in custom and in ceremony
Are innocence and beauty born?
Ceremony's a name for the rich horn,
And custom for the spreading laurel tree.

June 1919

W. B. YEATS   1865–1939   Ireland

Father
to
Son

A Child is Something Else Again

A child is something else again. Wakes up
in the afternoon and in an instant he's full of words,
in an instant he's humming, in an instant warm,
instant light, instant darkness.

A child is Job. They've already placed their bets on him
but he doesn't know it. He scratches his body
for pleasure. Nothing hurts yet.
They're training him to be a polite Job,
to say 'Thank you' when the Lord has given,
to say 'You're welcome' when the Lord has taken away.

A child is vengeance.
A child is a missile into the coming generations.
I launched him: I'm still trembling.

A child is something else again: on a rainy spring day
glimpsing the Garden of Eden through the fence,
kissing him in his sleep,
hearing footsteps in the wet pine needles.
A child delivers you from death.
Child, Garden, Rain, Fate.

YEHUDA AMICHAI *b.* 1924, Germany   Israel
Translated by Chana Bloch and Stephen Mitchell

A Sympathy, A Welcome

Feel for your bad fall how could I fail,
poor Paul, who had it so good.
I can offer you only: this world like a knife.
Yet you'll get to know your mother
and humorless as you do look you will laugh
and all the others

will NOT be fierce to you, and loverhood
will swing your soul like a broken bell
deep in a forsaken wood, poor Paul,
whose wild bad father loves you well.

JOHN BERRYMAN   1914–1972   USA

To My Son

Those flaxen locks, those eyes of blue,
Bright as thy mother's in their hue;
Those rosy lips, whose dimples play
And smile to steal the heart away,
Recall a scene of former joy,
And touch thy father's heart, my Boy!

And thou canst lisp a father's name —
Ah, William, were thine own the same, —
No self-reproach — but, let me cease —
My care for thee shall purchase peace;
Thy mother's shade shall smile in joy,
And pardon all the past, my Boy!

Her lowly grave the turf has prest,
And thou hast known a stranger's breast;
Derision sneers upon thy birth,
And yields thee scarce a name on earth;
Yet shall not these one hope destroy, —
A Father's heart is thine, my Boy!

Why, let the world unfeeling frown,
Must I fond Nature's claims disown?
Ah, no — though moralists reprove,
I hail thee, dearest child of love,
Fair cherub, pledge of youth and joy —
A Father guards thy birth, my Boy!

Oh, 'twill be sweet in thee to trace,
Ere age has wrinkled o'er my face,
Ere half my glass of life is run,
At once a brother and a son;
And all my want of years employ
In justice done to thee, my Boy!

Although so young thy heedless sire,
Youth will not damp parental fire;
And, wert thou still less dear to me,
While Helen's form revives in thee,
The breast which beat to former joy,
Will ne'er desert its pledge, my Boy!

1807 (first publ. 1830)

GEORGE GORDON, LORD BYRON*   1788–1824   England

Epitaph for François

The two doors of the world
stand open:
opened by you
in the twinight.
We hear them slam and slam
and carry the thing that's uncertain
and carry the green thing into your Ever.

PAUL CELAN*   1920–1970   Romania
Translated by Michael Hamburger

The Father and the Son

I nick my chin while shaving;
my son bares his wrist,
searches for the rustiest blade,
sorrow pooling in his eyes.

I scold; he thrusts his hand
into ice, fire, calls himself
'Forever Second Best,' climbs
the cross, singing 'It is finished.'

I grow comic; he invents love,
the erection, children.
He watches as I go ashen,
fall backwards into the casket.

We trade places; I bring flowers,
light memory's candles with
his last breath. We trade places.
This goes on forever and ever.

DAVID CITINO   b. 1947   USA

Frost at Midnight

The frost performs its secret ministry,
Unhelped by any wind. The owlet's cry
Came loud – and hark, again! loud as before.
The inmates of my cottage, all at rest,
Have left me to that solitude, which suits
Abstruser musings: save that at my side
My cradled infant slumbers peacefully.
'Tis calm indeed! so calm, that it disturbs
And vexes meditation with its strange
And extreme silentness. Sea, hill, and wood,

This populous village! Sea, and hill, and wood,
With all the numberless goings on of life,
Inaudible as dreams! the thin blue flame
Lies on my low burnt fire, and quivers not;
Only that film, which fluttered on the grate,
Still flutters there, the sole unquiet thing.
Methinks, its motion in this hush of nature
Gives it dim sympathies with me who live,
Making it a companionable form,
Whose puny flaps and freaks the idling Spirit
By its own moods interprets, every where
Echo or mirror seeking of itself,
And makes a toy of Thought.

                      But O! how oft,
How oft, at school, with most believing mind,
Presageful, have I gazed upon the bars,
To watch that fluttering stranger! and as oft
With unclosed lids, already had I dreamt
Of my sweet birth-place, and the old church-tower,
Whose bells, the poor man's only music, rang
From morn to evening, all the hot Fair-day,
So sweetly, that they stirred and haunted me
With a wild pleasure, falling on mine ear
Most like articulate sounds of things to come!
So gazed I, till the soothing things I dreamt
Lulled me to sleep, and sleep prolonged my dreams!
And so I brooded all the following morn,
Awed by the stern preceptor's face, mine eye
Fixed with mock study on my swimming book:
Save if the door half opened, and I snatched
A hasty glance, and still my heart leaped up,
For still I hoped to see the stranger's face,
Townsman, or aunt, or sister more beloved,
My play-mate when we both were clothed alike!

   Dear Babe, that sleepest cradled by my side,
Whose gentle breathings, heard in this deep calm,
Fill up the interspersed vacancies
And momentary pauses of the thought!
My babe so beautiful! it thrills my heart
With tender gladness, thus to look at thee,

And think that thou shalt learn far other lore
And in far other scenes! For I was reared
In the great city, pent 'mid cloisters dim,
And saw nought lovely but the sky and stars.
But thou, my babe! shalt wander like a breeze
By lakes and sandy shores, beneath the crags
Of ancient mountain, and beneath the clouds,
Which image in their bulk both lakes and shores
And mountain crags: so shalt thou see and hear
The lovely shapes and sounds intelligible
Of that eternal language, which thy God
Utters, who from eternity doth teach
Himself in all, and all things in himself.
Great universal Teacher! he shall mould
Thy spirit, and by giving make it ask.

  Therefore all seasons shall be sweet to thee,
Whether the summer clothe the general earth
With greenness, or the redbreast sit and sing
Betwixt the tufts of snow on the bare branch
Of mossy apple-tree, while the night thatch
Smokes in the sun-thaw; whether the eve-drops fall
Heard only in the trances of the blast,
Or if the secret ministry of frost
Shall hang them up in silent icicles,
Quietly shining to the quiet Moon.

SAMUEL TAYLOR COLERIDGE 1772–1834 England

Little Brown Baby

Little brown baby wif spa'klin' eyes,
 Come to yo' pappy an' set on his knee.
What you been doin', suh – makin' san' pies?
 Look at dat bib – you's ez du'ty ez me.
Look at dat mouf – dat's merlasses, I bet;
 Come hyeah, Maria, an' wipe off his han's.

Bees gwine to ketch you an' eat you up yit,
  Bein' so sticky an sweet – goodness lan's!

Little brown baby wif spaklin' eyes,
  Who's pappy's darlin' an' who's pappy's chile?
Who is it all de day nevah once tries
  Fu' to be cross, er once loses dat smile?
Whah did you git dem teef? My, you's a scamp!
  Whah did dat dimple come f'om in yo' chin?
Pappy do' know you – I b'lieves you's a tramp;
  Mammy, dis hyeah's some ol' straggler got in!

Let's th'ow him outen de do' in de san',
  We do' want stragglers a-layin' roun' hyeah;
Let's gin him 'way to de big buggah-man;
  I know he's hidin' erroun' hyeah right neah.
Buggah-man, buggah-man, come in de do',
  Hyeah's a bad boy you kin have fu' to eat.
Mammy an' pappy do' want him no mo',
  Swaller him down f'om his haid to his feet!

Dah, now, I t'ought dat you'd hug me up close.
  Go back, ol' buggah, you sha'n't have dis boy.
He ain't no tramp, ner nor straggler, of co'se;
  He's pappy's pa'dner an' playmate an' joy.
Come to you' pallet now – go to yo' res';
  Wisht you could allus know ease an' cleah skies;
Wisht you could stay jes' a chile on my breas' –
  Little brown baby wif spaklin' eyes!

PAUL LAURENCE DUNBAR 1872–1906 USA

My Son My Executioner

My son, my executioner,
  I take you in my arms,
Quiet and small and just astir,
  And whom my body warms.

Sweet death, small son, our instrument
   Of immortality,
Your cries and hungers document
   Our bodily decay.

We twenty-five and twenty-two,
   Who seemed to live forever,
Observe enduring life in you
   And start to die together.

DONALD HALL   *b.* 1928   USA

Nightmare Begins Responsibility

I place these numbed wrists to the pane
watching white uniforms whisk over
him in the tube-kept
prison
fear what they will do in experiment
watch my gloved stickshifting gasolined hands
breathe *boxcar-information-please* infirmary tubes
distrusting white-pink mending paperthin
silkened end hairs, distrusting tubes
shrunk in his *trunk-skincapped*
shaven head, in thighs
distrusting-white-hands-picking-baboon-light
on this son who will not make his second night
of this wardstrewn intensive airpocket
where his father's asthmatic
hymns of *night-train*, train done gone
his mother can only know that he has flown
up into essential calm unseen corridor
going boxscarred home, *mamaborn, sweetsonchild*
gonedowntown into *researchtestingwarehousebatteryacid*
mama-son-done-gone/me telling her 'nother
train tonight, no music, no breathstroked
heartbeat in my infinite distrust of them:

and of my distrusting self
white-doctor-who-breathed-for-him-all-night
say it for two sons gone,
say nightmare, say it loud
pane-breaking heartmadness:
nightmare begins responsibility.

MICHAEL S. HARPER   *b.* 1938   USA

To My Son

My dead dear, you refused to shut your eyes
open like two swallows to the sky:
June-crowned, their color soon turned to dew
drifting toward certain patches of morning.

Today, like a day underground, is dim,
rainy, deserted, as if underground
in the sunless damp of my body-to-be
as I'd like to have carried you underground.

Since you died mornings haven't breathed,
robbed of the fire of your sun-like eyes:
a rainy October beating on our windows,
you made way for autumn, turning seas into night.

The sun, your only rival, devoured you deep
as the far shadow did which launched you aflame;
light shoved you down, bore you to the bottom,
engulfing you; now it's as if you never were born.

Ten months in the light, the revolving sky,
dead sun blackened, eclipsed, and buried.
Your skin shriveled, without reaching daylight;
your flesh evening-dim along with the dawn.

The bird's east-facing body asks for you,
newborn flesh needs sunrise and joy;
my child, who just knew laughter so fully
only some flowers die with your smile.

Gone, gone, gone like the swallow,
summer bird shunning life touched by frost;
swallow no sooner trying its delicate wings
than clipped by scissors hostile to flight.

Flower too young to harden its teeth
or grasp the slightest feel for the wild,
life like a bud of incipient lips,
leaf that shrivels before it could rustle.

Useless to you were the sea's admonitions . . .
I've just stabbed a tender young sun,
buried a piece of bread in oblivion,
strewn over eyes a handful of nothingness.

Green, red, brown. Green, blue and gold —
latent colors of life, gardens,
core of flowers meant for your footsteps,
of sad bleak blacks, of grave stiff whites.

Wife backed in a corner, look up: it's day.
(Oh, eyes never setting on dawn forever!)
But in your womb, but in your eyes, dear wife,
the desolate night continues to fall.

MIGUEL HERNANDEZ   1910–1942   Spain
Translated by Edwin Honig

On My First Sonne

Farewell, thou child of my right hand, and joy;
My sinne was too much hope of thee, lov'd boy,
Seven yeeres tho' wert lent to me, and I thee pay,
Exacted by thy fate, on the just day.

O, could I loose all father, now. For why
Will man lament the state he should envie?
To have so soone scap'd worlds, and fleshes rage,
And, if no other miserie, yet age?
Rest in soft peace, and, ask'd, say here doth lye
Ben Jonson his best piece of poetrie.
For whose sake, hence-forth, all his vows be such,
As what he loves may never like too much.

BEN JONSON   c. 1572—1637   England

To My Child Carlino

Carlino! What art thou about, my boy?
Often I ask that question, though in vain;
For we are far apart: ah! therefore 'tis
I often ask it; not in such a tone
As wiser fathers do, who know too well.
Were we not children, you and I together?
Stole we not glances from each other's eyes?
Swore we not secrecy in such misdeeds?
Well could we trust each other. Tell me, then,
What thou art doing. Carving out thy name,
Or haply mine, upon my favourite seat,
With the new knife I sent thee over-sea?
Or hast thou broken it, and hid the hilt
Among the myrtles, starr'd with flowers, behind?
Or under that high throne whence fifty lilies
(With sworded tuberoses dense around)
Lift up their heads at once . . . not without fear
That they were looking at thee all the while.
   Does Cincirillo follow thee about?
Inverting one swart foot suspensively,
And wagging his dread jaw, at every chirp
Of bird above him on the olive branch?
Frighten him then away! 'twas he who slew
Our pigeons, our white pigeons, peacock-tailed,

That fear'd not you and me . . . alas, nor him!
I flattened his striped sides along my knee,
And reasoned with him on his bloody mind,
Till he looked blandly, and half-closed his eyes
To ponder on my lecture in the shade.
I doubt his memory much, his heart a little,
And in some minor matters (may I say it?)
Could wish him rather sager. But from thee
God hold back wisdom yet for many years!
Whether in early season or in late
It always comes high priced. For thy pure breast
I have no lesson; it for me has many.
Come, throw it open then! What sports, what cares
(Since there are none too young for these) engage
Thy busy thoughts? Are you again at work,
Walter and you, with those sly labourers,
Geppo, Giovanni, Cecco and Poeta,
To build more solidly your broken dam
Among the poplars, whence the nightingale
Inquisitively watched you all day long?
I was not of your council in the scheme,
Or might have saved you silver without end,
And sighs too without number. Art thou gone
Below the mulberry, where that cold pool
Urged to devise a warmer, and more fit
For mighty swimmers, swimming three abreast?
Or art thou panting in this summer noon
Upon the lowest step before the hall,
Drawing a slice of watermelon, long
As Cupid's bow athwart thy wetted lips
(Like one who plays Pan's pipe) and letting drop
The sable seeds from all their separate cells,
And leaving bays profound and rocks abrupt,
Redder than coral round Calypso's cave?

WALTER SAVAGE LANDOR*   1775–1864   England

Night Thoughts over a Sick Child

Numb, stiff, broken by no sleep,
I keep night watch. Looking for
signs to quiet fear, I creep
closer to his bed and hear
his breath come and go, holding
my own as if my own were
all I paid. Nothing I bring,
say, or do has meaning here.

Outside, ice crusts on river
and pond; wild hare come to my
door, pacified by torture.
No less ignorant than they
of what grips and why, I am
moved to prayer, the quaint gestures
which ennoble beyond shame
only the mute listener.

No one hears. A dry wind shifts
dry snow, indifferently;
the roof, rotting beneath drifts,
sighs and holds. Terrified by
sleep, the child strives toward
consciousness and the known pain.
If it were mine by one word
I would not save any man,

Myself or the universe
at such cost: reality.
Heir to an ancestral curse
Though fallen from Judah's tree,
I take up into my arms my hopes,
my son, for what it's worth give
bodily warmth. When he escapes
his heritage, then what have

I left but false remembrance
and the name. Against that day
there is no armor or stance,
only the frail dignity
of surrender, which is all
that can separate me now
or then from the dumb beast's fall,
unseen in the frozen snow.

PHILIP LEVINE   *b.* 1928   USA

Lament for Siôn y Glyn

One boy, Saint Dwyn, my bauble:
His father rues he was born!
Sorrow was bred of fondness,
Lasting pain, lacking a son.
My two sides, dead is my die,
For Siôn y Glyn are aching.
I moan everlastingly
For a baron of boyhood.

A sweet apple and a bird
The boy loved, and white pebbles,
A bow of a thorntree twig,
And swords, wooden and brittle;
Scared of pipes, scared of scarecrows,
Begging mother for a ball,
Singing to all his chanting,
Singing 'Oo-o' for a nut.
He would play sweet, and flatter,
And then turn sulky with me,
Make peace for a wooden chip
Or the dice he was fond of.

Ah that Siôn, pure and gentle,
Cannot be a Lazarus!
Beuno once brought back to life
Seven who'd gone to heaven;
My heart's sorrow, it's doubled,
That Siôn's soul is not the eighth.

Mary, I groan, he lies there,
And my sides ache by his grave.
The death of Siôn stands by me
Stabbing me twice in the chest.
My boy, my twirling taper,
My bosom, my heart, my song,
My prime concern till my death,
My clever bard, my daydream,
My toy he was, my candle,
My fair soul, my one deceit,
My chick learning my singing,
My Iseult's chaplet, my kiss,
My strength, in grief he's left me,
My lark, my weaver of spells,
My bow, my arrow, my love,
My beggar, O my boyhood.
Siôn is sending his father
A sword of longing and love.

Farewell, the smile on my mouth,
Farewell to my lips' laughter,
Farewell, sweet consolation,
Farewell, the begging for nuts,
Farewell, far-off the ballgame,
Farewell to the high-pitched song,
Farewell, while I stay earthbound,
My gay darling, Siôn my son.

LEWIS GLYN COTHI   *fl.* 1447–1486   Wales
Translated by Joseph P. Clancy

Walking Away
for Sean

It is eighteen years ago, almost to the day —
A sunny day with the leaves just turning,
The touch-lines new-ruled — since I watched you play
Your first game of football, then, like a satellite
Wrenched from its orbit, go drifting away

Behind a scatter of boys. I can see
You walking away from me towards the school
With the pathos of a half-fledged thing set free
Into a wilderness, the gait of one
Who finds no path where the path should be.

That hesitant figure, eddying away
Like a winged seed loosened from its parent stem,
Has something I never quite grasp to convey
About nature's give-and-take — the small, the scorching
Ordeals which fire one's irresolute clay.

I have had worse partings, but none that so
Gnaws at my mind still. Perhaps it is roughly
Saying what God alone could perfectly show —
How selfhood begins with a walking away,
And love is proved in the letting go.

C DAY LEWIS   1904–1972   England

Mongol

Beside me, on the stroke of twelve,
He comes into his own,
Choosing this midnight exactly.
The whole house strains to his cry.

Heaters tick and contract.
He starts again with a vengeance
An inexorable, absorbed rocking
In the sagged cot —

His shadow jetting like water —
Till I hoist and dangle him,
Damp in his bleached pyjama top
On which a dolphin smashes

Paper hooplas. I would mould
Tractable fictions for him,
Words in their warm spittle,
Yet still make nothing at all

Of a head hung slackly,
Its oblong, injured gravities
Beyond reach of my pet-names,
My watchful appeasements.

His stable, Indian smiling
Fastens and holds. I pronounce him
Christened, tricked in white,
Fondled and intolerable,

Made docile in a cot piled high
With stuffed ducks, glove puppets,
Cloth animals he scatters fiercely,
A staring, upended cheetah.

His is a botched script, effaced letters.
Though, clear as day at the window,
The moon makes no mistake.
Knowing him by sight and to hum to.

AIDAN CARL MATHEWS   *b.* 1956   Ireland

'This is a poem to my son Peter'

this is a poem to my son Peter
whom I have hurt a thousand times
whose large and vulnerable eyes
have glazed in pain at my ragings
thin wrists and fingers hung
boneless in despair, pale freckled back
bent in defeat, pillow soaked
by my failure to understand.
I have scarred through weakness
and impatience your frail confidence forever
because when I needed to strike
you were there to be hurt and because
I thought you knew
you were beautiful and fair
your bright eyes and hair
but now I see that no one knows that
about himself, but must be told
and retold until it takes hold
because I think anything can be killed
after a while, especially beauty
so I write this for life, for love, for
you, my oldest son Peter, age 10,
going on 11.

PETER MEINKE   *b.* 1932   USA

A Child in Winter

*Where is the man who does not feel his heart softened ... [by] these so
helpless and so perfectly innocent little creatures?*   COBBETT

When the trees have given up,
snowberries come into their own,
winter grapes, albino
settlers of the dark.

With their milky blobs
they lined our doorstep
that November dusk
we swung your basket

up the gravel-path
and home. Child-Moses,
prince of the changing-mat,
heir of furry ducklings,

your babygros in drifts
on the clothes-rack,
we anoint your body's
rashes and folds.

When you cry it's like
some part of ourselves
breaking off and filling
these rooms with its pain.

Your breath's a matchflame
certain to go out,
we're at the cot hourly
holding our own.

In the shush of night-time
snowflakes crowd the window
like our own pale faces,
a shedding of old skins,

a blown seedhead,
paper pellets thrown down
by the gods to mark
your fiftieth day.

Lorries flounder on the hill.
We're out there watching
with a babysling
while the world goes under wool.

Little one, limpet,
resented stranger,
who has no time for me
and does not know time,

your home's the cradle
of a snowy hillfort
with pink turrets
and underground springs.

Daylight bores you: all night
you otter in our bed until
we wake to find you with us,
hands folded like a saint

accepting his death.
If it's we who must die first
that seems less costly now,
having you here like wheat.

Spring comes, measured
in light and celandines
and your first tooth, faint
as a rock at low tide,

headstone for these trials
with cottonbuds and nappies,
your silver lips tracking
for comfort in the dark.

BLAKE MORRISON   *b.* 1950   England

It Allows a Portrait in Line Scan at Fifteen

He retains a slight 'Martian' accent, from the years of single
  phrases.
He no longer hugs to disarm. It is gradually allowing him
  affection.
It does not allow proportion. Distress is absolute, shrieking, and
  runs him at frantic speed through crashing doors.
He likes cyborgs. Their taciturn power, with his intonation.
It still runs him around the house, alone in the dark, cooing and
  laughing.
He can read about soils, populations and New Zealand. On
  neutral topics he's illiterate.
Arnie Schwarzenegger is an actor. He isn't a cyborg really, is he,
  Dad?
He lives on forty acres, with animals and trees, and used to
  draw it continually.
He knows the map of Earth's fertile soils, and can draw it
  freehand.
He can only lie in a panicked shout *SorrySorryIdidn'tdoit!*
  warding off conflict with others and himself.
When he ran away constantly it was to the greengrocers to
  worship stacked fruit.
His favourite country was the Ukraine: it is nearly all deep
  fertile soil.
Giggling, he climbed all over the dim Freudian psychiatrist
  who told us how autism resulted from 'refrigerator'
  parents.
When asked to smile, he photographs a rictus-smile on his face.
It long forbade all naturalistic films. They were Adult movies.
If they (that is, he) *are bad the police will put them in hospital.*
He sometimes drew the farm amid Chinese or Balinese rice
  terraces.
When a runaway, he made uproar in the police station, playing
  at three times adult speed.
Only animated films were proper. *Who Framed Roger Rabbit*
  then authorized the rest.
Phrases spoken to him he would take as teaching, and repeat,

When he worshipped fruit, he screamed as if poisoned when it
     was fed to him.
A one-word first conversation: *Blane. — Yes! Plane, that's right,
     baby! — Blane.*
He has forgotten nothing, and remembers the precise quality of
     experiences.
It requires rulings: *Is stealing very playing up, as bad as murder?*
He counts at a glance, not looking. And he has never been lost.
When he ate only nuts and dried fruit, words were for dire
     emergencies.
He knows all the breeds of fowls, and the counties of Ireland.
He'd begun to talk, then returned to babble, then silence. It
     withdrew speech for years.
Is that very autistic, to play video games in the day?
He is anger's mirror, and magnifies any near him, raging it
     down.
It still won't allow him fresh fruit, or orange juice with bits in it.
He swam in the midwinter dam at night. It had no rules about
     cold.
He was terrified of thunder and finally cried as if in explanation
     It — angry!
He grilled an egg he'd broken into bread. Exchanges of
     soil-knowledge are called *landtalking.*
He lives in objectivity. I was sure Bell's palsy would leave my
     face only when he said it had begun to.
Don't say word! when he was eight forbade the word 'autistic' in
     his presence.
Bantering questions about girlfriends cause a terrified look and
     blocked ears.
He sometimes centred the farm in a furrowed American
     midwest.
Eye contact, Mum! means he truly wants attention. It dislikes
     I-contact.
He is equitable and kind, and only ever a little jealous. It was a
     relief when that little arrived.
He surfs, bowls, walks for miles. For many years he hasn't
     trailed his left arm while running.
I gotta get smart! looking terrified into the years. *I gotta get
     smart!*

LES MURRAY   *b.* 1938   Australia

Subway Psalm

It's the first storm of the winter
and the worst since 1888,
the girl on television said.

I keep slipping in my leather-soled shoes.
Twice I've turned into a windmill
in my efforts to keep from falling.

At the top of the stairs leading down
to the subway, Johnnie watches me,
not just with his eyes but with his arms and legs.
He'll do his best to save the old man.

That's how I must have looked at him
when he was five or six years old.
Now he's twenty-six, and it seems
we've traded places.
                   Why are you laughing?

he asks me.
             The honest answer is:
Because you look so funny, standing there
like that, my beautiful son,
and because I've loved you
for such a long time and because this
is the finest storm I've ever seen
and everything is exactly as it should be.

ALDEN NOWLAN   1933–1983   Canada

Departing Words to a Son

We choose to say good-bye against our will
Home will take on stillness when you're gone
Remember us — but don't dwell on the past
Here — wear this watch my father gave to me

Home will take on stillness when you're gone
We'll leave your room as is — at least for now
Here — wear this watch my father gave to me
His face dissolves within the whirling snow

We'll leave your room as is — at least for now
I'll dust the model boats that sail your wall
His face dissolves within the whirling snow
It's hard to picture someone else's life

I'll dust the model boats that sail your wall
Don't lose the watch — the inside is engraved
It's hard to picture someone else's life
Your window's full of icicles again

Don't lose the watch — the inside is engraved
A wedge of geese heads somewhere out of sight
Your window's full of icicles again
Look how the icicles reflect the moon

A wedge of geese heads somewhere out of sight
My father knew the distances we keep
Look how the icicles reflect the moon
The moonlight shimmers wavelike on your wall

My father knew the distances we keep
Your mother sometimes cries out in the night
Look how the icicles reflect the moon
The moonlight shimmers wavelike on your wall.

My father knew the distances we keep
Your mother sometimes cries out in the night
The moonlight shimmers wavelike on your wall
One June I dove too deep and nearly drowned

Your mother sometimes cries out in the night
She dreams the windy snow has covered her
One June I dove too deep and nearly drowned
She says she's watched me shudder in my sleep

She dreams the windy snow has covered her
She's heard your lost scream stretch across the snow
She says she's watched me shudder in my sleep
We all conceive the loss of what we love

She's heard your lost scream stretch across the snow
My need for her clenched tighter at your birth
We all conceive the loss of what we love
Our love for you has given this house breath

My need for her clenched tighter at your birth
Stillness deepens pulsing in our veins
Our love for you has given this house breath
Some day you'll pass this watch on to your son

Stillness deepens pulsing in our veins
My father's words still speak out from the watch
Some day you'll pass this watch on to your son
Repeating what the goldsmith has etched there

My father's words still speak out from the watch
As moonlit icicles drip on your sill
Repeating what the goldsmith has etched there
We choose to say good-bye against our will

ROBERT PACK   *b.* 1929   USA

The Toys

My little Son, who look'd from thoughtful eyes
And moved and spoke in quiet grown-up wise,
Having my law the seventh time disobey'd,
I struck him, and dismiss'd
With hard words and unkiss'd,

— His Mother, who was patient, being dead.
Then, fearing lest his grief should hinder sleep,
I visited his bed,
But found him slumbering deep,
With darken'd eyelids, and their lashes yet
From his late sobbing wet.
And I, with moan,
Kissing away his tears, left others of my own;
For, on a table drawn beside his head,
He had put, within his reach,
A box of counters and a red-vein'd stone,
A piece of glass abraded by the beach.
And six or seven shells,
A bottle with bluebells,
And two French copper coins, ranged there with careful art,
To comfort his sad heart.
So when that night I pray'd
To God, I wept, and said:
Ah, when at last we lie with tranced breath,
Not vexing Thee in death,
And thou rememberest of what toys
We made our joys,
How weakly understood
Thy great commanded good,
Then, fatherly not less
Than I whom Thou hast moulded from the clay,
Thou'lt leave thy wrath, and say,
'I will be sorry for their childishness.'

COVENTRY PATMORE   1823–1896   England

The Young Conquistador, 15

The young conquistador, 15, is growing:
wears amulets of ivory, has given up shoes,
& smokes everything.
Begging to be kissed, girls introduce themselves

in stores. And men make proposals
when he dozes in parks.
He yearns for Tokyo or France
but won't fly kites
or dance in the dark.
His only hero talks to God in public on the telephone.

Happily in debt, nearsighted
& born shameless

He sleeps on the beach, preferably alone.
'Love,' he says, 'is an ordeal for two.'

ROBERT PETERSON   *b*. 1924   USA

With Stephen in Maine

The huge mammalian rocks in front of the lawn,
domestic between the grass and the low tide –
Stephen has set his boat in one of the pools,
his hand the little god that makes it move.
It is cold, the sky the rough wool and gaberdine
of pictures someone almost talented has painted.
Off and on the sun, then Stephen is wading . . .

Yesterday we saw two gulls shot out of the sky.
One of them drifted into shore, broken, half-eaten,
green with the sea. When I found it this morning
all I could think to do was throw it back. One wing.
Its thin blood spread enough that Stephen is finger-
printed and painted with washing and wiping dry.
Even his boat, at the watermark, is stained.

I lift him, put him up on top of my shoulders.
From here he can watch the deep water pile, turn over.
He says, with wonder, that it looks like the ocean
killing itself. He wants to throw stones, he wants
to see how far this boat can sail, will float.

The mile or more from here to there is an order of color,
pitched white and black and dove- or green-gray, blue,

but far and hurt from where he is seeing.

STANLEY PLUMLY   *b.* 1939   USA

Rising Late and Playing with A-ts'ui, Aged Two

All the morning I have lain perversely in bed;
Now at dusk I rise with many yawns.
My warm stove is quick to get ablaze;
At the cold mirror I am slow in doing my hair.
With melted snow I boil fragrant tea;
Seasoned with curds I cook a milk-pudding.
At my sloth and greed there is no one but me to laugh;
My cheerful vigour none but myself knows.
The taste of my wine is mild and works no poison;
The notes of my harp are soft and bring no sadness.
To the Three Joys in the book of Mencius
I have added the fourth of playing with my baby-boy.

Written in 831

PO CHU-I   772–846   China
Translated by Arthur Waley

Daedalus

My son has birds in his head.

I know them now. I catch
the pitch of their calls, their shrill
cacophonies, their chitterings, their coos.
They hover behind his eyes and come to rest
on a branch, on a book, grow still,
claws curled, wings furled.
His is a bird world.

I learn the flutter of his moods,
his moments of swoop and soar.
From the ground I feel him try
the limits of the air –
sudden lift, sudden terror –
and move in time to cradle
his quivering, feathered fear.

At evening, in the tower,
I see him to sleep and see
the hooding-over of eyes,
the slow folding of wings,
I wake to his morning twitterings,
to the *croomb* of his becoming.

He chooses his selves – wren, hawk,
swallow or owl – to explore
the trees and rooftops of his heady wishing.
Tomtit, birdwit.
Am I to call him down, to give him
a grounding, teach him gravity?
Gently, gently.

Time tells us what we weigh, and soon enough
his feet will reach the ground.
Age, like a cage, will enclose him.
So the wise men said.

My son has birds in his head.

ALASTAIR REID   *b.* 1926   Scotland

To William Shelley

I

The billows on the beach are leaping around it,
    The bark is weak and frail,
The sea looks black, and the clouds that bound it
    Darkly strew the gale.
Come with me, thou delightful child,
Come with me, though the wave is wild,
And the winds are loose, we must not stay,
Or the slaves of the law may rend thee away.

II

They have taken thy brother and sister dear,
    They have made them unfit for thee;
They have withered the smile and dried the tear
    Which should have been sacred to me.
To a blighting faith and a cause of crime
They have bound them slaves in youthly prime,
And they will curse my name and thee
Because we fearless are and free.

III

Come thou, belovèd as thou art;
    Another sleepeth still
Near thy sweet mother's anxious heart,
    Which thou with joy shalt fill,

With fairest smiles of wonder thrown
On that which is indeed our own,
And which in distant lands will be
The dearest playmate unto thee.

IV

Fear not the tyrants will rule for ever,
    Or the priests of the evil faith;
They stand on the brink of that raging river,
    Whose waves they have tainted with death.
It is fed from the depths of a thousand dells,
Around them it foams and rages and swells;
And their swords and their sceptres I floating see,
Like wrecks on the surge of eternity.

V

Rest, rest, and shriek not, thou gentle child!
    The rocking of the boat thou fearest,
And the cold spray and the clamour wild? —
    There, sit between us two, thou dearest —
Me and thy mother — well we know
The storm at which thou tremblest so,
With all its dark and hungry graves,
Less cruel than the savage slaves
Who hunt us o'er these sheltering waves.

VI

This hour will in thy memory
    Be a dream of days forgotten long.
We soon shall dwell by the azure sea
Of serene and golden Italy,
Or Greece, the Mother of the free;
    And I will teach thine infant tongue
To call upon those heroes old
In their own language, and will mould
Thy growing spirit in the flame
Of Grecian lore, that by such name
A patriot's birthright thou mayst claim!

PERCY BYSSHE SHELLEY* 1792–1822 England

Death of a Son

(who died in a mental hospital aged one)

Something has ceased to come along with me.
Something like a person: something very like one.
    And there was no nobility in it
        Or anything like that.

Something was there like a one year
Old house, dumb as stone. While the near buildings
    Sang like birds and laughed
        Understanding the pact

They were to have with silence. But he
Neither sang nor laughed. He did not bless silence
    Like bread, with words.
        He did not forsake silence.

But rather, like a house in mourning
Kept the eye turned in to watch the silence while
    The other houses like birds
        Sang around him.

And the breathing silence neither
Moved nor was still.

I have seen stones: I have seen brick
But this house was made up of neither bricks nor stone
    But a house of flesh and blood
        With flesh of stone

And bricks for blood. A house
Of stones and blood in breathing silence with the other
    Birds singing crazy on its chimneys.
        But this was silence,

This was something else, this was
Hearing and speaking though he was a house drawn
    Into silence, this was
        Something religious in his silence.

Something shining in his quiet.
This was different this was altogether something else:
    Though he never spoke, this
        Was something to do with death.

    And then slowly the eye stopped looking
Inward. The silence rose and became still.
The look turned to the outer place and stopped,
    With the birds still shrilling around him.
        And as if he could speak.

He turned over on his side with his one year
Red as a wound
He turned over as if he could be sorry for this
And out of his eyes two great tears rolled, like
                stones, and he died.

JON SILKIN   1930–1997   England

Axe Handles

One afternoon the last week in April
Showing Kai how to throw a hatchet
One-half turn and it sticks in a stump.
He recalls the hatchet-head
Without a handle, in the shop
And go gets it, and wants it for his own.
A broken-off axe handle behind the door
Is long enough for a hatchet,
We cut it to length and take it
With the hatchet head
And working hatchet, to the wood block.
There I begin to shape the old handle
With the hatchet, and the phrase
First learned from Ezra Pound
Rings in my ears!
'When making an axe handle
      the pattern is not far off.'

And I say this to Kai
'Look: We'll shape the handle
By checking the handle
Of the axe we cut with —'
And he sees. And I hear it again:
It's in Lu Ji's *Wen Fu*, fourth century
AD 'Essay on Literature' — in the
Preface: 'In making the handle
Of an axe
By cutting wood with an axe
The model is indeed near at hand.'
My teacher Shih-hsiang Chen
Translated that and taught it years ago
And I see: Pound was an axe,
Chen was an axe, I am an axe
And my son a handle, soon
To be shaping again, model
And tool, craft of culture,
How we go on.

GARY SNYDER   *b.* 1930   USA

At Bedtime

Reading you the story you cannot understand
any more than another, before the light
goes out, I am distracted by the hand
turning the page too early or too late —

as I was in the bookshop, hearing today
that other father with the small son say:
'We need a book. What would you recommend
for a four-year-old starting to read?'

And a dam in my head broke under the thought
of things your simple hands would never make:
toys, love, and poems scattering the comfort
of commandments you can never break.

JON STALLWORTHY *b.* 1935 England

For My Child

Was it from some hunger
or from greater love —
but your mother is a witness to this:
I wanted to swallow you, my child,
when I felt your tiny body losing its heat
in my fingers
as though I were pressing
a warm glass of tea,
feeling its passage to cold.

You're no stranger, no guest,
for in this earth one does not
        give birth to aliens.
You reproduce yourself like a ring
and the rings fit into chains.

My child,
what else may I call you but: love.
Even without the word that is who you are,
you — seed of my every dream,
hidden third one,
who came from the world's corner
with the wonder of an unseen storm,
you who brought, rushed two together
to create you and rejoice: —

Why have you darkened creation
with the shutting of your tiny eyes
and left me begging outside
in the snow swept world
to which you have returned?

No cradle gave you pleasure
whose rocking
conceals in itself the pulse of the stars.
Let the sun crumble like glass
since you never beheld its light.
That drop of poison extinguished your faith —
you thought
it was warm sweet milk.

I wanted to swallow you, my child,
to feel the taste
of my anticipated future.
Perhaps in my blood
you will blossom as before.

But I am not worthy to be your grave.
So I bequeath you
to the summoning snow,
the snow — my first respite,
and you will sink
like a splinter of dusk
into its quiet depths
and bear greetings from me
to the frozen grasslands ahead —

Vilna Ghetto, 18 January 1943

ABRAHAM SUTZKEVER* *b.* 1913, Estonia   Israel
Translated by Seymour Mayne

The Son

It was your mother wanted you;
you were already half-formed
when I entered. But can I deny
the hunger, the loneliness bringing me in
from myself? And when you appeared
before me, there was no repentance
for what I had done, as there was shame
in the doing it; compassion only
for that which was too small to be called
human. The unfolding of your hands
was plant-like, your ear was the shell
I thundered in; your cries, when they came,
were those of a blind creature
trodden upon; pain not yet become grief.

R. S. THOMAS   *b.* 1913   Wales

Ways of Day

I have come all this way.
I am sitting in the shade.
Book on knee and mind on nothing,
I now fix my gaze
On my small son playing in the afternoon's blaze.

Convulsive and cantankerous,
Night heaved, and burning, the star
Fell. Oh, what do I remember?
I heard the swamp owl, night-long, call.
The far car's headlight swept the room wall.

I am the dark and tricky one.
I am watching from my shade.
Your tousled hair-tips prickle the sunlight.
I watch you at your sunlit play.
Teach me, my son, the ways of day.

ROBERT PENN WARREN   1905–1988   USA

Anecdote for Fathers

I have a boy of five years old;
His face is fair and fresh to see;
His limbs are cast in beauty's mould,
And dearly he loves me.

One morn we strolled on our dry walk,
Our quiet home all full in view,
And held such intermitted talk
As we are wont to do.

My thoughts on former pleasures ran;
I thought of Kilve's delightful shore,
Our pleasant home when spring began,
A long, long year before.

A day it was when I could bear
Some fond regrets to entertain;
With so much happiness to spare,
I could not feel a pain.

The green earth echoed to the feet
Of lambs that bounded through the glade,
From shade to sunshine, and as fleet
From sunshine back to shade.

Birds warbled round me – and each trace
Of inward sadness had its charm;
Kilve, thought I, was a favoured place,
And so is Liswyn farm.

My boy beside me tripped, so slim
And graceful in his rustic dress!
And, as we talked, I questioned him,
In very idleness.

'Now tell me, had you rather be,'
I said, and took him by the arm,
'On Kilve's smooth shore, by the green sea,
Or here at Liswyn farm?'

In careless mood he looked at me,
While still I held him by the arm,
And said, 'At Kilve I'd rather be
Than here at Liswyn farm.'

'Now, little Edward, say why so:
My little Edward, tell me why.' —
'I cannot tell, I do not know.' —
'Why, this is strange,' said I;

'For here are woods, hills smooth and warm:
There surely must some reason be
Why you would change sweet Liswyn farm
For Kilve by the green sea.'

At this my boy hung down his head,
He blushed with shame, nor made reply;
And three times to the child I said,
'Why, Edward, tell me why?'

His head he raised — there was in sight,
It caught his eye, he saw it plain —
Upon the house-top, glittering bright,
A broad and gilded vane.

Then did the boy his tongue unlock,
And eased his mind with this reply:
'At Kilve there was no weather-cock;
And that's the reason why.'

O dearest, dearest boy! my heart
For better lore would seldom yearn,
Could I but teach the hundredth part
Of what from thee I learn.

WILLIAM WORDSWORTH 1770–1850 England

Father
to
Child

'It Out-Herods Herod. Pray You, Avoid It'

Tonight my children hunch
Toward their Western, and are glad
As, with a Sunday punch,
The Good casts out the Bad.

And in their fairy tales
The warty giant and witch
Get sealed in doorless jails
And the match-girl strikes it rich.

I've made myself a drink.
The giant and witch are set
To bust out of the clink
When my children have gone to bed.

All frequencies are loud
With signals of despair;
In flash and morse they crowd
The rondure of the air.

For the wicked have grown strong,
Their numbers mock at death,
Their cow brings forth its young,
Their bull engendereth.

Their very fund of strength,
Satan, bestrides the globe;
He stalks its breadth and length
And finds out even Job.

Yet by quite other laws
My children make their case;
Half God, half Santa Claus,
But with my voice and face,

A hero comes to save
The poorman, beggarman, thief,
And make the world behave
And put an end to grief.

And that their sleep be sound
I say this childermas
Who could not, at one time,
Have saved them from the gas.

ANTHONY HECHT   *b.* 1923   USA

The Children in Our Midst

(Akbaadunaa tamshi 'ala l'ardi)

From on high, the grand design of providence
    reduced me to nothing on this earth.
This same providence robbed me of its store of riches
    and honour is all I have as wealth.
I might have had the world's arena to myself
    in its full length and breadth.
This same providence offered the gift of laughter
    but I have had to weep for grief,
Except that my young daughters run to and fro together,
    each as soft as the down of a dove.
Yes our children are our living lights,
    as they make their way in our midst.
Were the wind to blow even slightly against them,
    my eyes would refuse to close.

HITTAAN BIN AL-MU'ALLAA   7th–8th century   Arabia
Translated by David Pryce-Jones

My Thoughts

My thoughts?
                Far from the roof
sheltering you, my thoughts
are of you, my children, and the hopes
that lie in you. My summer days
have ripened and the sun
has started its decline. Each year
the shadow of your branches
creeps further up my wall
yet some furled petals still retain
the secret dazzle of your dawn.

I think of the two younger ones
laughing as they cry.
The threshold must be green
where they babble mingling
games with quarrels both with charm –
two flowers occasionally
rub against each other as they sway.

All fathers worry and I think
about the two older ones
already further from the shore
among deeper waves. They lean
their heads to one side now, the boy
all curiosity, the girl all thought.

Alone here, sad, I think these things
while sailors sing beneath the cliff.
The sea at evening
seems to breathe and sigh
when waves advance, recede.
The wind blends salt into the air
that stirs with strange
echoes of land and water.

I think of you, my children, seeing
a table surrounded with laughter,
a fireplace crackling,

all the piety and care
your mother and her father shed
in tenderness.
Here at my feet the clear sea spreads
set with sails and mirroring the stars.
Boatmen casually
glance from the unending
sea to the unending
sky and I think of you, my children,
trying to sound
the depth of love I have for you,
its gentleness, its power —
and in comparison how small the sea!

15 July 1837
by the sea at Fécamp

VICTOR HUGO* 1802–1885 France
Translated by Harry Guest

Parenthood

I have held what I hoped would become the best minds of a
    generation
Over the gutter outside an Italian coffee shop watching the
    small
Warm urine splatter on the asphalt — impatient to rejoin
An almond torta and a cappuccino at a formica table.
I have been a single parent with three children at a Chinese
    restaurant
The eldest five years old and each in turn demanding
My company as they fussed in toilets and my pork satay went
    cold.
They rarely went all at once; each child required an individual
Moment of inspiration — and when their toilet pilgrimage was
    ended
I have tried to eat the remains of my meal with twisting
    children

Beneath the table, screaming and grabbing in a scrimmage.
I have been wiping clean the fold between young buttocks as a
   pizza
I hoped to finish was removed from a red and white checked
   table cloth.
I have been pouring wine for women I was hoping to impress
When a daughter ran for help through guests urgently holding
   out
Her gift, a potty, which I took with the same courtesy
As she gave it, grateful to dispose of its contents so simply
In a flurry of water released by the pushing of a button.
I have been butted by heads which have told me to go away
   and I have done so,
My mouth has been wrenched by small hands wanting to reach
   down to my tonsils
As I lay in bed on Sunday mornings and the sun shone through
   the slats
Of dusty blinds. I have helpfully carried dilly-dalliers up steps
Who indignantly ran straight down and walked up by
   themselves.
My arms have become exhausted, bouncing young animals until
   they fell asleep
In my lap listening to Buxtehude. 'Too cold,' I have been told,
As I handed a piece of fruit from the refrigerator, and for weeks
   had to warm
Refrigerated apples in the microwave so milk teeth cutting
   green
Carbohydrate did not chill. I have pleasurably smacked small
   bottoms
Which have climbed up and arched themselves on my lap
   wanting the report
And tingle of my palm. I have known large round heads that
   bumped
And rubbed themselves against my forehead, and affectionate
   noses
That loved to displace inconvenient snot from themselves onto
   me.
The demands of their bodies have taken me to unfamiliar
   geographies.
I have explored the white tiles and stainless steel benches of
   restaurant kitchens

And guided short legs across rinsed floors smelling of detergent
Past men in white with heads lowered and cleavers dissecting
    and assembling
Mounds of sparkling pink flesh – and located the remote dark
    shrine
Of a toilet behind boxes of coarse green vegetables and long
    white radishes.
I have badgered half-asleep children along backstreets at night,
    carrying
Whom I could to my van. I have stumbled with them sleeping
    in my arms
Up concrete steps on winter nights after eating in Greek
    restaurants,
Counting each body, then slamming the door of my van and
    taking
My own body, the last of my tasks, to a cold bed free of
    arguments.
I have lived in the extreme latitudes of child rearing, the
    blizzard
Of the temper tantrum and my own not always wise or
    honourable response,
The midnight sun of the child calling for attention late at
    night,
And I have longed for the white courtyards and mediterranean
    calm of middle age.
Now these small bodies are becoming civilized people claiming
    they are not
Ashamed of a parent's overgrown garden and unpainted ceilings
Which a new arrival, with an infant's forthrightness, complains
    are 'old'.
And the father of this tribe sleeps in a bed which is warm with
    arguments.
Their bones elongate and put on weight and they draw away
    into space.
Their faces lengthen with responsibility and their own concerns.
I could clutch as they recede and fret for the push of miniature
    persons.
And claim them as children of my flesh – but my own body is
    where I must live.

GEOFFREY LEHMANN   *b.* 1940   Australia

Two Trinities

Are you ready? soul said again
smiling deep in the dark
where mind and I live passionately
grain rasping across grain
in a strangled question-mark
— or so we have lived lately.

I looked through the hollow keyhole
at my wife not young any more
with my signature on her forehead
and her spirit hers and whole
unsigned by me — as before
we knew each other, and wed.

I looked at my grown daughter
cool and contained as a flower
whose bees I shall not be among —
vivid as white spring water
full of womanish power
like the first phrases of a song.

I looked at my son, and wept
in my mouth's cave to see
the seed ready for sowing
and the harvest unready to be reaped —
green fruit shocked from the tree,
the bird killed on the wing.

Well? soul said and I said,
Mind and I are at one
to go with you now — finally
joined now to be led —
for our place here is gone:
we are not among those three.

Soul said, *Now come with me.*

KENNETH MACKENZIE   1913–1955   Australia

In Modern Dress

A pair of blackbirds
warring in the roses,
one or two poppies

losing their heads,
the trampled lawn
a battlefield of dolls.

Branch by pruned branch,
a child has climbed
the family tree

to queen it over us:
we groundlings search
the flowering cherry

till we find her face,
its pale prerogative
to rule our hearts.

Sir Walter Raleigh
trails his comforter
about the muddy garden,

a full-length Hilliard
in miniature hose
and padded pants.

How rakishly upturned
his fine moustache
of oxtail soup,

foreshadowing, perhaps,
some future time
of altered favour,

stuck in the high chair
like a pillory, features
pelted with food.

So many expeditions
to learn the history
of this little world:

I watch him grub
in the vegetable patch
and ponder the potato

in its natural state
for the very first time,
or found a settlement

of leaves and sticks,
cleverly protected
by a circle of stones.

But where on earth
did he manage to find
that cigarette end?

Rain and wind.
The day disintegrates.
I observe the lengthy

inquisition of a worm
then go indoors to face
a scattered armada

of picture hooks
on the dining room floor,
the remains of a ruff

on my glass of beer,
Sylvia Plath's *Ariel*
drowned in the bath.

Washing hair, I kneel
to supervise a second rinse
and act the courtier:

tiny seed pearls,
tingling into sight,
confer a kind of majesty.

And I am author
of this toga'd tribune
on my aproned lap,

who plays his part
to an audience of two,
repeating my words.

CRAIG RAINE *b.* 1944 England

The Green Tree

Ever since my daughters started to walk
I have had increasing difficulty with my eyes.
I remember the day Wendy took her first steps, when
she said 'bamboo' and waddled over to pat the rusty
      bumper

of a truck, I could barely make out the writing
scrawled in dirt on the trailer and had trouble focusing
as she stepped into its shadow.
The morning in Maine when she raced down the beach

and splashed into the ocean before I could reach her,
I actually mistook her for another little girl in pink
whom – I am sorry to say – I began leading slowly out of
      the water.
Then there is Jill: when she first walked I remember

looking at her and thinking, 'I am a camera fading back,
      back.'
Years later when she would go rollerskating with Wendy
my eyes were so bad I could no longer tell
where the sidewalks left off and my daughters began.

By now everything has faded into fine print. I
have been to a doctor who says he is also troubled,
but has sons. My only son died one day after
birth, weighing two pounds. His name was

Jeffrey, but I have always preferred to call him
    'Under-the-Earth'
or, especially on rainy days, 'Under-the-Sod'. In fact,
sometimes I catch myself repeating these words: 'My
    only son,
Under-the-Sod, is playing over there by the green tree.'

JAMES REISS   *b.* 1941   USA

'God gave to me a child in part'

God gave to me a child in part,
Yet wholly gave the father's heart;
Child of my soul, O whither now,
Unborn, unmothered, goest thou?

You came, you went, and no man wist;
Hapless, my child, no breast you kist;
On no dear knees, a privileged babbler, clomb,
Nor knew the kindly feel of home.

My voice may reach you, O my dear, –
A father's voice perhaps the child may hear;
And, pitying, you may turn your view
On that poor father whom you never knew.

Alas! alone he sits, who then,
Immortal among mortal men
Sat hand in hand with love, and all day through
With your dear mother wondered over you.

ROBERT LOUIS STEVENSON   1850–1894   Scotland

Before A Birth

Hear the finger of God, that has fixed the pole of the heavens.
There the Pleiades spin, and Orion, that great hunter.
Stars silver the night, where Hercules moves with Arcturus.
Spawning systems amaze: they respond to an ordered music.
Ultimate distance vibrates, close to that intimate spring.

Stoop, for nothing can weigh the inscrutable movement of
 beech leaves
Silken, of brightest green, which May has transfigured like
 music
Born of their trumpet-like buds; this movement, ever so little,
Hangs on a leaf-hidden breath, so near to the nest of the
 greenfinch;
Nothing so secret as this, under the shadows of Spring.

Love, your measure is full: the stars of infinite distance,
Needing the shade of a bird to knit our time to the timeless,
Fell to-night through the dusk. Ear close to the ground-root, I
 listened,
Feeling the sunlight fall through May's untranslatable evening;
Then, upon earth, my pulse beat with the pulse of the dead.

Guests go into the house. On the floor, attended by shadows,
Late I can hear one walk, a step, and a fruitful silence.
Touch, finger of Wine, this well of crystalline water
And this earthenware jug, that knows the language of silence;
Touch, for darkness is near, that brings your glory to bed.

VERNON WATKINS 1906–1967 Wales

Mother
to
Daughter

In the Distance

In the distance, O my lady,
　　Little lady, turned of three!
Will the woodland seem as shady?
　　Will the sunshine seem as free?
Will the primrose buds come peeping
　　Quite as bright beneath the tree?
And the brook sing in its leaping
　　As they do for you and me?

O my darling, O my daisy,
　　In the days that are to be,
In the distance dim and hazy
　　With its lights far out at sea;
When you're tall and fair and stately,
　　Will you ever care for me?
Will you prize my coming greatly
　　As you did when you were three?

CECIL FRANCES ALEXANDER　1818–1895　England

The Pomegranate

The only legend I have ever loved is
The story of a daughter lost in hell.
And found and rescued there.
Love and blackmail are the gist of it.
Ceres and Persephone the names.
And the best thing about the legend is
I can enter it anywhere. And have.
As a child in exile in
A city of fogs and strange consonants,

I read it first and at first I was
An exiled child in the crackling dusk of
The underworld, the stars blighted. Later
I walked out in a summer twilight
Searching for my daughter at bedtime.
When she came running I was ready
To make any bargain to keep her.
I carried her back past whitebeams.
And wasps and honey-scented buddleias.
But I was Ceres then and I knew
Winter was in store for every leaf
On every tree on that road.
Was inescapable for each one we passed.
And for me.
It is winter
And the stars are hidden.
I climb the stairs and stand where I can see
My child asleep beside her teen magazines,
Her can of Coke, her plate of uncut fruit.
The pomegranate! How did I forget it?
She could have come home and been safe
And ended the story and all
Our heartbroken searching but she reached
Out a hand and plucked a pomegranate.
She put out her hand and pulled down
The French sound for apple and
The noise of stone and the proof
That even in the place of death,
At the heart of legend, in the midst
Of rocks full of unshed tears
Ready to be diamonds by the time
The story was told, a child can be
Hungry. I could warn her. There is still a chance.
The rain is cold. The road is flint-coloured.
The suburb has cars and cable television.
The veiled stars are above ground.
It is another world. But what else
Can a mother give her daughter but such
Beautiful rifts in time?
If I defer the grief I will diminish the gift.
The legend must be hers as well as mine.

She will enter it. As I have.
She will wake up. She will hold
The papery, flushed skin in her hand.
And to her lips. I will say nothing.

EAVAN BOLAND   *b.* 1944   Ireland

After Reading Mickey in the Night Kitchen
for the Third Time Before Bed

'I'm in the milk and
the milk's in me! . . . I'm Mickey!'

My daughter spreads her legs
to find her vagina:
hairless, this mistaken
bit of nomenclature
is what a stranger cannot touch
without her yelling. She demands
to see mine and momentarily
we're a lopsided star
among the spilled toys,
my prodigious scallops
exposed to her neat cameo.

And yet the same glazed
tunnel, layered sequences.
She is three; that makes this
innocent. *We're pink!*
she shrieks, and bounds off.

Every month she wants
to know where it hurts and
what the wrinkled string means
between my legs. *This is good blood*
I say, but that's wrong, too.

How to tell her that it's what makes us —
black mother, cream child.
That we're in the pink
and the pink's in us.

RITA DOVE   *b.* 1952   USA

On Visiting the Grave of My Stillborn Little Girl
Sunday July 4th 1836

I made a vow within my soul, O Child,
When thou wert laid beside my weary heart,
With marks of death on every tender part
That, if in time a living infant smiled,
Winning my ear with gentle sounds of love
In sunshine of such joy, I still would save
A green rest for thy memory, O Dove!
And oft times visit thy small, nameless grave.
Thee have I not forgot, my firstborn, though
Whose eyes ne'er opened to my wistful gaze,
Whose sufferings stamped with pain thy little brow;
I think of thee in these far happier days,
And thou, my child, from thy bright heaven see
How well I keep my faithful vow to thee.

ELIZABETH GASKELL   1810–1865   England

Iva's Pantoum

We pace each other for a long time.
I packed my anger with the beef jerky.
You are the baby on the mountain. I am
in a cold stream where I led you.

I packed my anger with the beef jerky.
You are the woman sticking her tongue out
in a cold stream where I led you.
You are the woman with spring water palms.

You are the woman sticking her tongue out.
I am the woman who matches sounds.
You are the woman with spring water palms.
I am the woman who copies.

You are the woman who matches sounds.
You are the woman who makes up words.
You are the woman who copies
her cupped palm with her fist in clay.

I am the woman who makes up words.
You are the woman who shapes
a drinking bowl with her fist in clay.
I am the woman with rocks in her pockets.

I am the woman who shapes.
I was a baby who knew names.
You are the child with rocks in her pockets.
You are the girl in a plaid dress.

You are the woman who knows names.
You are the baby who could fly.
You are the girl in a plaid dress
upside-down on the monkey bars.

You are the baby who could fly
over the moon from a swinging perch
upside-down on the monkey bars.
You are the baby who eats meat.

Over the moon from a swinging perch
the feather goblin calls her sister.
You are the baby who eats meat
the bitch wolf hunts and chews for you.

The feathery goblin calls her sister:
'You are braver than your mother.
The bitch wolf hunts and chews for you.
What are you whining about now?'

You are braver than your mother
and I am not a timid woman:
what are you whining about now?
My palms itch with slick anger,

and I'm not a timid woman.
You are the woman I can't mention;
my palms itch with slick anger.
You are the heiress of scraped knees.

You are the woman I can't mention
to a woman I want to love.
You are the heiress of scraped knees:
scrub them in mountain water.

To a woman, I want to love
women you could turn into,
scrub them in mountain water,
stroke their astonishing faces.

Women you could turn into
the scare mask of Bad Mother
stroke their astonishing faces
in the silver-scratched sink mirror.

The scare mask of Bad Mother
crumbles to chunked, pinched clay,
sinks in the silver-scratched mirror.
You are the Little Robber Girl, who

crumbles the clay chunks, pinches
her friend, gives her a sharp knife.
You are the Little Robber Girl, who
was any witch's youngest daughter.

Our friend gives you a sharp knife,
shows how the useful blades open.
Was any witch's youngest daughter
golden and bold as you? You run and

show how the useful blades open.
You are the baby on the mountain. I am
golden and bold as you. You run and
we pace each other for a long time.

MARILYN HACKER   *b.* 1942   USA

Dialogue

If an angel came with one wish
I might say, deliver that child
who died before birth, into life.
Let me see what she might have become.
He would bring her into a room
fair skinned   the bones of her hands
would press on my shoulderblades
in our long embrace
                              we would sit
with the albums spread on our knees:
now here are your brothers   and here
your sister   here the old house
among trees and espaliered almonds.

– But where am I?
                              Ah my dear
I have only one picture
                                    here
in my head   I saw you lying
still folded   one moment   forever
your head bent down to your heart
eyes closed on unspeakable wisdom
your delicate frog-pale fingers
                                        spread
apart as if you were playing
a woodwind instrument.
       – My name?
                              It was never given.
       – Where is my grave?
                              in my head   I suppose
the hospital burnt you.
       – Was I beautiful?
                              To me.
       – Do you mourn for me every day?
Not at all   it is more than thirty years
I am feeling the coolness of age
the perspectives of memory change.
Pearlskull   what lifts you here
from night-drift to solemn ripeness?
Mushroom dome? Gourd plumpness?
The frog in my pot of basil?
       – It is none of these, but a rhythm
         the bones of my fingers   dactylic
         rhetoric smashed from your memory.
         Forget me again.
                              Had I lived
         no rhythm would be the same
         nor my brothers and sister feast
         in the world's eternal house.

Overhead   wings of cloud
         burning   and under my feet
              stones marked with demons' teeth.

GWEN HARWOOD   b. 1920   New Zealand

Mothers, Daughters

Through every night we hate,
preparing the next day's
war. She bangs the door.
Her face laps up my own
despair, the sour, brown eyes,
the heavy hair she won't
tie back. She's cruel,
as if my private meanness
found a way to punish us.
We gnaw at each other's
skulls. Give me what's mine.
I'd haul her back, choking
myself in her, herself
in me. There is a book
called *Poisons* on her shelf.
Her room stinks with incense,
animal turds, hamsters
she strokes like silk. They
exercise on the bathroom
floor, and two drop through
the furnace vent. The whole
house smells of the accident,
the hot skins, the small
flesh rotting. Six days
we turn the gas up then
to fry the dead. I'd fry
her head if I could until
she cried love, love me!

All she won't let me do.
Her stringy figure in
the windowed room shares
its thin bones with no one.
Only her shadow on the glass
waits like an older sister.

Now she stalks, leans forward,
concentrates merely on getting
from here to there. Her feet
are bare. I hear her breathe
where I can't get in. If I
break through to her, she will
drive nails into my tongue.

SHIRLEY KAUFMAN   *b.* 1923   USA

The Dead to the Living

Work while it is day: the night cometh, when no man can work

In the childhood of April, while purple woods
    With the young year's blood in them smiled,
I passed through the lanes and the wakened fields,
    And stood by the grave of the child.
And the pain awoke that is never dead
    Though it sometimes sleeps, and again
It set its teeth in this heart of mine,
    And fastened its claws in my brain:
For it seemed so hard that the little hands
    And the little well-loved head
Should be out of reach of my living lips,
    And be side by side with the dead —
Not side by side with us who had loved,
    But with these who had never seen
The grace of the smile, the gold of the hair,
    And the eyes of my baby-queen.
Yet with trees about where the brown birds build,
    And with long green grass above,
She lies in the cold, sweet breast of earth
    Beyond the reach of our love;
Whatever befalls in the coarse, loud world,
    We know she will never wake.

When I thought of the sorrow she might have known,
  I was almost glad for her sake . . .
Tears might have tired those kiss-closed eyes,
  Grief hardened the mouth I kissed;
I was almost glad that my dear was dead
  Because of the pain she had missed.
Oh, if I could but have died a child
  With a white child-soul like hers,
As pure as the wind-flowers down in the copse,
  Where the soul of the spring's self stirs;
Or, if I had only done with it all,
  And might lie by her side unmoved!
I envied the very clods of earth
  Their place near the child I loved!

And my soul rose up in revolt at life,
  As I stood dry-eyed by her grave,
When sudden the grass of the churchyard sod
  Rolled back like a green, smooth wave;
The brown earth looked like the brown sea rocks,
  The tombstones were white like spray,
And white like surf were the curling folds
  Of the shrouds where the dead men lay;
For each in his place with his quiet face
  I saw the dead lie low,
Who had worked and suffered and found life sad,
  So many sad years ago.
Unchanged by time I saw them lie
  As when first they were laid to rest,
The tired eyes closed, the sad lips still,
  And the work-worn hands on the breast.
There were some who had found the green world so grey
  They had left it before their time,
And some were little ones like my dear,
  And some had died in their prime;
And some were old, they had had their fill
  Of bitter, unfruitful hours,
And knew that none of them, none, had known
  A flower of a hope like ours!

Through their shut eyelids the dead looked up,
    And without a voice they said:
'We lived without hope, without hope we died,
    And hopeless we lie here dead;
And death *is* better than life that draws
    Pain in, as it draws in breath,
If life never dreams of a coming day
    When life shall not envy death.
Through the dark of our hours and our times we lived,
    Uncheered by a single ray
Of such hope as lightens the lives of you
    Who are finding life hard to-day;
With our little lanterns of human love
    We lighted our dark, warm night —
But you in the chill of the dawn are set
    With your face to the eastern light.
Freedom is waiting with hands held out
    Till you tear the veil from her face —
And when once men have seen the light of her eyes,
    And felt her divine embrace,
The light of the world will be risen indeed,
    And will shine in the eyes of men,
And those who come after will find life fair,
    And their lives worth living then!
Will you strive to the light in your loud, rough world,
    That these things may come to pass,
Or lie in the shadow beside the child,
    And strive to the sun through the grass?'
'My world while I may,' I cried; 'but you
    Whose lives were as dark as your grave?'
'We too are a part of the coming night,'
    They called through the smooth, green wave.
Their white shrouds gleamed as the flood of green
    Rolled over and hid them from me —
Hid all but the little hands and the hair,
    And the face that I always see.

EDITH NESBIT   1858–1924   England

A Natal Address to My Child, March 19th 1844

Hail to thy puggy nose, my Darling,
Fair womankind's last added scrap,
That, callow as an unfledg'd starling,
Liest screaming in the Nurse's lap.

No locks thy tender cranium boasteth,
No lashes veil thy gummy eye
And, like some steak gridiron toasteth,
Thy skin is red and crisp and dry.

Thy mouth is swollen past describing,
Its corners twisted as in scorn
Of all the Leech is now prescribing
To doctor thee, the newly born.

Sweet little lump of flannel binding,
Thou perfect cataract of clothes,
Thy many folds there's no unwinding
Small mummy without arms or toes!

And am I really then thy Mother?
My very child I cannot doubt thee,
Rememb'ring all the fuss and bother
And moans and groans I made about thee!

'Tis now thy turn to groan and grumble,
As if afraid to enter life,
To dare each whipping scar and tumble
And task and toil with which 'tis rife.

O baby of the wise round forehead,
Be not too thoughtful ere thy time;
Life is not truly quite so horrid –
Oh! how she squalls! – she can't bear rhyme!

ELIZA OGILVY 1822–1912 England

The Month of June: 13½

As my daughter approaches graduation and
puberty at the same time, at her
own calm deliberate serious rate,
she begins to kick up her heels, jazz out her
hands, thrust out her hip-bones, chant
I'm great! I'm great! She feels 8th grade coming
open around her, a chrysalis cracking and
letting her out, it falls behind her and
joins the other husks on the ground,
7th grade, 6th grade, the
purple rind of 5th grade, the
hard jacket of 4th when she had so much pain,
3rd grade, 2nd, the dim cocoon of
1st grade back there somewhere on the path, and
kindergarten like a strip of thumb-suck blanket
taken from the actual blanket they wrapped her in at birth.
The whole school is coming off her shoulders like a
cloak unclasped, and she dances forth in her
jerky sexy child's joke dance of
self, self, her throat tight and a
hard new song coming out of it, while her
two dark eyes shine
above her body like a good mother and a
good father who look down and
love everything their baby does, the way she
lives their love.

SHARON OLDS   *b.* 1942   USA

To a Daughter at Fourteen Forsaking the Violin

All year, Mozart went under
the sea of rock punk reggae
that crashed into your room every
night and wouldn't recede however
I sandbagged our shore
and swore to keep the house dry.
Your first violin, that halfsize
rented model, slipped out of tune
as you played Bach by ear
Suzuki method with forty other virtuosos
who couldn't tie their shoes.
Then such progress: your own
fiddle, the trellised notes you read,
recitals where I sat on hard chairs.
Your playing made me the kid.
If I had those fingers! . . .
Five of yours grasped my pinky,
the world before you grew teeth.
OK. They're your fingers.
To paint the nails of, put rings on,
hold cigarettes in, make obscene
gestures or farewells with.

CAROLE SIMMONS OLES *b.* 1939 USA

Darwin's Great-great-great-granddaughter Smiles

Involuntary at first, they say —
a muscle-spasm, relaxation after wind —
this is smile from outer space, slowly engraving
individual, karma, race. It will end as courtesy's ghost
on quarried cheeks. A hundred years old,
your great-grandmother over the fen
responds to no pattern now but smile,
forgets the orchid she discovered,
the aquilegia named after her.

This minute change of face will draw you in
with the rest of us, to ambiguity.
Skeletons smile into earth while you
my winter daughter on a ruthless planet
struggle to make your new smile social.
Neurology sketches community's coin.
After this the meanings of smile
will not leave you alone.
It's a form of suffering too

and I, to whom you give this first
extraordinary signal, cannot guess
how you will use it. Who will be there
to undo it, say Yes, or misunderstand,
as I, growing separately older,
watch chalk and lemon leaves
flick over your ambiguous
no longer baby face
under tents of waving trees?

RUTH PADEL   *b.* 1944   England

Double Ritual

for Baby Thérèse and Grandpa Mendel

Death thresholded old man hold
Upon your uncertain lap – here, hold!
Upon your near centuried lap
Your golden child.

And smile your ancient heartworn ache:
There is no place for an old man.

This is the dance of youth and old age,
Kick high!
You wear death in place of the features
We knew. Kick high! Kick high!

Death's intervening face affronts my gaze,
Oh no. This is no place.

Too late: it scarcely seems worth the journey's weight
To bring the child's gaiety for your poor sight.
Dim old man, dear grandpa, homeless and confined,
I grieve years long with an enduring grief

For you, earth ridden, wandering and shackled, in the hospital
Of an old age home. There is no place for an old man.

That she may look upon the earth
I cast her on, and weep for all the shipwrecks,
All the castaways,
That she may view the sorrow

Of unalterable loneliness
Before her infant mind can penetrate its mysteries,

To inoculate her spirit
Against the dreadful vagaries
Of brutal man, I bring her here,
And for your benedictine touch, your glance, your winging
    wishes.

Where there is no place for an old man
There is no place for anyone.

But, there! she moves upon your lap
As though the great wheel on which we all ride
Stirred her, as though wheels, worlds, the moving years
Of centuries leaned upon her tiny thoughtful form

As she sits, gazing out from the bright rim of all the heavens
Upon the shell of night.

DACHINE RAINER   *b.* 1921   USA

Rebeca in a Mirror

Our little tantrum, flushed and misery-hollow,
sits having it out
in a mirror; drawn stiff as it
till her joke of a body, from flat,
flaps with the spasms of crying.
The small eyes frighten
the small eyes clutching
out of such puffed intensity of rage.
She will not look at people about, or follow
a dangled toy. No one can budge her huge
fury of refusal; being accustomed
to orchards of encouraging faces rolled in her lap,
cloud-bursts of ministering teats and spoons
and the pair of deft pin-welding scavengers
that keep her clean,
she is appalled by her own lonely image.
And we, that she's into
this share of knowledge,
and is ridiculously
comic in her self-feeding anger,
her frantic
blindness by now to the refuge
of a dozen anchoring shoulders and outheld hands,
vassals,
her multitudes . . .

Yet who can be more alone, months walled
in her cot's white straw,
the family hushed
and hovering, afraid to touch
so small
a trigger of uproar;
or so much as flutter
one of her million or more
petulant rufflers spoiling for noise and action
around the nerve-end flares that signal ruction?
And think, she has not long come
through a year of twilight time in one gradual place
further and faster
than death, or the endless relays
of causeless disaster;
frail-cauled, a hero, past perils vaster than space
she has come —
and can never re-enter
the unasked bodily friendship
of her first home.

JUDITH RODRIGUEZ   *b.* 1936   Australia

Broken Moon

(for Emma)

Twelve, small as six,
strength, movement, hearing
all given in half measure,
my daughter,
child of genetic carelessness,
walks uphill, always.

I watch her morning face;
precocious patience as she hooks each sock,
creeps it up her foot,
aims her jersey like a quoit.
My fingers twitch;
her private frown deters.

Her jokes can sting:
'My life is like dressed crab
— lot of effort, rather little meat.'
Yet she delights in seedlings taking root,
finding a fossil,
a surprise dessert.

Chopin will not yield to her stiff touch;
I hear her cursing.
She paces Bach exactly,
firm rounding of perfect cadences.
Somewhere inside
she is dancing a courante.

In dreams she skims the sand,
curls toes into the ooze of pools,
leaps on to stanchions.
Awake, her cousins take her hands;
they lean into the waves,
stick-child between curved sturdiness.

She turns away from stares,
laughs at the boy who asks
if she will find a midget husband.
Ten years ago, cradling her,
I showed her the slice of silver in the sky.
'Moon broken,' she said.

CAROLE SATYAMURTI *b.* 1939 England

Pain for a Daughter

Blind with love, my daughter
has cried nightly for horses,
those long-necked marchers and churners
that she has mastered, any and all,
reigning them in like a circus hand –
the excitable muscles and the ripe neck;
tending this summer, a pony and a foal.
She who is too squeamish to pull
a thorn from the dog's paw,
watched her pony blossom with distemper,
the underside of the jaw swelling
like an enormous grape.
Gritting her teeth with love,
she drained the boil and scoured it
with hydrogen peroxide until pus
ran like milk on the barn floor.

Blind with loss all winter,
in dungarees, a ski jacket and a hard hat,
she visits the neighbours' stable,
our acreage not zoned for barns;
they who own the flaming horses
and the swan-whipped thoroughbred
that she tugs at and cajoles,
thinking it will burn like a furnace
under her small-hipped English seat.

Blind with pain she limps home.
The thoroughbred has stood on her foot.
He rested there like a building.
He grew into her foot until they were one.
The marks of the horseshoe printed
into her flesh, the tips of her toes ripped
off like pieces of leather,
three toenails swirled like shells
and left to float in blood in her riding boot.

Blind with fear, she sits on the toilet,
her foot balanced over the washbasin,
her father, hydrogen peroxide in hand,
performing the rites of the cleansing.
She bites on a towel, sucked in breath,
sucked in and arched against the pain,
her eyes glancing off me where
I stand at the door, eyes locked
on the ceiling, eyes of a stranger,
and then she cries . . .
Oh my God, help me!
Where a child would have cried *Mama!*
Where a child would have believed *Mama!*
she bit the towel and called on God
and I saw her life stretch out . . .
I saw her torn in childbirth,
and I saw her, at that moment,
in her own death and I knew that she knew.

ANNE SEXTON   1928–1974   USA

After the Death of Her Daughter in Childbirth, Looking at the Child

Leaving us behind,
Whom will she have pitied more –
Infant or mother?
My child it was for me:
Her child it must have been.

Recklessly
I cast myself away;
Perhaps
A heart in love
Becomes a deep ravine?

Never could I think
Our love a worldly commonplace
On this morning when
For the first time my heart
Is filled with many thoughts.

As the rains of spring
Fall, day after day, so I
Fare on through time
While by the fence the grasses grow
And green spreads everywhere.

From that first night,
Although I have not wept
Cold, rainy tears upon my bed,
Yet I have recklessly
Slept in strange places and strange ways.

From darkness
Into the path of darkness
Must I enter:
Shine upon me from afar,
O moon above the mountain crest.

IZUMI SHIKIBU   10th century   Japan
Translated by Edwin A. Cranston

Sonnet

There's one I miss. A little questioning maid
   That held my finger, trotting by my side,
   And smiled out of her pleased eyes open wide,
Wondering and wiser at each word I said.
And I must help her frolics if she played,
   And I must feel her trouble if she cried;
   My lap was hers past right to be denied;
She did my bidding, but I more obeyed.

Dearer she is to-day, dearer and more;
   Closer to me, since sister womanhoods meet;
Yet, like poor mothers some long while bereft,
I dwell on toward ways, quaint memories left,
   I miss the approaching sound of pit-pat feet,
The eager baby voice outside my door.

AUGUSTA WEBSTER   1837—1894   England

*Mother
to
Son*

On a Son Returned to New Zealand

He is my green branch growing in a far plantation.
He is my first invention.

No one can be in two places at once.
So we left Athens on the same morning.
I was in a hot railway carriage, crammed
between Serbian soldiers and peasant
women, on sticky seats, with nothing to
drink but warm mineral water.
                         He was
in a cabin with square windows, sailing
across the Mediterranean, fast,
to Suez.
          Then I was back in London
in the tarnished summer, remembering,
as I folded his bed up, and sent the
television set away. Letters came
from Aden and Singapore, late.
                         He was
already in his father's house, on the
cliff-top, where the winter storms roll across
from Kapiti Island, and the flax bends
before the wind. He could go no further.

He is my bright sea-bird on a rocky beach.

FLEUR ADCOCK *b.* 1934, New Zealand England

Shards

You cannot leave your mother an orphan.   JOYCE

I

For me, deprived of fire and water,
Separated from my only son . . .
Being on the infamous scaffold of misfortune
Is like being beneath the canopy of a throne . . .

II

How well he's succeeded, this fierce debater,
All the way to the Yenisey plains . . .
To you he's a vagabond, rebel, conspirator —
To me he is — an only son.

III

Seven thousand and three kilometers . . .
Don't you hear your mother's call
In the north wind's frightful howl?
Cooped up, surrounded by adversity,
You grow wild there, you grow savage — you are dear,
You are the last and the first, you — are ours.
Over my Leningrad grave
Spring wanders indifferently.

IV

When and to whom did I talk?
Why didn't I hide from people
That my son was rotting in the camps,
That they flogged my Muse to death.
I am more guilty than anyone on earth
Who ever was, is now, or ever will be.
And to lie about in a madhouse
Would be a great honor for me.

V

You raised me up, like a slain beast
On a bloody hook,
So that sniggering, and not believing,
Foreigners wandered in
And wrote in their respectable papers
That my incomparable gift had died out,
That I had been a poet among poets,
But my thirteenth hour had struck.

ANNA AKHMATOVA*   1889–1966   USSR
Translated by Judith Hemschemeyer

On My Son's Return out of England, July 17, 1661

All praise to Him who hath now turned
My fears to joys, my sighs to song,
My tears to smiles, my sad to glad;
He's come for whom I waited long.

Thou didst preserve him as he went,
In raging storms didst safely keep,
Didst that ship bring to quiet port.
The other sank low in the deep.

From dangers great Thou didst him free
Of pirates who were near at hand,
And order'st so the adverse wind
That he before them got to land.

In country strange Thou didst provide,
And friends raised him in every place,
And courtesies of sundry sorts
From such as 'fore ne'er saw his face.

In sickness when he lay full sore,
His help and his physician wert.
When royal ones that time did die,
Thou healed'st his flesh and cheered his heart.

From trouble and encumbers Thou
Without all fraud didst set him free,
That without scandal he might come
To th'land of his nativity.

On eagles' wings him hither brought
Through want and dangers manifold,
And thus hath granted my request
That I Thy mercies might behold.

O help me pay Thy vows, O Lord,
That ever I may thankful be
And may put him in mind of what
Thou'st done for him, and so for me.

In both our hearts erect a frame
Of duty and of thankfulness,
That all Thy favours great received
Our upright walking may express.

O Lord, grant that I may never forget Thy loving kindness in
    this particular, and how graciously Thou hast answered my
    desires.

ANNE BRADSTREET   1612–1672   USA

A Little Child's Wreath

in memoriam R. M.

Our Roger loved the fields, the flowers, the trees;
Great London jarred him; he was ill at ease
And alien in the stir, the noise, the press;
The city vexed his perfect gentleness.

So, loving him, we sent him from the town
To where the autumn leaves were falling brown,
And the November primrose, pale and dim,
In his own garden-plot delighted him.

There, like his flowers, he would thrive and grow,
We in our fondness thought. But God said: No,
Your way is loving, but not wholly wise;
My way is best — to give him Paradise.

Turn where I will, I miss, I miss my sweet;
By my lone fire, or in the crowded way
Once so familiar to his joyous feet,
I miss, I hunger for him all the day.

This is the house wherefrom his welcome rang;
These are the wintry walks where he and I
Would pause to mark if a stray robin sang,
Or some new sunset-flame enriched the sky.

Here, where we crossed the dangerous road, and where
Unutterably desolate I stand,
How often, peering though the sombre air,
I felt the sudden tightening of his hand!

Round me the city looms, void, waste and wild,
Wanting the presence of one little child.

ELIZABETH RACHEL CHAPMAN   1827–1896   England

How Lies Grow

The first time I lied to my baby, I told him that it was his face
on the baby food jar. The second time I lied to my baby, I told
him that he was the best baby in the world, that I hoped he'd
never leave me. Of course I want him to leave me someday. I
don't want him to become one of those fat shadows who live in
their mother's houses watching game shows all day. The third
time I lied to my baby I said, 'Isn't she nice?' of the woman who'd

caressed him in his carriage. She was old and ugly and had a disease. The fourth time I lied to my baby, I told him the truth, I thought. I told him how he'd have to leave me someday or risk becoming a man in a bow tie who eats macaroni on Fridays. I told him it was for the best, but then I thought, I want him to live with me forever. Someday he'll leave me: then what will I do?

MAXINE CHERNOFF *b.* 1952 USA

The Scholar

You often went to breathe a timeless air
And walk with those you loved, perhaps the most.
You spoke to Plato. You were native there.
Like one who made blind Homer sing to him,
You visited the caves where sirens swim
Their deep indented coast
                        With us you seemed
A quiet happy sailor come of late
From those strange seas you best could navigate,
Knowing a world that others only dreamed.
Almost we looked for spray upon your hair,
Who met you, silent-footed on the stair,
Like an Elysian ghost.
                        So on that day
You left us on a deep withdrawing tide,
We dared not beg you, with one sigh, to stay
Or turn from your discoveries aside.

FRANCES CORNFORD* 1886–1960 England

The Apple Trees

Your son presses against me
his small intelligent body.

I stand beside his crib
as in another dream
you stood among trees hung
with bitten apples
holding out your arms.
I did not move
but saw the air dividing
into panes of color — at the very last
I raised him to the window saying
See what you have made
and counted out the whittled ribs,
the heart on its blue stalk
as from among the trees
the darkness issued:

In the dark room your son sleeps.
The walls are green, the walls
are spruce and silence.
I wait to see how he will leave me.
Already on his hand the map appears
as though you carved it there,
the dead fields, women rooted to the river.

LOUISE GLÜCK   *b.* 1943   USA

Mother Stone

My father was a tall man who approved of beating,
but my mother, like a mother stone,
preferred us to be sitting in a small room
lined with damson-coloured velvet
thinking quietly to ourselves, undisturbed;
everything was slow and beautiful
when we were being punished: all we had to do
was watch the dark-red petals' roses
press against each other in the slight breeze
on the window pane, and blossoms fall
in silence from the cherry-tree;

and now my son is lying in a long white shirt
across our eiderdown, trying to stay awake,
and fingering my spine's shell pink as if I were a beach
and he were blades of marram grass in drifts of sand.
I dab my face with cream that smells of cucumber
and whisper in a distant milky voice
Of course I'll wake you up when he comes;
and then his eyelids close,
and in his self-created darkness he is following
a big car on a motorway at night,
it turns into the driveway to the house,
and presently the driver gets out:
it is only a bear in the moonlight,
walking on the lavender beds.

SELIMA HILL   *b.* 1945   England

A War Film

I saw,
With a catch of the breath and the heart's uplifting,
Sorrow and pride,
 The 'week's great draw' —
The Mons Retreat;
The 'Old Contemptibles' who fought, and died,
The horror and the anguish and the glory.

As in a dream,
Still hearing machine-guns rattle and shells scream,
I came out into the street.
When the day was done,
My little son
Wondered at bath-time why I kissed him so,
Naked upon my knee.
How could he know
The sudden terror that assaulted me? . . .
The body I had borne
Nine moons beneath my heart,
A part of me . . .
If, someday,
It should be taken away
To war. Tortured. Torn.
Slain.
Rotting in No Man's Land, out in the rain —
My little son . . .
Yet all those men had mothers, every one.

How should he know
Why I kissed and kissed and kissed him, crooning his name?
He thought that I was daft.
He thought it was a game,
And laughed, and laughed.

TERESA HOOLEY* 1888–1973 England

The Tay Moses

What can I fashion
for you but a woven
creel of river-
rushes, a golden
oriole's nest, my gift
wrought from the Firth —

and choose my tide; either
the flow, when water-tight,
you'll drift to the uplands —
my favourite hills; held
safe in eddies, where salmon,
wisdom and guts
withered in spawn,
rest between moves: that
slither of body as you were born;

or the ebb, when the water
will birl you to snag
on reeds, the river-
pilot leaning over the side:
'Name o God!' and you'll change hands
tractor-man, grieve,
to the farm-wife, who
takes you into her
competent arms

even as I drive, slamming
the car's gears;
spitting gravel on tracks
down between berry-fields,
engine still racing, the door wide,
as I run toward her, crying
LEAVE HIM! Please,
it's okay, he's mine.

KATHLEEN JAMIE   *b.* 1962   Scotland

Bestiary

Nostrils flared, ears pricked,
our son asks me if people can mate
with animals. I say it hardly
ever happens. He frowns, fur and
skin and hooves and slits and pricks and
teeth and tails whirling in his brain.
You *could* do it, he says, not wanting the
world to be closed to him in any
form. We talk about elephants
and parakeets, until we are rolling on the
floor, laughing like hyenas. Too late,
I remember love – I backtrack
and try to slip it in, but that is
not what he means. Seven years old,
he is into hydraulics, pulleys, doors which
fly open in the side of the body,
entrances, exits. Flushed, panting,
hot for physics, he thinks about lynxes,
eagles, pythons, mosquitoes, girls,
casting a glittering eye of use
over creation, wanting to know
exactly how the world was made to receive him.

SHARON OLDS   *b.* 1942   USA

For a Fatherless Son

You will be aware of an absence, presently,
Growing beside you, like a tree,
A death tree, colour gone, an Australian gum tree –
Balding, gelded by lightning – an illusion,
And a sky like a pig's backside, an utter lack of attention.

But right now you are dumb.
And I love your stupidity,
The blind mirror of it. I look in
And find no face but my own, and you think that's funny.
It is good for me

To have you grab my nose, a ladder rung.
One day you may touch what's wrong
The small skulls, the smashed blue hills, the godawful hush.
Till then your smiles are found money.

SYLVIA PLATH   1932–1963   USA

Sick Boy

Illness falls like a cloud upon
    My little frisking son:
He lies like a plant under a blight
    Dulling the bright leaf-skin.
Our culture falls away, the play
    That apes, and grows, a man,
Falters, and like the wounded or
    Sick animal, his kin,
He curls to shelter the flame of life
    And lies close in his den.

Children in patient suffering
    Are sadder to see than men
Because more humble and more bewildered:
    What words can there explain
Why all pleasures have lost their savour,
    Or promise health again?
Kindness speaks from a far mountain –
    Cannot touch their pain.

ANNE RIDLER   b. 1912   England

Child Waking

The child sleeps in the daytime,
With his abandoned, with his jetsam look,
On the bare mattress, across the cot's corner;
Covers and toys thrown out, a routine labour.

Relaxed in sleep and light,
Face upwards, never so clear a prey to eyes;
Like a walled town surprised out of the air –
All life called in, yet all laid bare

To the enemy above –
He has taken cover in daylight, gone to ground
In his own short length, his body strong in bleached
Blue cotton and his arms outstretched.

Now he opens eyes but not
To see at first; they reflect the light like snow,
And I wait in doubt if he sleeps or wakes, till I see
Slight pain of effort at the boundary

And hear how the trifling wound
Of bewilderment fetches a caverned cry
As he crosses out of sleep – at once to recover
His place and poise, and smile as I lift him over.

But I recall the blue-
White snowfield of his eyes empty of sight
High between dream and day, and think how there
The soul might rise visible as a flower.

E. J. SCOVELL   b. 1907   England

The Victory

I thought you were my victory
though you cut me like a knife
when I brought you out of my body
into your life.

Tiny antagonist, gory,
blue as a bruise. The stains
of your cloud of glory
bled from my veins.

How can you dare, blind thing,
blank insect eyes?
You barb the air. You sting
with bladed cries.

Snail! Scary knot of desires!
Hungry snarl! Small son.
Why do I have to love you?
How have you won?

ANNE STEVENSON   *b.* 1933   USA

Mother
to
Child

To a Little Invisible Being Who is Expected Soon to Become Visible

Germ of new life, whose powers expanding slow
For many a moon their full perfection wait —
Haste, precious pledge of happy love, to go
Auspicious borne through life's mysterious gate.

What powers lie folded in thy curious frame —
Senses from objects locked, and mind from thought!
How little canst thou guess thy lofty claim
To grasp at all the worlds the Almighty wrought!

And see, the genial season's warmth to share,
Fresh younglings shoot, and opening roses glow!
Swarms of new life exulting fill the air —
Haste, infant bud of being, haste to blow!

For thee the nurse prepares her lulling songs,
The eager matrons count the lingering day;
But far the most thy anxious parent longs
On thy soft cheek a mother's kiss to lay.

She only asks to lay her burden down,
That her glad arms that burden may resume;
And nature's sharpest pangs her wishes crown,
That free thee living from thy living tomb.

She longs to fold to her maternal breast
Part of herself, yet to herself unknown;
To see and to salute the stranger guest,
Fed with her life through many a tedious moon.

Come, reap thy rich inheritance of love!
Bask in the fondness of a mother's eye!
Nor wit nor eloquence her heart shall move
Like the first accents of thy feeble cry.

Haste, little captive, burst thy prison doors!
Launch on the living world, and spring to light!
Nature for thee displays her various stores,
Opens her thousand inlets of delight.

If charmed verse or muttered prayers had power
With favouring spells to speed thee on thy way,
Anxious I'd bid my beads each parting hour,
Till thy wish'd smile thy mother's pangs o'erpay.

ANNA LAETITIA BARBAULD   1743–1825   England

The Mother

Abortions will not let you forget.
You remember the children you got that you did not get,
The damp small pulps with a little or with no hair,
The singers and workers that never handled the air.
You will never neglect or beat
Them, or silence or buy with a sweet.
You will never wind up the sucking-thumb
Or scuttle off ghosts that come.
You will never leave them, controlling your luscious sigh,
Return for a snack of them, with gobbling mother-eye.

I have heard in the voices of the wind the voices of my dim
        killed children.
I have contracted. I have eased
My dim dears at the breasts they could never suck.

I have said, Sweets, if I sinned, if I seized
Your luck
And your lives from your unfinished reach,
If I stole your births and your names,
Your straight baby tears and your games,
Your stilted or lovely loves, your tumults, your marriages, aches,
        and your deaths,
If I poisoned the beginnings of your breaths,
Believe that even in my deliberateness I was not deliberate.
Though why should I whine,
Whine that the crime was other than mine? –

Since anyhow you are dead.
Or rather, or instead,
You were never made.
But that too, I am afraid,
Is faulty: oh, what shall I say, how is the truth to be said?
You were born, you had body, you died.
It is just that you never giggled or planned or cried.

Believe me, I loved you all.
Believe me, I knew you, though faintly, and I loved, I loved you
All.

GWENDOLYN BROOKS   *b.* 1917   USA

The Mother

I feel within myself a life
That holds 'gainst death a feeble strife;
They say 'tis destined that the womb
Shall be its birthplace and its tomb.
O child! if it be so, and thou
Thy native world must never know,
Thy Mother's tears will mourn the day
    When she must kiss thy Death-born face.
But oh! how lightly thou wilt pay
    The forfeit due from Adam's race!
Thou wilt have lived, but not have wept,
    Have died, and yet have known no pain;
And sin's dark presence will have swept
    Across thy soul, yet left no stain.
Mine is thy life; my breath thy breath:
    I only feel the dread, the woe;
And in thy sickness or thy death,
    Thy Mother bears the pain, not thou.

Life nothing means for thee, but still
It is a living thing, I feel;
A sex, a shape, a growth are thine,
A form and human face divine;
A heart with passions wrapp'd therein,
A nature doom'd, alas! to sin;
A mind endow'd with latent fire,
To glow, unfold, expand, aspire;
Some likeness from thy father caught,
Or by remoter kindred taught;
Some faultiness of mind or frame,
To wake the bitter sense of shame;
Some noble passions to unroll,
   The generous deed, the human tear;
Some feelings which thy Mother's soul
   Has pour'd on thine, while dwelling near.
All this must pass unbloom'd away
To worlds remote from earthly day;
Worlds whither we by paths less brief,
Are journeying on through joy and grief,
And where thy Mother, now forlorn,
May learn to know her child unborn;
Oh, yes! created thing, I trust
Thou too wilt rise with Adam's dust.

CAROLINE CLIVE   1810–1873   England

Transformation

I see you dart into the world
pearly pink like the inside of a shell
streaked with silver.

Look! Look!
I am shouting with joy, rising up
like a phoenix from my pain

With my eyes I behold you
In the flesh I behold you

So a holy man waking into death
from a life of devotion or
martyrdom in flames

might look into the shining face of god
and see at once
he had never believed.

I see you with my eyes
I see you in glory.

From a tatter of flesh I watch them work.
From a pinnacle of joy.
The placenta, purplish liver meat

sails out of my body like a whale
rubbery hands turn it inside out
hold it up to the light.

The sinewy pulsing cord.
In a haze of peace they cut and stitch
my threaded body like scarlet linen

the midwife chatting comfortably
seated at her work, the needle threaded,
the thimble, the green thread

in and out, in and out.
Then washed and trim in clean sheets
they leave us: mother father child

three folded together.
I see your sleeping face
eyelids crescent lines, lips curled translucent

in stillness like a cowrie shell
whirlpool of your hair. I see you breathe.
In a still pool the moon lies quiet.

JENI COUZYN   b. 1942   South Africa

Changing the Children

Anger does this.
Wishing the furious wish
turns the son into a crow,
the daughter, a porcupine.

Soon enough, no matter how
we want them to be happy
our little loved ones, no
matter how we prod them
into our sun that it may
shine on them, they whine
to stand in the dry-goods store.
Fury slams in.
The willful fury befalls.

Now the varnish-black son in a tree
crow the berater, denounces the race
of fathers, and the golden daughter
all arched bristle and quill
leaves scribbles on the tree bark
writing how The Nameless One
accosted her in the dark.

How put an end to this cruel spell?
Drop the son from the tree with a rifle.
Introduce maggots under his feathers
to eat down to the pure bone of boy.

In spring when the porcupine comes
all stealth and waddle to feed on the willows
stun her with one blow of the sledge
and the entrapped girl will fly out
crying Daddy! or Danny!
or is it Darling?

And we will live all in bliss
for a year and a day until
the legitimate rage of parents
speeds the lad off this time
in the uniform of a toad
who spews a contagion of warts
while the girl contracts to a spider
forced to spin from her midseam
the saliva of false repentance.

Eventually we get them back.
Now they are grown up.
They are much like ourselves.
They wake mornings beyond cure,
not a virgin among them.
We are civil to one another.
We stand in the kitchen
slicing bread, drying spoons,
and tuning in to the weather.

MAXINE KUMIN   *b.* 1925   USA

Pregnancy after Forty

More than half an average lifetime
I have waited for you, bleeding uselessly every month,
a womanhood denied. And now I cradle you,
my miracle chance, within me where, for a while
you are safe. Learning to float and dance through worlds
that, within the lure of visual images, inspire
your growth, you seem far more advanced than I.
And keep me in the hope where I keep you.

Desperate for the seven remaining months to pass
without a hitch, I refrain from carrying heavy weights,
cool the water in my bath and, instead of eating,
nourish you with vitamins and minerals untasted before.

I wish on you your father's temperament, his hair
which straightens to silk in the rain; not to be born,
like me, over aware, with hair that bumps in depressions.
But to take things in your stride – as I hope

to take you, reciprocal in virtue. There are books
I could read to tell, in detail, of your development,
tests I could have to rule out handicap
and prove you curled up cosily, not dangling
from a precipice, ready to drop because your fingertips
have had no chance to form. Yet, in a way, I'd rather
not know. And trust in the nature we are both pushing
to extremes as it pushes us: mother and daughter

or mother and son, linked for as long as wishes dare
the substantial. Do you realize you make me
tired and queasy on seas that give you no qualms –
whitening to break on my surprise Holy Land?
That you must be careful of me lest I lose you
to outer years before they peel off their age inside?
For it is in my youth that you grow, in my youth
that I dare call myself, however temporarily, 'woman'.

PATRICIA MCCARTHY   20th century   England

Child Burial

Your coffin looked unreal,
fancy as a wedding cake.

I chose your grave clothes with care,
your favourite stripey shirt,

your blue cotton trousers.
They smelt of woodsmoke, of October,

your own smell there too.
I chose a gansy of handspun wool,

warm and fleecy for you. It is
so cold down in the dark.

No light can reach you and teach you
the paths of wild birds,

the names of the flowers,
the fishes, the creatures.

Ignorant you must remain
of the sun and its work,

my lamb, my calf, my eaglet,
my cub, my kid, my nestling,

my suckling, my colt. I would spin
time back, take you again

within my womb, your amniotic lair,
and further spin you back

through nine waxing months
to the split seeding moment

you chose to be made flesh,
word within me.

I'd cancel the love feast
the hot night of your making.

I would travel alone
to a quiet mossy place,

you would spill from me into the earth
drop by bright red drop.

PAULA MEEHAN   *b.* 1955   Ireland

The Moment the Two Worlds Meet

That's the moment I always think of — when the
slick, whole body comes out of me,
when they pull it out, not pull it but steady it
as it pushes forth, not catch it but keep their
hands under it as it pulses out,
they are the first to touch it,
and it shines, it glistens with the thick liquid on it.
That's the moment, while it's sliding, the limbs
compressed close to the body, the arms
bent like a crab's rosy legs, the
thighs closely packed plums in heavy syrup, the
legs folded like the white wings of a chicken —
that is the center of life, that moment when the
juiced bluish sphere of the baby is
sliding between the two worlds,
wet, like sex, it *is* sex,
it is my life opening back and back
as you'd strip the reed from the bud, not strip it but
watch it thrust so it peels itself and the
flower is there, severely folded, and
then it begins to open and dry
but by then the moment is over,
they wipe off the grease and wrap the child in a blanket and
hand it to you entirely in this world.

SHARON OLDS   *b.* 1942   USA

Invocation

from *For a Christening*

Blessing, sleep and grow taller in sleeping.
Lie ever in kind keeping.
Infants curl in a cowrie of peace
And should lie lazy. After this ease,
When the soul out of its safe shell goes,
Stretched as you stretch those knees and toes,
What should I wish you? Intelligence first,
In a credulous age by instruction cursed.
Take from us both what immunity
We have from the germ of the printed lie.
Your father's calm temper I wish you, and
The shaping power of his confident hand.
Much, too, that is different and your own;
And may we learn to leave you alone.
For your part, forgive us the pain of living,
Grow in that harsh sun great-hearted and loving.
Sleep, little honey, then; sleep while the powers
Of the Nine Bright Shiners and the Seven Stars
Harmless, encircle: the natural world
Lifegiving, neutral, unless despoiled
By our greed or scorn. And wherever you sleep –
My arms outgrown – or waking weep,
Life is your lot: you lie in God's hand,
In his terrible mercy, world without end.

ANNE RIDLER   *b.* 1912   England

'The spirit is too blunt an instrument'

The spirit is too blunt an instrument
to have made this baby.
Nothing so unskillful as human passions
could have managed the intricate
exacting particulars: the tiny
blind bones with their manipulative tendons,
the knee and the knucklebones, the resilient
fine meshings of ganglia and vertebrae
in the chain of the difficult spine.

Observe the distinct eyelashes and sharp crescent
fingernails, the shell-like complexity
of the ear with its firm involutions
concentric in miniature to the minute
ossicles. Imagine the
infinitesimal capillaries, the flawless connections
of the lungs, the invisible neural filaments
through which the completed body
already answers to the brain.

Then name any passion or sentiment
possessed of the simplest accuracy.
No. No desire or affectation could have done
with practice what habit
has done perfectly, indifferently,
through the body's ignorant precision.
It is left to the vagaries of the mind to invent
love and despair and anxiety
and their pain.

ANNE STEVENSON *b.* 1933 USA

Song: Time Drawes Neere

Time drawes neere
    love adornes you
        pours down autumn sunne

Babye I follow you
    sweete offspringe of
        nighte & sleepe

Pangs of the babye
    tossed in a bellie:
        birdies & woodlands cheer!

Eies gaze with delighte
    I hope I fear I laugh
        call you 'rolling mountain'

Your roote is deepe, be you englishe
    rosie fayre or german darkly
        call you boy or girl?

I must have pillowes & musicke
    I must have raspberry leaf tea
        I needs must groan Ah me!

Ah thee! a secret growing
    I go no more a-maying
        I settle into my tent shift

Bursting at seams
    big tub, water barrel
        tossed as boat or cloud, gravid

Powre to claime my hart in
    bodye roome, powre to keepe
        me waking all nighte a-peeing

I ride you unseene wave
    wee rise together
        under daddye's roof & hand.

ANNE WALDMAN   *b.* 1945   USA

To an Infant Expiring the Second Day of Its Birth

Tender, softness, infant mild,
Perfect, purest, brightest child;
Transient lustre, beauteous clay,
Smiling wonder of a day:
Ere the last convulsive start
Rends thy unresisting heart;
Ere the long-enduring swoon
Weighs thy precious eyelids down;
Oh! regard a mother's moan,
Anguish deeper than thy own!
Fairest eyes, whose dawning light
Late with rapture blessed my sight,
Ere your orbs extinguished be,
Bend their trembling beams on me,
Drooping sweetness, verdant flower,
Blooming, withering in an hour,
Ere thy gentle breast sustains
Latest, fiercest, vital pains,
Hear a suppliant! Let me be
Partner in thy destiny!

MEHETABEL WRIGHT* 1697–1750 England

Daughter
to
Father

Assembler

My twentieth summer I got a job in Door Locks
at the Ford plant where my father has worked
for twenty years. Five in the morning
we'd stand tired in the glare and old heat
of the kitchen, my father fiddling with
the radio dial, looking for a clear station.

There weren't any women in my department.
At first the men would ask me to lift
what I couldn't, would speed up the turntable,
juggling the greasy washers and bolts,
winking at each other, grinning at me.
In the break room they would buy me coffee,
study my check to see if I got shorted.
They were glad I was in school and told me
to finish, they said I'd never regret it.
Once I got loaned to Air Conditioners,
worked three days in a special enclosure,
quiet and cool and my hands stayed clean.
Out the window I could see Door Locks,
the men taking salt pills, 110 degrees.

In rest rooms there were women sleeping
on orange vinyl couches, oven timers ticking
next to their heads.

At lunch I'd take the long walk to my father.
I'd see him from a distance, wearing safety glasses
like mine, and earphones, bright slivers of brass
in his hair — him standing alone in strange sulfur light
amidst machines the size of small buildings.
Every twenty minutes he worked a tumbler,
in between he read from his grocery bag of paperbacks.
He would pour us coffee from a hidden pot,
toast sandwiches on a furnace. We sat
on crates, shouting a few things and laughing
over the roar and banging of presses.

Mostly I remember the back-to-back heat waves,
coffee in paper cups that said Safety First,
my father and I hurrying away from the time clocks,
proud of each other. And my last day, moving shy past
their *Good Lucks*, out into 5:00, shading my eyes.

DEBRA ALLBERY *b.* 1957 USA

Your Father will Disown You

I swim out as far as I dare,
reckless in salt water.
Ocean muffles my great scream;
the caique will keelhaul me
straight to wherever he may be.
It was the sob of bouzouki
that pushed me into the dream,
rocked me with him in his cradle
of a small boat tearing toward light.

I'm home, beside my green hearth
and he spiders between my breasts,
across my heart; it's Daddy Long Legs,
his smell of woodsmoke and shaving soap
returns like the repressed until
I don't know whether I am hearing
nightingales or violins.

The voice in my head is a last seduction
it teases, it cajoles, it caresses,
it needs reassurance, it follows me
into the intimacy of my bath
for a moment of disbelief;
I shave my legs, mummy never did.

Yes I will go with you all the way
until only a handful of ash remains.
Yes, I will look after her in her grief
No, I won't tell her you love her.
Fresh rosemary flowers mimic
The baby-blue of his shroud,
Shocked by it she refuses me a look
that might have told me my body
is real which his is not.
I'm in my cot again, rattling.

LIZ ALMOND *b.* 1949 England

Amoebaean for Daddy

I was a pretty baby.
White folks used to stop
My mother
Just to look at me.
(All black babies
Are Cute.) Mother called me
Bootsie and Daddy said . . .
(Nobody listened to him).

On the Union Pacific, a
Dining-car waiter, bowing and scraping,
Momma told him to
Stand up straight, he shamed her
In the big house
(Bought from tips) in front of her
Nice club ladies.

His short legs were always
Half bent. He could have posed as
The Black jockey Mother found
And put on the lawn.
He sat silent when
We ate from the good railroad china
And stolen silver spoons.
Furniture crowded our
Lonely house.

But I was young and played
In the evenings under a blanket of
Licorice sky. When Daddy came home
(I might be forgiven) that last night,
I had been running in the
Big backyard and
Stood sweating above the tired old man,
Panting like a young horse,
Impatient with his lingering. He said
'All I ever asked, all I ever asked, all I ever –'
Daddy, you should have died
Long before I was a
Pretty baby, and white
Folks used to stop
Just to look at me.

MAYA ANGELOU *b.* 1928 USA

John Milton and My Father

Milton was not my father's favourite poet.
Shakespeare was. And you got marks for that
In the Victorian classroom with the brown
Trusses of the pointed roof and the black fat
Stove with the turtle, and always blowing through it
The smell of clothes muggy with country rain.

Milton came second. You earned marks for that.
My father, a conformist to his death,
Would have believed even at the age of ten
This value judgement to be gospel truth.
But when he spoke of Milton to us, we got
Much more than the right answer from his tone.

Seated on his high Dickensian stool
From puberty to impotence, a clerk
(The chief clerk in the corner in his glass
Box of authority), he felt that work
And the world were a less smelly school
Where seraphim and angels knew their place.

He tasted hierarchy as Milton did
And was enchanted by it; jewelled stairs
And thrones and powers and principalities.
Each night he knelt but glanced up through his prayers
To the mountain where sat golden almighty God
With nothing over him but empty space.

PATRICIA BEER   *b.* 1919   England

Equality, Father

Equality, father! Your dream has come true.
I glimpse you dimly, still see you walking
next to Roth the man of property who refused us
a little cottage cheese for the holidays,
Klein the shoemaker who wouldn't resole your only shoes
on credit, Goldberg the butcher
with his trimmed goatee who dragged you
into court for selling meat without a license,
Stein the teacher who gave us Hebrew lessons
in expectation of a heavenly reward and directed us
like a demoniac conductor
breaking dozens of pointers over the heads
of your children, illiterate in Hebrew, destined to hell.

And you, the poorest, most recognizable
by those skinny buttocks! The most agile,
most exploitable in forced labor.
Forward, father! You've been tried by every eventuality,
armed with experience.
You know the front lines, rifles, trenches,
the daily struggle even in good times.
You know prison, the hard plank in the dark cell
where you picked off lice, licked your wounds,
unrolled cigarette butts.
You know the taste of blood in your mouth
from a rotten tooth
from a Fascist's fist
from a bullet you caught defending the homeland
you stubbornly believed was yours.

You know death lurking in ambush
the meanness of men
the power game
the bosses' exploitation.
You know the whole gamut of humiliation
the dark street with menacing shadows
ravenous wolves and skittish horses
on sleepless nights during your solitary trips
in the illusion of business deals
doomed to fail
the promises not kept
except for Jehovah's wrath!

Forward, father! You know the marches,
the cold, hunger! Hold your head high!
you no longer have to hide from your creditors:
they're all there, naked!

Ah, you turn toward me? Don't you know me?
I've grown up, my breasts are firm,
the down on my skin is pure and soft
like mama's when they brought her to you
as a bride. Take me, father!

I'll give you pleasure, not children,
love, not obligations,
love, not reproaches,
love undreamed of by you,
imagined by me. Run:
It is the time of the Apocalypse!
Let us commit a mortal sin
worthy of death.

EDITH BRÜCK*   *b.* 1932, Hungary   Italy
Translated by Ruth Feldman

To Charles Burney

Oh author of my being! – far more dear
To me than light, than nourishment, or rest,
Hygeia's blessings, Rapture's burning tear,
Or the life-blood that mantles in my breast!

If in my heart the love of Virtue glows,
'Twas planted there by an unerring rule;
From thy example the pure flame arose,
Thy life, my precept – thy good works, my school.

Could my weak powers thy numerous virtues trace,
By filial love each fear should be repressed;
The blush of Incapacity I'd chase,
And stand, recorder of thy worth, confessed:

But since my niggard stars that gift refuse,
Concealment is the only boon I claim;
Obscure be still the unsuccessful Muse,
Who cannot raise, but would not sink, your fame.

Oh! of my life at once the source and joy!
If e'er thy eyes these feeble lines survey,
Let not their folly their intent destroy;
Accept the tribute — but forget the lay.

FRANCES BURNEY   1752—1840   England

Mirror Image

Tonight I saw myself in the dark window as
the image of my father, whose life
was spent like this,
thinking of death, to the exclusion
of other sensual matters,
so in the end that life
was easy to give up, since
it contained nothing: even
my mother's voice couldn't make him
change or turn back
as he believed
that once you can't love another human being
you have no place in the world.

LOUISE GLÜCK   *b.* 1943   USA

Father and Child

I BARN OWL

Daybreak: the household slept.
I rose, blessed by the sun.
A horny fiend, I crept
out with my father's gun.

Let him dream of a child
obedient, angel-mild —

old No-Sayer, robbed of power
by sleep. I knew my prize
who swooped home at this hour
with daylight-riddled eyes
to his place on a high beam
in our old stables, to dream

light's useless time away.
I stood, holding my breath,
in urine-scented hay,
master of life and death,
a wisp-haired judge whose law
would punish beak and claw.

My first shot struck. He swayed,
ruined, beating his only
wing, as I watched, afraid
by the fallen gun, a lonely
child who believed death clean
and final, not this obscene

bundle of stuff that dropped,
and dribbled through loose straw
tangling in bowels, and hopped
blindly closer. I saw
those eyes that did not see
mirror my cruelty

while the wrecked thing that could
not bear the light nor hide
hobbled in its own blood.
My father reached my side,
gave me the fallen gun.
'End what you have begun.'

I fired. The blank eyes shone
once into mine, and slept.
I leaned my head upon
my father's arm, and wept,
owl-blind in early sun
for what I had begun.

II NIGHTFALL

Forty years, lived or dreamed:
what memories pack them home.
Now the season that seemed
incredible is come.
Father and child, we stand
in time's long-promised land.

Since there's no more to taste
ripeness is plainly all.
Father, we pick our last
fruits of the temporal.
Eighty years old, you take
this late walk for my sake.

Who can be what you were?
Link your dry hand in mine,
my stick-thin comforter.
Far distant suburbs shine
with great simplicities.
Birds crowd in flowering trees,

sunset exalts its known
symbols of transience.
Your passionate face is grown
to ancient innocence.
Let us walk for this hour
as if death had no power

or were no more than sleep.
Things truly named can never
vanish from earth. You keep
a child's delight for ever
in birds, flowers, shivery-grass —
I name them as we pass.

'Be your tears wet?' You speak
as if air touched a string
near breaking-point. Your cheek
brushes on mine. Old king,
your marvellous journey's done.
Your night and day are one

as you find with your white stick
the path on which you turn
home with the child once quick
to mischief, grown to learn
what sorrows, in the end,
no words, no tears can mend.

GWEN HARWOOD   *b.* 1920   New Zealand

Thrall

The room is sparsely furnished:
A chair, a table and a father.

He sits in the chair by the window.
There are books on the table.
The time is always just past lunch.

You tiptoe past as he eats his apple
And reads. He looks up, angry.
He has heard your asthmatic breathing.

He will read for years without looking up
Until your childhood is over:

Smells, untidiness and boring questions;
Blood, from the first skinned knees
To the first stained thighs;
The foolish tears of adolescent love.

One day he looks up, pleased
At the finished product.
Now he is ready to love you!

So he coaxes in the voice reserved
For reading Keats. You agree to everything.

Drilled in silence and duty.
You will give him no cause for reproach.
He will boast of you to strangers.

When the afternoon is older
Shadows in a smaller room
Fall on the bed, the books, the father.

You read aloud to him
'La Belle Dame sans Merci'.
You feed him his medicine.
You tell him you love him.

You wait for his eyes to close at last
So you may write this poem.

CAROLYN KIZER   *b.* 1925   USA

Elegy for an Irish Speaker

Numbered day,
night only just beginning,
be born very slowly, stay
with me, impossible to name.

Do I know you, Miss Death,
by your warrant, your heroine's head
pinned against my hero's shoulder?
The seraphim are as cold
to each other in Paradise:
and the room of a dying man
is open to everyone.
The knitting together of your two spines
is another woman
reminding of a wife, his life
surrounds you as a sun,
consumes your light.

Are you waiting to be fertilized,
dynamic death, by his dark company?
To be warmed in your wretched
overnight lodgings
by his kind words and small talk
and powerful movements?
He breaks away from your womb
to talk to me,
he speaks so with my consciousness
and not with words, he's in danger
of becoming a poetess.

Roaming root of multiple meanings,
he shouts himself out
in your narrow amphora,
your tasteless, because immortal, wine.
The instant of recognition
is unsweet to him, scarecrow word
sealed up, second half
of a poetic simile lost somewhere.

Most foreign and cherished reader,
I cannot live without
your trans-sense language,
the living furrow of your spoken words
that plough up time.
Instead of the real past
with its deep roots,
I have yesterday,
I have minutes when
you burn up the past
with your raspberry-coloured farewell
that shears the air. Bypassing
everything, even your frozen body,
with your full death, the no-road-back
of your speaking flesh.

MEDBH MCGUCKIAN   *b.* 1950   Ireland

A Father of Women

. .

'Thy father was transfused into thy blood.'
DRYDEN, *Ode to Mrs Anne Killigrew*

Our father works in us,
The daughters of his manhood. Not undone
Is he, not wasted, though transmuted thus,
    And though he left no son.

Therefore on him I cry
To arm me: 'For my delicate mind a casque,
A breastplate for my heart, courage to die,
    Of thee, captain, I ask.

'Nor strengthen only; press
A finger on this violent blood and pale,
Over this rash will let thy tenderness
    A while pause, and prevail.

'And shepherd-father, thou
Whose staff folded my thoughts before my birth,
Control them now I am of earth, and now
    Thou art no more of earth.

'O liberal, constant, dear,
Crush in my nature the ungenerous art
Of the inferior; set me high, and here,
    Here garner up thy heart!'

Like to him now are they,
The million living fathers of the War –
Mourning the crippled world, the bitter day –
    Whose striplings are no more.

The crippled world! Come then,
Fathers of women with your honour in trust,
Approve, accept, know them daughters of men,
    Now that your sons are dust.

ALICE MEYNELL   1847–1922   England

Silence

My father used to say,
'Superior people never make long visits,
have to be shown Longfellow's grave
or the glass flowers at Harvard.
Self-reliant like the cat –
that takes its prey to privacy,
the mouse's limp tail hanging like a shoelace from its mouth –
they sometimes enjoy solitude,
and can be robbed of speech
by speech which has delighted them.
The deepest feeling always shows itself in silence;
not in silence, but restraint.'
Nor was he insincere in saying, 'Make my house your inn.'
Inns are not residences.

MARIANNE MOORE   1887–1972   USA

Blood

'A true Arab knows how to catch a fly in his hands,'
my father would say. And he'd prove it,
cupping the buzzer instantly
while the host with the swatter stared.

In the spring our palms peeled like snakes.
True Arabs believed watermelon could heal fifty ways.
I changed these to fit the occasion.

Years before, a girl knocked,
wanted to see the Arab.
I said we didn't have one.

After that, my father told me who he was,
'Shihab' – 'shooting star' –
a good name, borrowed from the sky.
Once I said, 'When we die, we give it back?'
He said that's what a true Arab would say.

Today the headlines clot in my blood.
A little Palestinian dangles a truck on the front page.
Homeless fig, this tragedy with a terrible root
is too big for us. What flag can we wave?
I wave the flag of stone and seed,
table mat stitched in blue.

I call my father, we talk around the news.
It is too much for him,
neither of his two languages can reach it.
I drive into the country to find sheep, cows,
to plead with the air:
Who calls anyone *civilized*?
Where can the crying heart graze?
What does a true Arab do now?

NAOMI SHIHAB NYE   *b.* 1952   USA

My Father Speaks to Me from the Dead

I seem to have woken up in a pot-shed,
on clay, on shards, the bright paths
of slugs kiss-crossing my body. I don't know
where to start, with this grime on me.
I take the spider glue-net, plug
of the dead, out of my mouth, let's see
if where I have been I can do this.
I love your feet. I love your knees,
I love your our my legs, they are so
long because they are yours and mine
both. I love your – what can I call it,

between your legs, we never named it, the
glint and purity of its curls. I love
your rear end, I changed you once,
washed the detritus off your tiny
bottom, with my finger rubbed
the oil on you; when I touched your little
anus I crossed wires with God for a moment.
I never hated your shit — that was
your mother. I love your navel, thistle
seed fossil, even though
it's her print on you. Of course I love
your breasts — did you see me looking up
from within your daughter's face, as she nursed?
I love your bony shoulders and you know I
love your hair, thick and live
as earth. And I never hated your face,
I hated its eruptions. You know what I love?
I love your brain, its halves and silvery
folds, like a woman's labia.
I love in you
even, what comes
from deep in your mother — your heart, that
        hard worker,
and your womb, it is a heaven to me,
I lie on its soft hills and gaze up
at its rosy vault.
I have been in a body without breath,
I have been in the morgue, in fire, in the slagged
chimney, in the air over the earth,
and buried in the earth, and pulled down
into the ocean — where I have been
I understand this life, I am matter,
your father, I made you, when I say now that I
        love you
I mean look down at your hand, move it,
that action is matter's love, for human
love go elsewhere.

SHARON OLDS   b. 1942   USA

Shadows

Each night this house sinks into the shadows
under its weight of love and fear and pity.
Each morning it floats up again so lightly
it seems attached to sky instead of earth,
a place where we will always go on living
and there will be no dead to leave behind.

But when we think of whom we've left behind
already in the ever hungry shadows,
even in the morning hum of living
we pause a minute and are filled with pity
for the lovely children of the earth
who run up and down the stairs so lightly

and who weave their careless songs so lightly
through the hedges which they play behind
that the fruits and flowers of the earth
rise up on their stems above the shadows.
Perhaps even an apple can feel pity;
perhaps the lilac wants to go on living.

In this house where we have all been living
we bind the family together lightly
with knots made equally of love and pity
and the knowledge that we'll leave behind
only partial memories, scraps of shadows,
trinkets of our years upon the earth.

I think about my father in the earth
as if it were a room in which he's living,
as if it were a house composed of shadows
where he remembers those he loved not lightly,
where he remembers what he left behind.
He had a great capacity for pity

but told me that I mustn't waste my pity
on him — he'd had his share of life on earth,
and he was happy just to leave behind
daughters of daughters who would go on living.
So he seemed to leave us almost lightly,
closing the curtains which were stitched with shadows.

Always save your pity for the living
who walk the eggshell crust of earth so lightly,
in front of them, behind them, only shadows.

LINDA PASTAN *b.* 1932 USA

The Colossus

I shall never get you put together entirely,
Pieced, glued, and properly jointed.
Mule-bray, pig-grunt and bawdy cackles
Proceed from your great lips.
It's worse than a barnyard.

Perhaps you consider yourself an oracle,
Mouthpiece of the dead, or of some god or other.
Thirty years now I have laboured
To dredge the silt from your throat.
I am none the wiser.

Scaling little ladders with gluepots and pails of lysol
I crawl like an ant in mourning
Over the weedy acres of your brow
To mend the immense skull-plates and clear
The bald, white tumuli of your eyes.

A blue sky out of the Oresteia
Arches above us. O father, all by yourself
You are pithy and historical as the Roman Forum.
I open my lunch on a hill of black cypress.
Your fluted bones and acanthine hair are littered

In their old anarchy to the horizon-line.
It would take more than a lightning-stroke
To create such a ruin.
Nights, I squat in the cornucopia
Of your left ear, out of the wind.

Counting the red stars and those of plum-colour.
The sun rises under the pillar of your tongue.
My hours are married to shadow.
No longer do I listen for the scrape of a keel
On the blank stones of the landing.

SYLVIA PLATH   1932–1963   USA

After Dark

1

You are falling asleep and I sit looking at you
old tree of life
old man whose death I wanted
I can't stir you up now.

Faintly a phonograph needle
whirs round in the last groove
eating my heart to dust.
That terrible record! how it played

down years, wherever I was
in foreign languages even
over and over, *I know you better*
than you know yourself   I know

you better than you know
yourself   I know
you   until, self-maimed,
I limped off, torn at the roots,

stopped singing a whole year,
got a new body, new breath,
got children, croaked for words,
forgot to listen

or read your *mene tekel* fading on the wall,
woke up one morning
and knew myself your daughter.
Blood is a sacred poison.

Now, unasked, you give ground.
We only want to stifle
what's stifling us already.
Alive now, root to crown, I'd give

— oh, — something — not to know
our struggles now are ended.
I seem to hold you, cupped
in my hands, and disappearing.

When your memory fails —
no more to scourge my inconsistencies —
the sashcords of the world fly loose.
A window crashes

suddenly down. I go to the woodbox
and take a stick of kindling
to prop the sash again.
I grow protective toward the world.

2

Now let's away from prison —
Underground seizures!
I used to huddle in the grave
I'd dug for you and bite

my tongue for fear it would babble
— *Darling* —
I thought they'd find me there
someday, sitting upright, shrunken,

my hair like roots and in my lap
a mess of broken pottery —
wasted libation —
and you embalmed beside me.

No, let's away. Even now
there's a walk between doomed elms
(whose like we shall not see much longer)
and something — grass and water —

an old dream-photograph.
I'll sit with you there and tease you
for wisdom, if you like,
waiting till the blunt barge

bumps along the shore.
Poppies burn in the twilight
like smudge pots.
I think you hardly see me

but — this is the dream now —
your fears blow out,
off, over the water.
At the last, your hand feels steady.

1964

ADRIENNE RICH *b.* 1929 USA

Papa Love Baby

My mother was a romantic girl
So she had to marry a man with his hair in curl
Who subsequently became my unrespected papa,
But that was a long time ago now.

What folly is it that daughters are always supposed to be
In love with papa. It wasn't the case with me
I couldn't take to him at all
But he took to me
What a sad fate to befall
A child of three.

I sat upright in my baby carriage
And wished mama hadn't made such a foolish marriage.
I tried to hide it, but it showed in my eyes unfortunately
And a fortnight later papa ran away to sea.

He used to come home on leave
It was always the same
I could not grieve
But I think I was somewhat to blame.

STEVIE SMITH   1902–1971   England

To Her Father

In vain, mistaken Sir, you boast
Your Frown can give me lasting Pain;
Your Rigour, when you threaten most,
Attempts to wound my Peace in vain.

With transient Grief you may oppress
A Mind that greater Griefs can bear.
To make Unkindness past Redress,
Your child must *love*, as well as *fear*!

If your kind Hand had fixt me sure
From Want and Shame's impending Harms
Or lodg'd my ripen'd Bloom, secure,
Within some worthy Husband's Arms;

Or when you saw me circled round
With ills that vex and shorten Life,
Had once your dear Condolence found
My sufferings when a wretched Wife;

Altho' *I* was not worth your *Love*,
Had *you* a Parent's *Care* exprest;
Or by one tender Action strove
To make the Life you gave me blest;

How should I mourn had this been so!
How ill your Rage I should endure!
But *gentler Hands* must give the Blow,
Which *rankles*, and *admits no Cure*.

If any Hand a Stroke could send
To vanquish and undo me quite;
'Tis where the *Guardian, Father, Friend,*
And ev'ry kinder name unite.

From such a Sire, rever'd an Age,
A *Look*, perchance, or *Word unkind,*
Might wound beyond your utmost Rage,
With ev'ry faithless Friend combin'd.

The shocks that must on Life attend,
We firmly bear, or shun their Pow'r:
But hard Reproaches from a Friend
Will *torture* to our *latest Hour.*

Refrain your needless Rages then:
Your Anger touches me no more
Than *needless wounds* on dying Men,
Who felt the *mortal pang* before.

As Caesar, bay'd by cruel Foes,
Dauntless, awhile defers his Fate:
He bears, or wards, repeated Blows;
Nor deigns to sink beneath their Weight,

Till, wounded in the tend'rest Part,
He finds his Life not worth his Care:
His hand disdains to guard his Heart,
And ev'ry Stab is welcome there.

MEHETABEL WRIGHT*   1697–1750   England

Photograph, 1958

My father and I play checkers
in profile. He sits on the couch,
leans forward on his elbow, there's
a low coffee table between us.
I am four, sit opposite on a hassock.
He concentrates on the board,
I am watching him, who
is winning?
I no longer know
the rules or object of the game.
Checkers on the board and off,
an open cigarette package, box of matches.
My father wears a loose white
shirt, work pants, my hair
is badly cut, these
are the details. Beyond the barely
furnished room I guess snow:
banked against the front
and back doors. Years later
we'll live in another city.
In an old farmhouse
rock at the green edge
of a golf course. My father
will pull a stove out of a wall
and hurl it across a kitchen
on my account. Boiling lobsters
will fly like wet birds.

In this photograph my face
tilts up toward his. I wait
for him to make his move
and I would gladly wait forever,
deaf to the screams, the scarlet tails
that will one day scatter.

PATRICIA YOUNG   *b.* 1954   Canada

*Daughter
to
Mother*

The Chiffonier

You're glad I like the chiffonier. But I
feel suddenly uneasy, scenting why
you're pleased I like this pretty thing you've bought,
the twin of one that stood beside your cot
when you were small: you've marked it down for me;
it's not too heavy to be sent by sea
when the time comes, and it's got space inside
to pack some other things you've set aside,
things that are small enough to go by water
twelve thousand miles to me, your English daughter.
I know your habits — writing all our names
in books and on the backs of picture-frames,
allotting antique glass and porcelain dishes
to granddaughters according to their wishes,
promising me the tinted photographs
of my great-grandmother. We used to laugh,
seeing how each occasional acquisition
was less for you than for later disposition:
'You know how Marilyn likes blue and white
china? I've seen some plates I thought I might
indulge in.' Bless you, Mother! But we're not
quite so inclined to laugh now that you've got
something that's new to you but not a part
of your estate: that weakness in your heart.
It makes my distance from you, when I go
back home next week, suddenly swell and grow
from thirty hours' flying to a vast
galactic space between present and past.
How many more times can I hope to come
to Wellington and find you still at home?
We've talked about it, as one has to, trying
to see the lighter aspects of your dying:
'You've got another twenty years or more'
I said, 'but when you think you're at death's door
just let me know. I'll come and hang about
for however long it takes to see you out.'

'I don't think it'll be like that' you said:
'I'll pop off suddenly one night in bed.'

How secretive! How satisfying! You'll
sneak off, a kid running away from school —
well, that at least's the only way I find
I can bring myself to see it in my mind.
But now I see you in your Indian skirt
and casual cornflower-blue lined shirt
in the garden, under your feijoa tree,
looking about as old or young as me.
Dear little Mother! Naturally I'm glad
you found a piece of furniture that had
happy associations with your youth;
and yes, I do admire it — that's the truth:
its polished wood and touch of Art Nouveau
appeal to me. But surely you must know
I value this or any other treasure
of yours chiefly because it gives you pleasure.
I have to write this now, while you're still here:
I want my mother, not her chiffonier.

FLEUR ADCOCK   *b.* 1934, New Zealand   England

The Lost Woman

My mother went with no more warning
Than a bright voice and a bad pain.
Home from school on a June morning
And where the brook goes under the lane
I saw the back of a shocking white
Ambulance drawing away from the gate.

She never returned and I never saw
Her buried. So a romance began.
The ivy-mother turned into a tree
That still hops away like a rainbow down
The avenue as I approach.
My tendrils are the ones that clutch.

I made a life for her over the years.
Frustrated no more by a dull marriage
She ran a canteen through several wars.
The wit of a cliché-ridden village
She met her match at an extra-mural
Class and the OU summer school.

Many a hero in his time
And every poet has acquired
A lost woman to haunt the home,
To be compensated and desired,
Who will not alter, who will not grow,
A corpse they need never get to know.

She is nearly always benign. Her habit
Is not to stride at dead of night.
Soft and crepuscular in rabbit-
Light she comes out. Hear how they hate
Themselves for losing her as they did.
Her country is bland and she does not chide.

But my lost woman evermore snaps
From somewhere else: 'You did not love me.
I sacrificed too much perhaps,
I showed you the way to rise above me
And you took it. You are the ghost
With the bat-voice, my dear. *I* am not lost.'

PATRICIA BEER   *b.* 1919   England

The Punishment

from *Christmas in Africa*

One autumn afternoon when I was nine
feeding the chickens near the grapevine, brooding
in sunshine, my mother asked me to choose

a christmas present that year.
Anything I said, but a doll. Whatever you choose
but not a doll

my faith in her to know
better than I could myself what gift would please me.
And so at the height of summer

we made our pilgrimage
to the earth's greenest riches and the ample ocean.
And christmas eve

was three white daughters
three bright angels singing silent night as my mother
lit the candles

the tree blooming
sea breathing, the beloved son in his cradle sleeping.
Over the hills and skies

on his sleigh the father
the awaited one, made his visitation. Weeks of dreaming
and wondering now

in a box in my hand.
Shoebox size. Not waterwings then or a time machine no
something the size

of a pair of shoes.
Not a pony then or a river canoe. Not a new dress no.
I pulled at the bright bowed ribbons

and little christmas angels
with trembling hands. Underneath the monkey-apple branch
dressed up in baubles and tinsel

and blobs of cotton wool
the sea soaring, stars and the fairy at the treetop
shining

his hand on my shoulder
my mother's eyes on my face two burning suns
piercing my mind and in the box

a doll.
A stupid pretty empty thing. Pink smiling girl. The world
rocked about my head

my face fell into a net
from that moment. My heart in me played possum
and never recovered.

I said I liked the wretched thing
joy broke over my face like a mirror cracking. I said it
so loud, so often

I almost believed it. All that christmas
a shameful secret bound me and the doll and my mother
irrevocably together

When I knew she was watching
I would grab for the doll in the night, or take it
tenderly with me to the beach

wrapped in a small towel.
At last on the last night of the journey home
staying at a hotel

my mother woke me early
to go out and find the maid. In my pyjamas, half asleep
I staggered out into the dawn

heat rising like mist
from the ground, birds making an uproar, snakes
not yet awake

a sense of something
about to happen under the heavy damp rustle
of the trees.

My feet left footprints
in the dew. When I returned I was clutching that precious
corpse to my chest

like one of the bereaved.
*Now I know, said my mother, that although you didn't
want a doll, you really do love her.*

I was believed!
Something fell from my face with a clatter –
my punishment was over

and in that moment
fell from my mother's face a particular smile, a kind of
dear and tender curling of the eyes

fell. Two gripped faces
side by side on the floor, smiled at each other
before we grabbed them back

and fitted them with a hollow rattle
to our love. And I laid the doll down in a suitcase
and slammed the lid on its face

and never looked at it again.
And in a sense my mother did the same, and in a sense
my punishment and hers

had always been, and just begun.

JENI COUZYN   *b.* 1942   South Africa

Litany

The soundtrack then was a litany – *candlewick
bedspread three piece suite display cabinet* –
and stiff-haired wives balanced their red smiles,
passing the catalogue. *Pyrex.* A tiny ladder
ran up Mrs Barr's American Tan leg, sly
like a rumour. Language embarrassed them.

The terrible marriages crackled, cellophane
round polyester shirts, and then The Lounge
would seem to bristle with eyes, hard
as the bright stones in engagement rings,
and sharp hands poised over biscuits as a word
was spelled out. An embarrassing word, broken

to bits, which tensed the air like an accident.
This was the code I learnt at my mother's knee, pretending
to read, where no one had cancer, or sex, or debts,
and certainly not leukaemia, which no one could spell.
The year a mass grave of wasps bobbed in a jam-jar;
a butterfly stammered itself in my curious hands.

A boy in the playground, I said, *told me
to fuck off;* and a thrilled, malicious pause
salted my tongue like an imminent storm. Then
uproar. *I'm sorry, Mrs Barr, Mrs Hunt, Mrs Emery,
sorry, Mrs Raine.* Yes, I can summon their names.
My mother's mute shame. The taste of soap.

CAROL ANN DUFFY   *b.* 1955   Scotland

Handbag

My mother's old handbag,
crowded with letters she carried
all through the war. The smell
of my mother's handbag: mints
and lipstick and Coty powder.
The look of those letters, softened
and worn at the edges, opened,
read, and refolded so often.
Letters from my father. Odour
of leather and powder, which ever
since then has meant womanliness,
and love, and anguish, and war.

RUTH FAINLIGHT   *b.* 1931, USA   England

Fanfare

from *Stations Underground*

for Winifred Fanthorpe, born 5 February 1895,
died 13 November 1978

You, in the old photographs, are always
The one with the melancholy half-smile, the one
Who couldn't quite relax into the joke.

My extrovert dog of a father,
With his ragtime blazer and his swimming togs
Tucked like a swiss roll under his arm,
Strides in his youth towards us down some esplanade,

Happy as Larry. You, on his other arm,
Are anxious about the weather forecast,
His overdraft, or early closing day.

You were good at predicting failure: marriages
Turned out wrong because you said they would.
You knew the rotations of armistice and war,
Watched politicians' fates with gloomy approval.

All your life you lived in a minefield,
And were pleased, in a quiet way, when mines
Exploded. You never actually said
I told you so, but we could tell you meant it.

Crisis was your element. You kept your funny stories
Your music-hall songs for doodlebug and blitz-nights.
In the next cubicle, after a car-crash, I heard you
Amusing the nurses with your trench wit through the blood.

Magic alerted you. Green, knives and ladders
Will always scare me through your tabus.
Your nightmare was Christmas; so much organized
Compulsory whoopee to be got through.

You always had some stratagem for making
Happiness keep its distance. Disaster
Was what you planned for. You always
Had hoarded loaves or candles up your sleeve.

Houses crumbled around your ears, taps leaked,
Electric light bulbs went out all over England,
Because for you homes were only provisional,
Bivouacs on the stony mountain of living.

You were best at friendship with chars, gypsies,
Or very far-off foreigners. Well-meaning neighbours
Were dangerous because they lived near.

Me too you managed best at a distance. On the landline
From your dugout to mine, your nightly
Pass, friend was really often quite jovial.

You were the lonely figure in the doorway
Waving goodbye in the cold, going back to a sink-full
Of crockery dirtied by those you loved. We
Left you behind to deal with our crusts and gristle.

I know why you chose now to die. You foresaw
Us approaching the Delectable Mountains,
And didn't feel up to all the cheers and mafficking.

But how, dearest, will even you retain your
Special brand of hard-bitten stoicism
Among the halleluyas of the triumphant dead?

U. A. FANTHORPE   *b.* 1929   England

The Fowlers of the Marshes

Three thousand years ago
they were fowling in the marshes
around Thebes – men in knotted skirts
and tiered faience collars,
who avoided the brown crocodile,
and loved the ibis, which they stalked
with long striped cats on strings,
under the eye of Nut, the goddess of the sky.

My mother's hushed peculiar world's the same:
she haunts it like the fowlers of the marshes,
tiptoeing gaily into history, sustained by gods
as strange to me as Lady Nut, and Anubis,
the oracular, the jackal-masked.
When I meet her at the station, I say
Hello, Mum! and think *Hello, Thoth,*
This is the Weighing of the Heart.

SELIMA HILL   *b.* 1945   England

The Intruder

My mother – preferring the strange to the tame:
Dove-note, bone marrow, deer dung,
Frog's belly distended with finny young,
Leaf-mould wilderness, hare-bell, toadstool,
Odd, small snakes roving through the leaves,
Metallic beetles rambling over stones: all
Wild and natural! – flashed out her instinctive love,
        and quick, she
Picked up the fluttering, bleeding bat the cat laid at her feet,
And held the little horror to the mirror, where
He gazed on himself, and shrieked like an old screen door
        far off.

Depended from her pinched thumb, each wing
Came clattering down like a small black shutter.
Still tranquil, she began, 'It's rather sweet . . .'
The soft mouse body, the hard feral glint
In the caught eyes. Then we saw,
And recoiled: lice, pallid, yellow,
Nested within the wing-pits, cosily sucked and snoozed.
The thing dropped from her hands, and with its thud,
Swiftly, the cat, with a clean careful mouth
Closed on the soiled webs, growling, took them out
        to the back stoop.

But still, dark blood, a sticky puddle on the floor
Remained, of all my mother's tender, wounding passion
For a whole wild, lost, betrayed and secret life
Among its dens and burrows, its clean stones,
Whose denizens can turn upon the world
With spitting tongue, an odor, talon, claw,
To sting or soil benevolence, alien
As our clumsy traps, our random scatter of shot.
She swept to the kitchen. Turning on the tap,
She washed and washed the pity from her hands.

CAROLYN KIZER   *b.* 1925   USA

The 90th Year
for Lore Segal

High in the jacaranda shines the gilded thread
of a small bird's curlicue of song – too high
for her to see or hear.
                              I've learned
not to say, these last years,
'O, look! – O, listen, Mother!'
as I used to.
                      (It was she
who taught me to look;
to name the flowers when I was still close to the ground,
my face level with theirs;
or to watch the sublime metamorphoses
unfold and unfold
over the walled back gardens of our street . . .

It had not been given her
to know the flesh as good in itself,
as the flesh of a fruit is good. To her
the human body has been a husk,
a shell in which souls were prisoned.

Yet, from within it, with how much gazing
her life has paid tribute to the world's body!
How tears of pleasure
would choke her, when a perfect voice,
deep or high, clove to its note unfaltering!)

She has swept the crackling seedpods,
the litter of mauve blossoms, off the cement path,
tipped them into the rubbish basket.
She's made her bed, washed up the breakfast dishes,
wiped the hotplate. I've taken the butter and milkjug
back to the fridge next door – but it's not my place,
visiting here, to usurp the tasks
that weave the day's pattern.
Now she is leaning forward in her chair,
        by the lamp lit in the daylight,
rereading *War and Peace*.
                        When I look up
from her wellworn copy of *The Divine Milieu*,
which she wants me to read, I see her hand
loose on the black stem of the magnifying glass,
she is dozing.
'I am so tired,' she has written to me, 'of appreciating
the gift of life.'

DENISE LEVERTOV   *b.* 1929, England   *d.* 1997, USA

After 37 Years My Mother Apologizes for My Childhood

When you tilted toward me, arms out
like someone trying to walk through a fire,
when you swayed toward me, crying out you were
sorry for what you had done to me, your
eyes filling with terrible liquid like
balls of mercury from a broken thermometer

skidding on the floor, when you quietly screamed
Where else could I turn? Who else did I have?, the
chopped crockery of your hands swinging toward me, the
water cracking from your eyes like moisture from
stones under heavy pressure, I could not
see what I would do with the rest of my life.
The sky seemed to be splintering like a window
someone is bursting into or out of, your
tiny face glittered as if with
shattered crystal, with true regret, the
regret of the body. I could not see what my
days would be, with you sorry, with
you wishing you had not done it, the
sky falling around me, its shards
glistening in my eyes, your old soft
body fallen against me in horror I
took you in my arms, I said *It's all right,
don't cry, it's all right,* the air filled with
flying glass, I hardly knew what I
said or who I would be now that I had forgiven you.

SHARON OLDS   *b.* 1942   USA

Medusa

Off that landspit of stony mouth-plugs,
Eyes rolled by white sticks,
Ears cupping the sea's incoherences,
You house your unnerving head — God-ball,
Lens of mercies,

Your stooges
Plying their wild cells in my keel's shadow,
Pushing by like hearts,
Red stigmata at the very centre,
Riding the rip tide to the nearest point of departure,

Dragging their Jesus hair.
Did I escape, I wonder?
My mind winds to you
Old barnacled umbilicus, Altantic cable,
Keeping itself, it seems, in a state of miraculous repair.

In any case, you are always there,
Tremulous breath at the end of my line,
Curve of water upleaping
To my water rod, dazzling and graceful,
Touching and sucking.

I didn't call you.
I didn't call you at all.
Nevertheless, nevertheless
You steamed to me over the sea,
Fat and red, a placenta

Paralyzing the kicking lovers.
Cobra light
Squeezing the breath from the blood bells
Of the fuchsia. I could draw no breath,
Dead and moneyless,

Overexposed, like an X-ray.
Who do you think you are?
A Communion wafer? Blubbery Mary?
I shall take no bite of your body,
Bottle in which I live,

Ghastly Vatican.
I am sick to death of hot salt.
Green as eunuchs, your wishes
Hiss at my sins.
Off, off, eely tentacle!

There is nothing between us.

SYLVIA PLATH* 1932–1963 USA

Heirloom

She gave me childhood's flowers,
Heather and wild thyme,
Eyebright and tormentil,
Lichen's mealy cup
Dry on wind-scored stone,
The corbies on the rock,
The rowan by the burn.

Sea-marvels a child beheld
Out in the fisherman's boat,
Fringed pulsing violet
Medusa, sea-gooseberries,
Starfish on the sea-floor,
Cowries and rainbow-shells
From pools on a rocky shore,

Gave me her memories,
But kept her last treasure:
'When I was a lass,' she said,
'Sitting among the heather,
'Suddenly I saw
'That all the moor was alive!
'I have told no one before.'

That was my mother's tale.
Seventy years had gone
Since she saw the living skein
Of which the world is woven,
And having seen, knew all;
Through long indifferent years
Treasuring the priceless pearl.

KATHLEEN RAINE   *b.* 1908   England

Mama's God

mama's God never was no white man.
her My Jesus, Sweet Jesus never was neither.
the color they had was the color of
her aches and trials, the tribulations of her heart
mama never had no saviour that would turn
his back on her because she was black
when mama prayed, she knew who she
was praying to and who she was praying to
didn't and ain't got
no color.

CAROLYN M. RODGERS *b.* 1945 USA

A Chilly Night

I rose at the dead of night,
    And went to the lattice alone
To look for my Mother's ghost
    Where the ghostly moonlight shone.

My friends had failed one by one,
    Middle-aged, young, and old,
Till the ghosts were warmer to me
    Than my friends that had grown cold.

I looked and I saw the ghosts
    Dotting plain and mound:
They stood in the blank moonlight,
    But no shadows lay on the ground:
They spoke without a voice
    And they leaped without a sound.

I called: 'O my Mother dear,' –
   I sobbed: 'O my Mother kind,
Make a lonely bed for me
   And shelter it from the wind.

'Tell the others not to come
   To see me night or day:
But I need not tell my friends
   To be sure to keep away.'

My Mother raised her eyes,
   They were blank and could not see:
Yet they held me with their stare
   While they seemed to look at me.

She opened her mouth and spoke;
   I could not hear a word,
While my flesh crept on my bones
   And every hair was stirred.

She knew that I could not hear
   The message that she told
Whether I had long to wait
   Or soon should sleep in the mould:
I saw her toss her shadowless hair
   And wring her hands in the cold.

I strained to catch her words,
   And she strained to make me hear;
But never a sound of words
   Fell on my straining ear.

From midnight to the cockcrow
   I kept my watch in pain
While the subtle ghosts grew subtler
   In the sad night on the wane.

From midnight to the cockcrow
   I watched till all were gone,
Some to sleep in the shifting sea
   And some under turf and stone:
Living had failed and dead had failed,
   And I was indeed alone.

CHRISTINA ROSSETTI   1830–1894   England

Passed On

Before, this box contained my mother.
For months she'd sent me out for index cards,
scribbled with a squirrel concentration
while I'd nag at her, seeing strength
drain, ink-blue, from her finger-ends
providing for a string of hard winters
I was trying not to understand.

Only after, opening it, I saw
how she'd rendered herself down from flesh
to paper, alphabetical; there for me
in every way she could anticipate
— *Acupuncture: conditions suited to*
— *Books to read by age twenty-one*
— *Choux pastry: how to make, when to use.*

The cards looked after me. I'd shuffle them
to almost hear her speak. Then, my days
were box-shaped (or was I playing safe?)
for every doubt or choice, a card that fitted
— *Exams: the best revision strategy*
— *Flowers: cut, how to make them last*
— *Greece: the men, what you need to know.*

But then they seemed to shrink. I'd turn them over,
find them blank; the edges furred, mute,
whole areas wrong, or missing. Had she known?
The language pointed to what wasn't said.
I'd add notes of my own, strange beside
Her urgent dogmatism, loosening grip
— *infinitives never telling love*
  lust single issue politics when
  don't hopeless careful trust

On the beach, I built a hollow cairn,
tipped in the cards. Then I let her go.
The smoke rose thin and clear, slowly blurred.
I've kept the box for diaries, like this.

CAROLE SATYAMURTI   *b.* 1939   England

Christmas Eve

Oh sharp diamond, my mother!
I could not count the cost
of all your faces, your moods —
that present that I lost.
Sweet girl, my deathbed,
my jewel-fingered lady,
your portrait flickered all night
by the bulbs of the tree.

Your face as calm as the moon
over a mannered sea,
presided at the family reunion,
the twelve grandchildren
you used to wear on your wrist,
a three-months-old baby,
a fat check you never wrote,
the red-haired toddler who danced the twist,
your aging daughters, each one a wife,
each one talking to the family cook,
each one avoiding your portrait,
each one aping your life.

Later, after the party,
after the house went to bed,
I sat up drinking the Christmas brandy,
watching your picture,
letting the tree move in and out of focus.
The bulbs vibrated.
They were a halo over your forehead.
Then they were a beehive,
blue, yellow, green, red;
each with its own juice, each hot and alive
stinging your face. But you did not move.
I continued to watch, forcing myself,
waiting, inexhaustible, thirty-five.

I wanted your eyes, like the shadows
of two small birds, to change.

But they did not age.
The smile that gathered me in, all wit,
all charm, was invincible.
Hour after hour I looked at your face
but could not pull the roots out of it.
Then I watched how the sun hit
your red sweater, your withered neck,
your badly painted flesh-pink skin.
You who led me by the nose,
I saw you as you were.
Then I thought of your body
as one thinks of murder . . .

Then I said Mary –
Mary, Mary, forgive me
and then I touched a present for the child,
the last I bred before your death;
and then I touched my breast
and then I touched the floor
and then my breast again as if,
somehow, it were one of yours.

ANNE SEXTON   1928–1974   USA

'for years I slept in the same room'

for years I slept in the same room
as my mother   every morning
I saw her wake up   lie silently awhile
struggle stiffly out of bed   struggle
to get her girdle on   saw the fat
on her waist   her ass   her thighs
squeezed mercilessly

saw her pull on her dress   groan
as she bent to put on her shoes
grimace into a mirror   pluck
a few hairs from her chin   (I
do that now)   put on
her makeup   her scarf   her hat   her coat
drink coffee standing   leave for work

the same gestures   every day for years
only stiffening
she was in pain   I found her graceless

I hated it when she called me
to the bathroom   to speak to me
while she was in the shower
her body repelled me
her broad freckled back
looked beaten
her scarred belly sagged
(I'd been a caesarian   and she often said
I wasn't worth the trouble)
she was flabby and worn

the flat was small
we watched television a lot
she talked   I had nothing to say
as she said   you could have cut the air with a knife

every night   I lay in bed   imagining
vividly   in intricate detail
all the ways I could kill her
or myself   anything that would stop that sound
as she   snored her exhaustion out

some nights   she didn't fall asleep
she spoke the perpetual litany of her aborted life
our uneasy bodies   found what comfort they could
I covered my head with the pillow   she repeated
that I was   an ungrateful bitch
that I had no heart   that although
I read so many books
I didn't know my ass from my elbow

that I was killing her   while
she was killing herself for me
that my only friend   was
taking advantage of me   was using me
for some unknown purpose of her own
and anyway I couldn't trust a friend

then she begged me   to confide in her

she wanted a normal daughter   married
with kids   a house   a good life
she got me   she tried   I tried
neither of us had a chance

SHEILA SHULMAN   *b.* 1936   USA

Daughter
to
Parents

To Father and Mother

When you return in dreams,
You smile, you are never cross with each other.
On the bizarre picnic, the fall-away cliff,
We dream together.

Often the fogs of war
Clogged my young breath, often you stood
Like two lighthouses, stabbing your powerful beams
Crosswise above my head.

You always smiled at me,
Never guessing at my built-in radar –
Hear beyond hearing, say nothing, think huge
(Children, the world over).

Your parent joy in me
Was not enough; I wanted you to smile so
One to the other – partners and relaxed,
As in finding mushrooms.

Now, in dreams, you do.

JEAN EARLE   *b.* 1909   England

I've Worked It Out

I've worked it out that when my parents parted
some time at the end of '43
I was about the size of a pea
eroding the lining of mum's womb.
He had been on compassionate leave
for grandfather's terminal illness, hence,
amid the stink of death that was Europe,
their chance to make life.

I know it like a memory, the walk to the station
with their arms hooked (that's how couples
walked those days), he in Luftwaffe uniform,
blue-grey, her favourite colour always,
she in the coat with the fox fur collar.
They talked of how it would be when it was over.
She saw the train out and walked back,
spent the rest of the pregnancy ducking bombs,
watching the city subside into rubble.

There was no news, but the letters stopped,
so he was listed missing. Someone claimed
to have seen him in Estonia, five hundred miles
from where he was last known to be.
She went to the fortune teller who said
he'd be back in '51, or if not, by '53.
Later, she had him declared dead
for the sake of the war widow's pension.
All the time, I spooned the hated potato soup –
one for mummy, one for sister, one for granny,
three for father starving in the camp.

In '55, Adenauer negotiated the release
of the last POWs in Soviet hands.
Aged eleven, I watched her watch the trains go by.
Leaning from open wagons other men waved to us,
excited so soon after crossing the border.
It was then she gave up and wept.

SUSANNE EHRHARDT   *b.* 1944, Germany   England

I was not there

The morning they set out from home
I was not there to comfort them
the dawn was innocent with snow
in mockery – it is not true
the dawn was neutral was immune
their shadows threaded it too soon
they were relieved that it had come
I was not there to comfort them

One told me that my father spent
a day in prison long ago
he did not tell me that he went
what difference does it make now
when he set out when he came home
I was not there to comfort him
and now I have no means to know
of what I was kept ignorant

Both my parents died in camps
I was not there to comfort them
I was not there they were alone
my mind refuses to conceive
the life the death they must have known
I must atone because I live
I could not have saved them from death
the ground is neutral underneath

Every child must leave its home
time gathers life impartially
I could have spared them nothing since
I was too young – it is not true
they might have lived to succour me
and none shall say in my defence
had I been there to comfort them
it would have made no difference

KAREN GERSHON*   *b.* 1923, Germany   *d.* 1993, Israel

'I can remember what my mother wore'

I can remember what my mother wore.
I knew that she was leaving and went on to school,
Pretending nothing happened.

She visited,
Sometimes my father hid these visits.
I'd been at school,
The door had closed before I opened it,
I couldn't hear her footsteps as I ran.
This was his act of kindness.

She would cry that she had left him,
And I listened, couldn't tell my father,
Nor tell her how my father was in pain,
Though both asked questions.

Now I would wish not to see my father again
If he were happy, and my mother,
Growing old in an always foreign country —
The refuge never home but better than another,
Still feels she's not arrived.

I cannot hope for footsteps with no meaning,
Nor want a noise which means I sleep in peace
And never hear the footsteps to the door.
I worry at the cost of waking late,
In ignorance of knowing what I missed,
All I know is waking wears me out,
And time's the cost I can't control or count.

A woman walked away from her small child,
And both are inconsolable.
So leave it.
The movement's not our will,
It happens anyway.

CAROLINE GRIFFIN   *b.* 1950   England

One Flesh

Lying apart now, each in a separate bed,
He with a book, keeping the light on late,
She like a girl dreaming of childhood,
All men elsewhere — it is as if they wait
Some new event: the book he holds unread,
Her eyes fixed on the shadows overhead.

Tossed up like flotsam from a former passion,
How cool they lie. They hardly ever touch,
Or if they do it is like a confession
Of having little feeling — or too much.
Chastity faces them, a destination
For which their whole lives were a preparation.

Strangely apart, yet strangely together,
Silence between them like a thread to hold
And not wind in. And time itself's a feather
Touching them gently. Do they know they're old,
These two who are my father and my mother
Whose fire, from which I came, has now grown cold?

ELIZABETH JENNINGS   *b.* 1926   England

The Red Graveyard

There are some stones that open in the night like flowers.
Down in the red graveyard where Bessie haunts her lovers.
There are stones that shake and weep in the heart of night
Down in the red graveyard where Bessie haunts her lovers.

Why do I remember the blues?
I am five or six or seven in the back garden;
the window is wide open;
her voice is slow motion through the heavy summer air.
Jelly roll. Kitchen man. Sausage roll. Frying pan.

Inside the house where I used to be myself,
her voice claims the rooms. In the best room even,
something has changed the shape of my silence.
Why do I remember her voice and not my own mother's?
Why do I remember the blues?

My mother's voice. What was it like?
A flat stone for skitting. An old rock.
Long long grass. Asphalt. Wind. Hail.
Cotton. Linen. Salt. Treacle.
I think it was a peach.
I heard it down to the ribbed stone.

I am coming down the stairs in my father's house.
I am five or six or seven. There is fat thick wallpaper
I always caress, bumping flower into flower.
She is singing. (Did they play anyone else ever?)
My father's feet tap a shiny beat on the floor.

Christ, my father says, that's some voice she's got.
I pick up the record cover. And now. This is slow motion.
My hand swoops, glides, swoops again.
I pick up the cover and my fingers are all over her face.
Her black face. Her magnificent black face.
That's some voice. His shoes dancing on the floor.

There are some stones that open in the night like flowers
Down in the red graveyard where Bessie haunts her lovers.
There are stones that shake and weep in the heart of night
Down in the red graveyard where Bessie haunts her lovers.

JACKIE KAY* *b.* 1961   Scotland

Outside

In the center of a harsh and spectrumed city
all things natural are strange.
I grew up in a genuine confusion
between grass and weeds and flowers
and what colored meant
except for clothes you couldn't bleach
and nobody called me nigger
until I was thirteen.
Nobody lynched my momma
but what she'd never been
had bleached her face of everything
but very private furies
and made the other children
call me yellow snot at school.

And how many times have I called myself back
through my bones confusion
black
like marrow meaning meat
and how many times have you cut me
and run in the streets
my own blood
who do you think me to be
that you are terrified of becoming
or what do you see in my face
you have not already discarded
in your own mirror
what face do you see in my eyes
that you will someday
come to
acknowledge your own?
Who shall I curse that I grew up
believing in my mother's face
or that I lived in fear of potent darkness
wearing my father's shape
they have both marked me
with their blind and terrible love
and I am lustful now for my own name.

Between the canyons of their mighty silences
mother bright and father brown
I seek my own shapes now
for they never spoke of me
except as theirs
and the pieces I stumble and fall over
I still record as proof
that I am beautiful
twice
blessed with the images
of who they were
and who I thought them once to be
of what I move
toward and through
and what I need
to leave behind me
most of all
I am blessed within my selves
who are come to make our shattered faces
whole.

AUDRE LORDE   1934–1992   USA

Their Bones are Silver

Their bones are silver and their winding sheets
are damask linen; I lock them away
pleased in their safety and anxious about them.

They will be knives and forks and table cloths
to whomever inherits them; and their photographs
will be camp decorations around somebody's room.

Only their voices, frail and tattered now,
will not survive me. Who'll listen to
good counsel and kind lies? They should have made

Some ballyhoo in dying. HAVE COURAGE
says her letter and her last; giving her number
(On her arm? Tattooed?) BEFORE I LEAVE, MY LOVE . . .

You saw them off, you say? – How were they then?
(Verzweifelt waren sie. Was sollten sie denn sein?)
Despairing! – O how else?

GERDA MAYER*   *b.* 1927, Czechoslovakia   England

I Go Back to May 1937

I see them standing at the formal gates of their colleges,
I see my father strolling out
under the ocher sandstone arch, the
red tiles glinting like bent
plates of blood behind his head,
I see my mother with a few light books at her hip
standing at the pillar made of tiny bricks with the
wrought-iron gate still open behind her, its
sword-tips black in the May air,
they are about to graduate, they are about to get married,
they are kids, they are dumb, all they know is they are
innocent, they would never hurt anybody.
I want to go up to them and say Stop,
don't do it – she's the wrong woman,
he's the wrong man, you are going to do things
you cannot imagine you would ever do,
you are going to do bad things to children,
you are going to suffer in ways you have not heard of,
you are going to want to die. I want to go
up to them there in the late May sunlight and say it,
her hungry pretty blank face turning to me,
her pitiful beautiful untouched body,
his arrogant handsome face turning to me,
his pitiful beautiful untouched body,

but I don't do it. I want to live. I
take them up like the male and female
paper dolls and bang them together
at the hips like chips of flint as if to
strike sparks from them, I say
Do what you are going to do, and I will tell about it.

SHARON OLDS   *b.* 1942   USA

Ptarmigans

My dad's bought her a cake.
We're doing the icing,
my daughter and I. A snake
of silver balls, the chocolate
leaves from Sainsbury's:
sycamore, willow, oak.

Six jellybabies for
her grandchildren, a crimson
seventy-seven for her years.

Last birthday with him?
Final cake he'll buy?
This is the kitchen
from which we radiate: a Kings
Cross of linkings
en route for destinations

that still may sabotage
or hurt, their titles mute
as ptarmigans in camouflage

of bland September leaves.
Chestnut, elm: a soft war-zone
where words you never think about
have squirreled away their bone.
What can he think of us? Daughter,
mother, father. Husband. Lover. Home.

RUTH PADEL   *b.* 1944   England

Mortal

There is a man of me that sows.
There is a woman of me that reaps.
One for good,
and one for fair,
And they cannot find me anywhere.

Father and Mother, shadowy ancestry,
Can you make no more than this of me?

LAURA RIDING   1901–1991   USA

A Child's Japan

1

Before we could call
America home,
In the days of exile,
My image of holiness
Was Kobo Daishi,

Young and beautiful,
Sitting on his lotus
In a thin gold circle
Of light.
He is with me still.

My father loved
Monasteries,
His fantasy, perhaps,
To abandon wife and child
And withdraw to a cell
Or an austere pavilion
With paper walls.

From my bed
Down the long dark hall
I could see him
Circled in light,
His back always bent
Over his desk,
Motionless for hours.

My mother
Treated flowers as individuals,
Hated clutter and confusion,
Invented marvelous games —
Paper skaters
Blown across a lacquer tray —
Knew how to make a small room
Open and quiet.

We lived in austere style
Through necessity
And because it suited us,
An artist, a scholar,
And their one child.
How Japanese the rain looked
In Cambridge,
Slanting down in autumn!
How Japanese the heavy snow in lumps
On the black branches!

It is clear to me now
That we were all three
A little in love with Japan.

2

When I flew out into the huge night,
Bearing with me a freight of memory,
My parents were dead.

I was going toward
All they had left behind
In the houses where we had lived,
In the artful measure
And sweet austerity
Of their lives —
That extravagance of work
And flowers,
Of work and music,
Of work and faith.

I was flying home to Japan —
A distant relative,
Familiar, strange,
And full of magic.

MAY SARTON   *b.* 1912   USA

Where Are You?

In this garden, after a day of rain,
a blackbird is making soundings,
flinging his counter-tenor line
into blue air, to where
an answering cadenza shows
the shape and depth of his own solitude.

Born in South London, inheritors
of brick, smoke, slate, tarmac,
uneasy with pastoral
as hill-billies with high-rise,
my parents called each other
in blackbird language:
my father's interrogative whistle
– 'where are you?'
my mother's note, swooping, dutiful
– 'here I am.'

There must have slid into the silences
the other questions,
blind, voiceless worms whose weight
cluttered his tongue:
questions I hear as, half a lifetime on,
I eavesdrop on blackbirds.

CAROLE SATYAMURTI   *b.* 1939   England

Flames

This is the black and white photograph
that I shall burn first, my young mother
in the wind at Margate,
self-conscious and smiling as the child
pulls back and away from her
and sulks, the silver-paper glitter of kite-tail
still streaming. These are the
flames, the crackling red and orange,
the hungry black ring that moves outwards.
And this one, with my father
standing on a mound to reach up
another two inches, as she looks laughing
over canal, trees, valley, the Dijon summer
colours disappearing in a stroke
of rising light, the transparent centre.

Or this one, taken much later,
the two of you always together,
against bulb-fields blazing
with red tulips, that I shall
leave until last, that perhaps I will not need
even to put a match to.

SUSAN WICKS *b.* 1947 England

Son
to
Father

A Song of Lies on Sabbath Eve

On a Sabbath eve, at dusk on a summer day
when I was a child,
when the odors of food and prayer drifted up from all the
    houses
and the wings of the Sabbath angels rustled in the air,
I began to lie to my father:
'I went to another synagogue.'

I don't know if he believed me or not
but the lie was very sweet in my mouth.
And in all the houses at night
hymns and lies drifted up together,
O taste and see,
and in all the houses at night
Sabbath angels died like flies in the lamp,
and lovers put mouth to mouth
and inflated one another till they floated in the air
or burst.

Since then, lying has tasted very sweet to me,
and since then I've always gone to another synagogue.
And my father returned the lie when he died:
'I've gone to another life.'

YEHUDA AMICHAI   *b.* 1924, Germany   Israel
Translated by Chana Bloch and Stephen Mitchell

In Memoriam W. R. A.

ob. *April 18th, 1963*

A *Cricket Match*, between
  The *Gentlemen of Cambridge*
And the *Hanover Club*, to be played
By the *Antient Laws of the Game*
[Two stumps, no boundaries, lobs,
Single wicket, no pads — all that]
    In *Antient Costume*
    For a *Good Cause*.

Leading the Gentlemen,
  I won the toss and batted.
With a bat like an overgrown spoon
And a racquets ball, runs came fast;
But as, in my ruffles and tights,
I marched to the crease, I was sad
    To see you nowhere
    About the field.

You would have got the point:
  'No boundaries' meant running
Literally each bloody run.
When I 'threw my wicket away'
And, puffing, limped back to my seat,
I wanted to catch your eye
    Half-shut with laughter
    (And pride and love).

Afterwards, over pints,
  Part of a chatting circle,
You would have said I was right
To declare about when I did;
Though the other chaps went for the runs
And got them with plenty in hand,
    What did it matter?
    The game's the thing.

Later: the two of us:
    'That time – do you remember? –
We watched Wally Hammond at Lord's,
And you said you wished you were him,
And I fixed up a coach, but you said
You were working too hard for exams?
    Oh well. A pity
    You never tried.'

I know. And I foresee
    (As if this were not fancy)
The on-and-on of your talk,
My gradually formal response
That I could never defend
But never would soften enough,
    Leading to silence,
    And separate ways.

Forgive me if I have
    To see it as it happened:
Even your pride and your love
Have taken this time to become
Clear, to arouse my love.
I'm sorry you had to die
    To make me sorry
    You're not here now.

KINGSLEY AMIS   1922–1995   England

'My father thought it bloody queer'

My father thought it bloody queer,
the day I rolled home with a ring of silver in my ear
half hidden by a mop of hair. 'You've lost your head.
If that's how easily you're led
you should've had it through your nose instead.'

And even then I hadn't had the nerve to numb
the lobe with ice, then drive a needle through the skin,
then wear a safety-pin. It took a jeweller's gun
to pierce the flesh, and then a friend
to thread a sleeper in, and where it slept
the hole became a sore, became a wound, and wept.

At twenty-nine, it comes as no surprise to hear
my own voice breaking like a tear, released like water,
cried from way back in the spiral of the ear. *If I were you,*
I'd take it out and leave it out next year.

SIMON ARMITAGE   *b.* 1963   England

Thoughts on My Father

You are boned clean now.
You are lost like dice and teeth.
Don't bother knock
I won't represent you.

A sound brain you were,
your body a mastery,
but no turning into any stepping stone
or handing anybody a key.

Simply it hurts that needing
we offended you
and I judge you by lack.

Playing some well shaped shadow
the sun alone moved,
you wouldn't be mixed with cash
or the world's cunning.

So perfectly exclusive,
you tantalized me.
You split our home in passions.
Every year we were more blunted.

I knew nowhere.
My eyes looked out from you
my first god.

Omnipotence breathed
come boy come
to hungrybelly revelations.

Lift your hat to doom
boy in the manner that roadside
weeds are indestructible.

Stubborn tides you echo.
I moved your sterile tones
from my voice.
I lifted your mole
from my back.

You scar me man,
but I must go over you again and again.
I must plunge my raging eyes
in all your steady enduring.

I must assemble material
of my own
for a new history.

JAMES BERRY   *b.* 1924   England

Dream Song 384

The marker slants, flowerless, day's almost done,
I stand above my father's grave with rage,
often, often before
I've made this awful pilgrimage to one
who cannot visit me, who tore his page
out: I come back for more,

I spit upon this dreadful banker's grave
who shot his heart out in a Florida dawn
O ho alas alas
When will indifference come, I moan & rave
I'd like to scrabble till I got right down
away down under the grass

and ax the casket open ha to see
just how he's taking it, which he sought so hard
we'll tear apart
the mouldering grave clothes ha & then Henry
will heft the ax once more, his final card,
and fell it on the start.

JOHN BERRYMAN* 1914–1972   USA

On a Portrait of a Deaf Man

The kind old face, the egg-shaped head,
    The tie, discreetly loud,
The loosely fitting shooting clothes,
    A closely fitting shroud.

He liked old City dining-rooms,
    Potatoes in their skin,
But now his mouth is wide to let
    The London clay come in.

He took me on long silent walks
    In country lanes when young,
He knew the name of ev'ry bird
    But not the song it sung.

And when he could not hear me speak
    He smiled and looked so wise
That now I do not like to think
    Of maggots in his eyes.

He liked the rain-washed Cornish air
   And smell of ploughed-up soil,
He liked a landscape big and bare
   And painted it in oil.

But least of all he liked that place
   Which hangs on Highgate Hill
Of soaked Carrara-covered earth
   For Londoners to fill.

He would have liked to say good-bye,
   Shake hands with many friends,
In Highgate now his finger-bones
   Stick through his finger-ends.

You, God, who treat him thus and thus,
   Say 'Save his soul and pray.'
You ask me to believe You and
   I only see decay.

JOHN BETJEMAN   1906–1984   England

Kew Gardens

in memory of Ian A. Black, died January 1971

Distinguished scientist, to whom I greatly defer
(old man moreover, whom I dearly love),
I walk today in Kew Gardens, in sunlight the colour of honey
which flows from the cold autumnal blue of the heavens to
     light these tans and golds,
these ripe corn and leather and sunset colours of the East Asian
     liriodendrons,
of the beeches and maples and plum-trees and the stubborn
     green banks of the holly hedges –
and you walk always beside me, you with your knowledge of
     names

and your clairvoyant gaze, in what for me is sheer panorama
seeing the net or web of connectedness. But today it is I who
　　　speak
(and you are long dead, but it is to you I say it):

'The leaves are green in summer because of chlorophyll
and the flowers are bright to lure the pollinators,
and without remainder (so you have often told me)
these marvellous things that shock the heart the head can
　　　account for;
but I want to sing an excess which is not so simply explainable,
to say that the beauty of the autumn is a redundant beauty,
that the sky had no need to be this particular shade of blue,
nor the maple to die in flames of this particular yellow,
nor the heart to respond with an ecstasy that does not beget
　　　children.
I want to say that I do not believe your science
although I believe every word of it, and intend to understand it;
that although I rate that unwavering gaze higher than almost
　　　everything
there is another sense, a hearing, to which I more deeply attend.
Thus I withstand and contradict you, I, your child,
who have inherited from you the passion which causes me to
　　　oppose you.'

D. M. BLACK　*b.* 1941, South Africa　Scotland

Rain

Quite suddenly the evening clears at last
as now outside the soft small rain is falling.
Falling or fallen. Rain itself is something
undoubtedly which happens in the past.

Whoever hears it falling has remembered
a time in which a curious twist of fate
brought back to him a flower whose name was 'rose'
and the perplexing redness of its red.

This rain which spreads its blind across the pane
must also brighten in forgotten suburbs
the black grapes on a vine across a shrouded

patio now no more. The evening's rain
brings me the voice, the dear voice of my father,
who comes back now, who never has been dead.

JORGE LUIS BORGES   1899—1986   Argentina
Translated by Alastair Reid

The Twins

he hinted at times that I was a bastard and I told him to listen
to Brahms, and I told him to learn to paint and drink and not be
dominated by women and dollars
but he screamed at me, For Christ's sake remember your
        mother,
remember your country,
you'll kill us all! . . .

I move through my father's house (on which he owes $8,000
        after 20
years on the same job) and look at his dead shoes
the way his feet curled the leather as if he were angry planting
        roses,
and he was, and I look at his dead cigarette, his last cigarette
and the last bed he slept in that night, and I feel I should
        remake it
but I can't, for a father is always your master even when he's
        gone;
I guess these things have happened time and again but I can't
        help
thinking
    to die on a kitchen floor at 7 o'clock in the morning
    while other people are frying eggs
    is not so rough
    unless it happens to you.

I go outside and pick an orange and peel back the bright skin;
things are still living: the grass is growing quite well,
the sun sends down its rays circled by a Russian satellite;
a dog barks senselessly somewhere, the neighbors peek behind
        blinds;
I am a stranger here, and have been (I suppose) somewhat the
        rogue,
and I have no doubt he painted me quite well (the old boy and
        I
fought like mountain lions) and they say he left it all to some
        woman
in Duarte but I don't give a damn – she can have it: he was my
        old
man
    and he died.

inside, I try on a light blue suit
much better than anything I have ever worn
and I flap the arms like a scarecrow in the wind
but it's no good:
I can't keep him alive
no matter how much we hated each other.
we looked exactly alike, we could have been twins
the old man and I: that's what they
said. he had his bulbs on the screen
ready for planting
while I was laying with a whore from 3rd street.

very well. grant us this moment: standing before a mirror
in my dead father's suit
waiting also
to die.

CHARLES BUKOWSKI   *b.* 1920, Germany   USA

Volare

Just as lights inside our living room
and steam from water boiling on the stove
erase Cleveland from the picture window,
father comes in,
stands in the kitchen, one shoulder thrust forward,
feet apart the way he's seen Lanza stand,
eyelids drooping like Dean Martin's or Como's,
Lucky Strike stuck to lower lip.
We can leave the confusion
and all disillusion behind.
And we know he got the raise,
his laborer's share of chemical company profits
from the Manhattan Project
and the revolution in plastics.
Four hundred a year. And that's not hay.
He grabs my mother
and spins with her before the stove,
wooden spoon brandished like the fine lady's fan
she saw that day in pages of *Life.*
Just like birds of a feather
a rainbow together we'll find.
Then he comes for me,
and I'm soaring above cauldrons
of rigatoni and sauce bubbling bright
as the scarlet cassocks altar boys wear
at Christmas and Easter.
He brings me back to earth
and twirls away to phone his mother.
That night when he comes home from moonlighting
in the credit department at Sears,
feet heavy as bricks,
he'll come to my bedroom and tell me again
how there'll be no promotion for him
because he couldn't go to college
but still he's risen higher than his father
who put in fifty years with the B & O.

He'll step out the door
and for a moment his head will be caught in light
like some raptured hoary saint drunk on love
in the window of Ascension of Our Lord
and the last thing I'll hear
will be his lovely forlorn baritone
fading, fading into stillness.
Volare. Wo-wo. Cantare. Wo-o-o-o.

DAVID CITINO   *b.* 1947   USA

To My Father

My body is buried, when I used to be my father,
In the overspill from the village churchyard
Into a field, where a single electrified wire
Keeps back the cows but not the grass or flowers.
Now he is I he waits for a worthwhile task
In which to succeed, better than the water towers
And colliery washers bulky as beer-drinkers
He built as foreman. Pity everyone
Who had, like him, to swim for it in the Thirties,
Fully clothed in the nation's economy.
Those days when he sat in his chair with nothing to smoke
And dressed in his best suit weekly to draw the dole
Pared people down to their character:
The poorest made spills from the *Daily Herald*
To sell to the not-so-poor to burn its bad news
And some who were mean who couldn't get odd jobs
Sneaked to the Means Test on those who could.
My Mother's wedding ring sold for old gold
But the tools my Father himself had made were a living:
Pieces of wood making passionate love
To each other in perfect joints,
Chisels holding out their healthy tongues of steel
And grooving planes with various long fingernails.

The back of my mind still looks for a sixpence of dole
I lost on an errand through swinging a gate
And weeded my footsteps for in remorse and vain.
Then, in better times, with a prospect of war
He spoilt the micrometer of his hand
On jobs that needed only hammer and nails.
No wonder that when they were lost in a fire
At his place of work he made no claim
For tools he used so seldom though fully insured
For forty years. He had willed his vision away –
The thought on a summer morning while colours still drowse
And the corn begins to turn in its bed in the breeze
That something must be done about the world –
Poet manage the image an appearance needed,
Scientist explain and engineer invent –
A creative force that would be wasted on women.
Father, you were uncommunicative
And lived like a hermit in your hopes
To whom it is too important that Heaven exists
For it to matter to him who goes there;
After the sack as yourself, your discarded hobbies
And unrepaired plans you try again as me.

STANLEY COOK   *b.* 1922   England

The Hospital Window

I have just come down from my father.
Higher and higher he lies
Above me in a blue light
Shed by a tinted window.
I drop through six white floors
And then step out onto pavement.

Still feeling my father ascend,
I start to cross the firm street,
My shoulder blades shining with all
The glass the huge building can raise.
Now I must turn round and face it,
And know his one pane from the others.

Each window possesses the sun
As though it burned there on a wick.
I wave, like a man catching fire.
All the deep-dyed windowpanes flash,
And, behind them, all the white rooms
They turn to the colour of Heaven.

Ceremoniously, gravely, and weakly,
Dozens of pale hands are waving
Back, from inside their flames.
Yet one pure pane among these
Is the bright, erased blankness of nothing.
I know that my father is there,

In the shape of his death still living.
The traffic increases around me
Like a madness called down on my head.
The horns blast at me like shotguns,
And drivers lean out, driven crazy —
But now my propped-up father

Lifts his arm out of stillness at last.
The light from the window strikes me
And I turn as blue as a soul,
As the moment when I was born.
I am not afraid for my father —
Look! He is grinning; he is not

Afraid for my life, either,
As the wild engines stand at my knees
Shredding their gears and roaring,
And I hold each car in its place
For miles, inciting its horn
To blow down the walls of the world

That the dying may float without fear
In the bold blue gaze of my father.
Slowly I move to the sidewalk
With my pin-tingling hand half dead
At the end of my bloodless arm.
I carry it off in amazement,

High, still higher, still waving,
My recognized face fully mortal,
Yet not; not at all, in the pale,
Drained, otherworldly, stricken,
Created hue of stained glass.
I have just come down from my father.

JAMES DICKEY   1923–1997   USA

Poem for My Father

I

He could feel, as he lay half-awake on his mat,
Not knowing if it were night or day,
The same black space behind the ears,
My nightmare is my family, and these hands of mine
Would wrench off my shoulders if they could,
But I am as the waters of my fate,
My father plunging through them to become me.

Outside, a commuter, refugee, goes leaping along the street
As by his fingertips he clings
To the broken glass of a late winter twilight sky.
Marked man, face up against the sky,
Riddled with aspirations.

II

I saw through my fingers a man in the sky
Moving out the bay:

Reality's Jack swaying out to sea.

What need to look back
Into the night at the root of it?
Who grips the twine to a poor man's kite
Grips me.

PAUL DURCAN   *b.* 1944   Ireland

The Father's Death

Since your loud voice has ebbed into
the cavern of a grief
the house sounds so vast and hollow
we dare not stir in it, who live

He who trampled down your ashes
trembles lest he hears your tread
the sole refuge without you is
where your presence has been laid

All elsewhere resounds with you
while here an anchored corpse you lie
no haven of escape from you
except your bed's periphery

I flood my memory with night
to be your assassin's lair
while the garden fountain's jet
gushes from an old well of tears

My stern judge now that you are gone
I can at last confess my crime
you were my tyrant and victim
you misjudged but the wrong was mine

Now I implore from your closed eyes
your anger's farewell flame,
father, when at last your face
shows me its goodness free of shame.

PIERRE EMMANUEL   1916–1984   France
Translated by Francis Scarfe

A Grand Night

When the film *Tell England* came
To Leamington, my father said,
'That's about Gallipoli – I was there.
'I'll call and see the manager . . .'

Before the first showing, the manager
Announced that 'a local resident . . .' etc.
And there was my father on the stage
With a message to the troops from Sir Somebody
Exhorting, condoling or congratulating.
But he was shy, so the manager
Read it out, while he fidgeted.
Then the lights went off, and I thought
I'd lost my father.
The Expedition's casualty rate was 50%.

But it was a grand night,
With free tickets for the two of us.

D. J. ENRIGHT   *b.* 1920   England

A Bill to My Father

I am typing up bills for a firm to be sent to their clients.
It occurs to me that firms are sending bills to my father
Who has that way an identity I do not always realize.
He is a person who buys, owes, and pays.
Not papa like he is to me.
His creditors reproach him for not paying on time
With a bill marked 'Please remit.'
I reproach him for never having shown his love for me
But only his disapproval.
He has a debt to me too
Although I have long since ceased asking him to come across;
He does not know how and so I do without it.
But in this impersonal world of business
He can be communicated with:
With absolute assurance of being paid
The boss writes 'Send me my money'
And my father sends it.

EDWARD FIELD   *b.* 1924   USA

Fathers

My father may be often in my dreams
Yet (since he died when I was young) play parts –
Or be himself – and stay unrecognized.

In any case dreaming often modifies
The features of the characters we know,
Though usually telling us who's really meant,

Like useful footnotes to an allegory.
This morning speckled foam fell in the basin:
Watching my father shave came flooding back

From over fifty years. His cut-throat razor,
Black beard, seemed things of fascinated love –
And now replace the visage and his speech.

Did he imagine (as I sometimes do)
His son would one day reach the age of sixty,
Himself being almost *ipso facto* dead?

Worse, in his final illness did he think
How he would leave a foolish child of eight,
Himself being hardly out of folly's years?

ROY FULLER   1912–1991   England

My Faither Sees Me

My faither sees me throu the gless;
why is he out there in the mirk?
His luik gaes throu me like a dirk,
and mine throu his, baith merciless.

Ta'en up aa wi my affairs,
what I maun spend, what I maun hain,[1]
I saw throu the blak shiny pane;
he tuik me geynear[2] unawares.

I see him, by the winnock-bar,[3]
yerkan[4] his heid as I yerk mine;
luik maikan[5] luik in double line,
ilk of the ither is made war.[6]

Yon luik has flasht frae my faither's een
in Edinbrugh, and hou faur hyne[7]
in Sutherland, and hou lang syne[8]
in Stromness, Dornoch, Aberdeen?

1 *hain:* save   2 *geynear:* almost   3 *winnock-bar:* sash-bar   4 *yerkan:* jerking
5 *maikan:* matching   6 *war:* aware   7 *hyne:* hence   8 *syne:* since

I beik⁹ about my cosy, bricht,
fluorescent electric warld.
He sees me yet, yon norland yarl;
I steik¹⁰ my shutters guid and ticht.

ROBERT GARIOCH   1909–1981   Scotland

9 *beik:* bask   10 *steik:* shut fast

Marked with D

When the chilled dough of his flesh went in an oven
not unlike those he fuelled all his life,
I thought of his cataracts ablaze with Heaven
and radiant with the sight of his dead wife,
light streaming from his mouth to shape her name,
'not Florence and not Flo but always Florrie'.
I thought how his cold tongue burst into flame
but only literally, which makes me sorry,
sorry for his sake there's no Heaven to reach.
I get it all from Earth my daily bread
but he hungered for release from mortal speech
that kept him down, the tongue that weighed like lead.

The baker's man that no one will see rise
and England made to feel like some dull oaf
is smoke, enough to sting one person's eyes
and ash (not unlike flour) for one small loaf.

TONY HARRISON   *b.* 1937   England

Those Winter Sundays

Sundays too my father got up early
and put his clothes on in the blueblack cold,
then with cracked hands that ached
from labor in the weekday weather made
banked fires blaze. No one ever thanked him.

I'd wake and hear the cold splintering, breaking.
When the rooms were warm, he'd call,
and slowly I would rise and dress,
fearing the chronic angers of that house,

Speaking indifferently to him,
who had driven out the cold
and polished my good shoes as well.
What did I know, what did I know
of love's austere and lonely offices?

ROBERT HAYDEN   1913–1980   USA

Man and Boy

I

'Catch the old one first,'
(My father's joke was also old, and heavy
And predictable.) 'Then the young ones
Will all follow, and Bob's your uncle.'

On slow bright river evenings, the sweet time
Made him afraid we'd take too much for granted
And so our spirits must be lightly checked.

Blessed be down-to-earth! Blessed be highs!
Blessed by the detachment of dumb love
In that broad-backed, low-set man
Who feared debt all his life, but now and then
Could make a splash like the salmon he said was
'As big as a wee pork pig by the sound of it'.

II

In earshot of the pool where the salmon jumped
Back through its own unheard concentric soundwaves
A mower leans forever on his scythe.

He has mown himself to the centre of the field
And stands in a final perfect ring
Of sunlit stubble.

'Go and tell your father,' the mower says
(He said it to my father who told me)
'I have it mowed as clean as a new sixpence.'

My father is a barefoot boy with news,
Running at eye-level with weeds and stooks
On the afternoon of his own father's death.

The open, black half of the half-door waits.
I feel much heat and hurry in the air.
I feel his legs and quick heels far away

And strange as my own — when he will piggyback me
At a great height, light-headed and thin-boned,
Like a witless elder rescued from the fire.

SEAMUS HEANEY   *b.* 1939   Ireland

The Means of Production

Like a man pleading for his life,
you put novels between yourself
and your pursuers – Atalanta,
always one step ahead of the game.

You gave me a copy of your second
with the dedication; *Michael,*
something else for you to read.
Your disparaging imperative

was too much resented for obedience . . .
You were a late starter at fiction,
but for ten years now, your family
has been kept at arm's length.

– We are as the warts on your elbows,
scratched into submission, but always
recrudescent. You call each of us
child, your wife and four children,

three of them grown-up. You have
the biblical manner; the indulgent patriarch,
his abused, endless patience; smiling
the absent smile of inattention . . .

Everything you need is at your desk:
glue-stained typewriter, match-sticks,
unravelled paper-clips – *Struwwelpeter* props!
With your big work-scissors, you snipe

at your nails, making the sparks fly.
The radio updates its bulletins
every hour, guarding you against surprises.
The living breath of the contemporary . . .

Once, you acceded to conversation,
got up to put on your black armband
and took your blood-pressure, as though
in the presence of an unacceptable risk.

MICHAEL HOFMANN*   *b.* 1957, Germany   England

The Course

My father, gasping, in his white calked shoes . . .
I serving irons to professionals . . .
He stumbles on the fairway. If he falls
No part of him meets turf trod on by Jews.

This is the course that I keep dreaming up:
Armstrong, Miss Libbey, moneyed Legionnaires.
The eighteenth green slopes toward 5000 shares
Of blue-chipped Bourbon boiling in the cup.

Mole spirits rise. Around me in their clans
The human blind posture a stiff approach.
Ground gophers retch. Poison tilts mouse and roach.
Miss Libbey, dying slower than she tans,

Afraid of what accrues with each divorce,
Snickers as Dad swings, sweating, in the traps
He'd keep me out of. When his body snaps
My spine cracks into puddles of remorse.

I used to drop the bag and fight these dreams
Until I found I couldn't beat this part.
My ears and eyes are older than my heart.
They will not change red hazards into streams.

I come upon him cursing my first book
For sentimental gawping: 'Lies, lies . . . lies —
Your mother, too, fawn-soft.' Before he dies:
'Watch for the doglegs, son; learn how to hook.

'But give 'em hell,' he gurgles, as the hand
That fed and gutted flails and flops about
And is at once his own and my first trout
Closing up finally on the wet trap sand.

I lift him in my arms and feel death quake
While, nine by nine, flags fall and geysers blow
The course to one black crater. Down we go,
Down, down together even as I wake.

ROBERT HUFF *b.* 1924 USA

From Father to Son

There is no limit to the number of times
Your father can come to life, and he is as tender as ever he was
And as poor, his overcoat buttoned to the throat,
His face blue from the wind that always blows in the outer
    darkness
He comes towards you, hesitant,
Unwilling to intrude and yet driven at the point of love
To this encounter.

You may think
That love is all that is left of him, but when he comes
He comes with all his winters and all his wounds.
He stands shivering in the empty street,
Cold and worn like a tramp at the end of a journey
And yet a shape of unquestioning love that you
Uneasy and hesitant of the cold touch of death
Must embrace.

Then, before you can touch him
He is gone, leaving on your fingers
A little more of his weariness
A little more of his love.

EMYR HUMPHREYS   *b.* 1919   Wales

Father and Son

Now in the suburbs and the falling light
I followed him, and now down sandy road
Whiter than bone-dust, through the sweet
Curdle of fields, where the plums
Dropped with their load of ripeness, one by one.

Mile after mile I followed, with skimming feet,
After the secret master of my blood,
Him, steeped in the odor of ponds, whose indomitable love
Kept me in chains. Strode years; stretched into bird;
Raced through the sleeping country where I was young,
The silence unrolling before me as I came,
The night nailed like an orange to my brow.

How should I tell him my fable and the fears,
How bridge the chasm in a casual tone,
Saying, 'The house, the stucco one you built,
We lost. Sister married and went from home,
And nothing comes back, it's strange, from where she goes.
I lived on a hill that had too many rooms:
Light we could make, but not enough of warmth,
And when the light failed, I climbed under the hill.
The papers are delivered every day;
I am alone and never shed a tear.'

At the water's edge, where the smothering ferns lifted
Their arms, 'Father!' I cried, 'Return! You know
The way. I'll wipe the mudstains from your clothes;
No trace, I promise, will remain. Instruct
Your son, whirling between two wars,
In the Gemara of your gentleness,
For I would be a child to those who mourn
And brother to the foundlings of the field
And friend of innocence and all bright eyes.
O teach me how to work and keep me kind.'

Among the turtles and the lilies he turned to me
The white ignorant hollow of his face.

STANLEY KUNITZ *b.* 1905 USA

The Escape from Youth

My father's discipline closed me like a box.
A hardness hammered shut the lid.
For fifteen years, no matter what he did,
I was unreachable. Venom sealed the locks.

Neutral beauty kept me company. Walking
through neighbours' cattle, from moving skies and trees
I learnt the slower, vaster intimacies.
Avoiding the world of men, I stopped talking,

Except intensely to myself. Rumours
of happiness sometimes seeped outside the box.
'Untrue!' I howled, and double-checked the locks.
In the dark, poetry grew like a tumour.

When the poems were big enough to break
their way out, dragging me behind, I saw
my father's face, more bitten than before,
a soft fist eaten by love, impossible to hate.

There is no forgiveness now, nor the need.
Silence bred rich fruits – a known self, those skies –
for which I thank my father. Amnesia lies
behind our peace. Neither of us dares to bleed.

1989

TONY LINTERMANS   *b.* 1948   Australia

Commander Lowell

1888–1949

There were no undesirables or girls in my set,
when I was a boy at Mattapoisett –
only Mother, still her father's daughter.
Her voice was still electric
with a hysterical, unmarried panic,
when she read to me from the Napoleon book.
Long-nosed Marie Louise
Hapsburg in the frontispiece
had a downright Boston bashfulness,
where she grovelled to Bonapart, who scratched his navel,
and bolted his food – just my seven years tall!
And I, bristling and manic,
skulked in the attic,
and got two hundred French generals by name,
from *A* to *V* – from Augereau to Vandamme.
I used to dope myself asleep,
naming those unpronounceables like sheep.

Having a naval officer
for my father was nothing to shout
about to the summer colony at 'Matt'.
He wasn't at all 'serious',
when he showed up on the golf course,
wearing a blue serge jacket and numbly cut
white ducks he'd bought
at a Pearl Harbor commissariat . . .
and took four shots with his putter to sink his putt.
'Bob,' they said, 'golf's a game you really ought to know how
      to play,
if you play at all.'
They wrote him off as 'naval',
naturally supposed his sport was sailing.
Poor Father, his training was engineering!
Cheerful and cowed
among the seadogs at the Sunday yacht club,
he was never one of the crowd.

'Anchors aweigh,' Daddy boomed in his bathtub,
'Anchors aweigh,'
when Lever Brothers offered to pay
him double what the Navy paid.
I nagged for his dress sword with gold braid,
and cringed because Mother, new
caps on all her teeth, was born anew
at forty. With seamanlike celerity,
Father left the Navy,
and deeded Mother his property.

He was soon fired. Year after year,
he still hummed 'Anchors aweigh' in the tub —
whenever he left a job,
he bought a smarter car.
Father's last employer
was Scudder, Stevens and Clark, Investment Advisors,
himself his only client.
While Mother dragged to bed alone,
read Menninger,
and grew more and more suspicious,
he grew defiant.
Night after night,
à la clarté déserte de sa lampe,
he slid his ivory Annapolis slide rule
across a pad of graphs —
piker speculations! In three years
he squandered sixty thousand dollars.
Smiling on all,
Father was once successful enough to be lost
in the mob of ruling-class Bostonians.
As early as 1928,
he owned a house converted to oil,
and redecorated by the architect
of St Mark's School . . . Its main effect
was a drawing room, 'longitudinal as Versailles',
its ceiling, roughened with oatmeal, was blue as the sea.
And once
nineteen, the younger ensign in his class,
he was 'the old man' of a gunboat on the Yangtze.

ROBERT LOWELL   1917–1977   USA

The Lesson

'Your father's gone,' my bald headmaster said.
His shiny dome and brown tobacco jar
Splintered at once in tears. It wasn't grief.
I cried for knowledge which was bitterer
Than any grief. For there and then I knew
That grief has uses – that a father dead
Could bind the bully's fist a week or two;
And then I cried for shame, then for relief.

I was a month past ten when I learnt this:
I still remember how the noise was stilled
In school-assembly when my grief came in.
Some goldfish in a bowl quietly sculled
Around their shining prison on its shelf.
They were indifferent. All the other eyes
Were turned towards me. Somewhere in myself
Pride, like a goldfish, flashed a sudden fin.

EDWARD LUCIE-SMITH   *b.* 1933   England

The Shell

Since the shell came and took you in its arms
    Whose body was fine bone
That walked in light beside a place of flowers,
        Why should your son
Years after the eclipse of those alarms
    Perplex this bitten stone
For some spent issue of the sea? Not one
Blue drop of drying blood I could call ours

In all that ocean that you were remains
    To move again. I come
Through darkness from a distance to your tomb
        And feel the swell
Where a dark flood goes headlong to the drains.
    I hear black hailstones drum
Like cold slugs on your skin. There is no bell
To tell what drowned king founders. Violets bloom

Where someone died. I dream that overhead
    I hear a bomber drone
And feel again stiff pumping of slow guns
        Then the All Clear's
Voice break, and the long summing of the dead
    Below the siren's moan
Subdue the salt flood of all blood and tears
To a prolonged strained weeping sound that stuns.

I turn in anger. By whatever stars
    Clear out of drifting rack
This winter evening I revive my claim
        To what has gone
Beyond your dying fall. Through these cold bars
    I feel your breaking back
And live again your body falling on
That flood of stone where no white Saviour came

On Christian feet to lift you to the verge
    Or swans with wings of fire
Whose necks were arched in mourning. Black as coal
        I turn to go
Out of the graveyard. Headstone shadows merge
    And blur. I see the spire
Lift over corpses. And I sense the flow
Of death like honey to make all things whole.

GEORGE MACBETH   1932–1992   Scotland

At My Father's Grave

The sunlicht still on me, you row'd in clood,
We look upon each ither noo like hills
Across a valley. I'm nae mair your son.
It is my mind, nae son o' yours, that looks,
And the great darkness o' your death comes up
And equals it across the way.
A livin' man upon a deid man thinks
And ony sma'er thocht's impossible.

HUGH MACDIARMID   1892–1978   Scotland

Yesterday

My friend says I was not a good son
you understand
I say yes I understand

he says I did not go
to see my parents very often you know
and I say yes I know

even when I was living in the same city he says
maybe I would go there once
a month or maybe even less
I say oh yes

he says the last time I went to see my father
he was asking me about my life
how I was making out and he
went into the next room
to get something to give me

oh I say
feeling again the cold
of my father's hand the last time

he says and my father turned
in the doorway and saw me
look at my wristwatch and he
said you know I would like you to stay
and talk with me

oh yes I say

but if you are busy he said
I don't want you to feel that you
have to
just because I'm here

I say nothing

he says my father
said maybe
you have important work you are doing
or maybe you should be seeing
somebody I don't want to keep you

I look out of the window
my friend is older than I am
he says and I told my father it was so
and I got up and left him then
you know

though there was nowhere I had to go
and nothing I had to do

W. S. MERWIN   *b.* 1927   USA

Fishermen 2

In late September on a school day
I take my father, failing, now past seventy
to the row boat on the reservoir, the waters
since July have gone down two hundred yards
below the shoreline.

The lake stretches before us — a secret,
we do not disturb a drifting branch, a single hawk.
For a moment nothing says, 'thou shalt not.'
If I could say anything to the sky and trees
I'd say things are best as they are.

It is more difficult for me to think
of my father's death than of my own.
He casts half the distance he used to.
I am trying to give him something,
to stuff a hill between his lips. I try
to spoon feed him nature, but an hour
in the evening on the lake does not nourish him,
the walk in the woods that comforts me
as it used to comfort him, makes him shiver.
I pretend to be cold.

We walk back along the old lake bottom,
our shoes sink into the cold mud —
where last spring there was ten foot of water,
where last summer I saw golden carp
coupling on the surface. It's after dark,
although I can barely see
I think I know where the fence is.
My father's hands tremble like the tail of a fish
resting in one place. As for me?
I have already become his ghost.

STANLEY MOSS   *b.* 1925   USA

A Dying Race

The less I visit, the more I think
myself back to your elegant house
I grew up in. The drive uncurled
through swaying chestnuts discovers it
standing four square, white-
washed unnaturally clear,
as if it were shown me by lightning.

It's always the place I see,
not you. You're somewhere outside,
waving goodbye where I left you
a decade ago. I've even lost sight
of losing you now; all I can find
are the mossy steps you stood on
– a visible loneliness.

I'm living four counties away, and still
I think of you driving south each night
to the ward where your wife is living.
How long will it last?
You've made that journey six years
already, taking comparative happinesses
like a present, to please her.

I can remember the fields you pass,
the derelict pill-boxes squatting
in shining plough. If I was still there,
watching your hand push back
the hair from her desperate face,
I might have discovered by now
the way love looks, its harrowing clarity.

ANDREW MOTION   *b.* 1952   England

The Last Hellos

Don't die, Dad —
but they die.

This last year he was wandery:
took off a new chainsaw blade
and cobbled a spare from bits.
Perhaps if I lay down
my head'll come better again.
His left shoulder kept rising
higher in his cardigan.

He could see death in a face.
Family used to call him in
to look at sick ones and say.
At his own time, he was told.

The knob found in his head
was duck-egg size. Never hurt.
Two to six months, Cecil.

I'll be right, he boomed
to his poor sister on the phone
I'll do that when I finish dyin.

             *

Don't die, Cecil.
But they do.

Going for last drives
in the bush, odd massive
board-slotted stumps bony white
in whipstick second growth.
I could chop all day.

*I could always cash
a cheque, in Sydney or anywhere.
Any of the shops.*

Eating, still at the head
of the table, he now missed
food on his knife's side.

*Sorry, Dad, but like
have you forgiven your enemies?
Your father and all of them?*
All his lifetime of hurt.

I must have (grin). *I don't
think about that now.*

*

People can't say goodbye
any more. They say last hellos.

Going fast, over Christmas,
He'd still stumble out
of his room, where his photos
hang over the other furniture,
and play host to his mourners.

The courage of his bluster,
firm big voice of his confusion.

Two last days in the hospital:
his long forearms were still
red mahogany. His hands
gripped steel frame. *I'm dyin.*

On the second day:
*You're bustin to talk
but I'm too busy dyin.*

*

Grief ended when he died,
the widower like soldiers who
won't live life their mates missed.

Good boy Cecil! No more Bluey dog.
No more cowtime. No more stories.
We're still using your imagination,
it was stronger than all ours.

Your grave's got littler
somehow, in the three months.
More pointy as the clay's shrivelled,
like a stuck zip in a coat.

Your cricket boots are in
the State museum! Odd letters
still come. Two more's died since you:
Annie, and Stewart. Old Stewart.

On your day there was a good crowd,
family, and people from away.
But of course a lot had gone
to their own funerals first.

Snobs mind us off religion
nowdays, if they can.
Fuck them. I wish you God.

LES MURRAY *b.* 1938 Australia

The Father

My blunt father comes back
from the trains.
We recognize
in the night
the whistle
of the locomotive
perforating the rain
with a wandering moan,
lament of the night,
and later
the door shivering open.
A rush of wind
came in with my father,
and between footsteps and drafts
the house
shook,

the surprised doors
banged with the dry
bark of pistols,
the staircase groaned,
and a loud voice,
complaining, grumbled
while the wild dark,
the waterfall rain
rumbled on the roofs
and, little by little,
drowned the world
and all that could be heard was the wind
battling with the rain.

He was, however, a daily happening.
Captain of his train, of the cold dawn,
and scarcely had the sun
begun to show itself
than there he was with his beard,
his red and green
flags, his lamps prepared,
the engine coal in its little inferno,
the station with trains in the mist,
and his duty to geography.
The railwayman is a sailor on earth
and in the small ports without a sea line –
the forest towns – the train runs, runs,
unbridling the natural world,
completing its navigation of the earth.
When the long train comes to rest,
friends come together,
come in, and the doors of my childhood open,
the table shakes
at the slam of a railwayman's hand,
the thick glasses of companions jump
and the glitter
flashes out
from the eyes of the wine.

My poor, hard father,
there he was at the axis of existence,
virile in friendship, his glass full.

His life was a running campaign,
and between his early risings and his traveling,
between arriving and rushing off,
one day, rainier than other days,
the railwaymen, José del Carmen Reyes,
climbed aboard the train of death and so far has not come back.

PABLO NERUDA   1904–1973   Chile
Translated by Alastair Reid

To My Dead Father

Don't call to me father
Wherever you are I'm
still your little son
running through the dark

I couldn't do what you
say even if I could hear
your roses no longer grow
my heart's black as their

bed their dainty thorns
have become my face's
troublesome stubble you
must not think of flowers

And do not frighten my
blue eyes with hazel flecks
or thicken my lips when
I face my mirror don't ask

that I be other than your
strange son understanding
minor miracles not death
father I am alive! father

forgive the roses and me

FRANK O'HARA   1926–1966   USA

The Boat

I dressed my father in his little clothes,
Blue sailor suit, brass buttons on his coat.
He asked me where the running water goes.

'Down to the sea,' I said; 'Set it afloat!'
Beside the stream he bent and raised the sail,
Uncurled the string and launched the painted boat.

White birds, flown like flags, wrenched his eyes pale.
He leaped on the tight deck and took the wind.
I watched the ship foam lurching in the gale,

And cried, 'Come back, you don't know what you'll find!'
He steered. The ship grew reddening the sky.
Water throbbed backward, blind stumbling after blind.

The rusty storm diminished in his eye.
And down he looked at me. A harbor rose.
I asked, 'What happens, father, when you die?'

He told where all the running water goes,
And dressed me gently in my little clothes.

ROBERT PACK   *b.* 1929   USA

My Papa's Waltz

The whiskey on your breath
Could make a small boy dizzy;
But I hung on like death:
Such waltzing was not easy.

We romped until the pans
Slid from the kitchen shelf;
My mother's countenance
Could not unfrown itself.

The hand that held my wrist
Was battered on one knuckle;
At every step you missed
My right ear scraped a buckle.

You beat time on my head
With a palm caked hard by dirt,
Then waltzed me off to bed
Still clinging to your shirt.

THEODORE ROETHKE   1908–1963   USA

Passing It On

I was three and already
my world shook with you.
Now I'm what's left. The eyes
I have are yours, your mouth.
That trick of your upper lip –
and those slurred l-syllables
you still slide
into a few of my words.

Now in my dreams again
and again your lacquered
casket sinks, becomes your door
into the grass. To one side
the clay heap waits to fall
a shovelful at a time.

I walk up close. I heft a clod,
then eat. Gnawing, I taste
the darkness between us
you suddenly died in. For years
it's been the red fist
of your heart that I've chewed
and gagged on, till I'm bled out
and odd of it.

And your small, thick hands.
Their anger has made my own hand
tremble, passing it on.

Already I'm hurt
by my son's look — the way
his eyes beat and grow secret
under this strange love
shaken into me.

REG SANER   *b.* 1931   USA

My Father's Face

Each morning, when I shave, I see his face,
Or something like a sketch of it gone wrong;
The artist caught, it seems, more than a trace
Of that uneasy boldness and the strong
Fear behind the stare which tried to shout
How tough its owner was, inviting doubt.

And though this face is altogether
Loosely put together, and indeed
A lot less handsome, weaker in the jaw
And softer in the mouth, I feel no need
To have it reassembled, made a better
Copy of the face of its begetter.

I do not mind because my mouth is not
That lipless hyphen, military, stern;
He had the face that faces blade and shot
In schoolboys' tales, and even schoolboys learn
To laugh at it. But they've not heard it speak
Those bayonet words that guard the cruel and weak.

For weakness was his own consistency;
And when I scrape the soapy fluff away
I see that he bequeathed this gift to me
Along with various debts I cannot pay.
But he gave, too, this mirror-misting breath
Whose mercy dims the looking-glass of death;

For which kind accident I thank him now
And, though I cannot love him, feel a sort
Of salty tenderness, remembering how
The prude and lecher in him moiled and fought
Their roughhouse in the dark ring of his pride
And killed each other when his body died.

This morning, as I shave, I find I can
Forgive the blows, the meanness and the lust,
The ricochetting arsenal of a man
Who groaned groin-deep in hope's ironic dust;
But these eyes in the glass regard the living
Features with distaste, quite unforgiving.

VERNON SCANNELL   *b.* 1922   England

Diplomacy: The Father

Your mission, in any disputed area, is to find
    (as in yourself)
which group, which element among the contending forces
    seems, by nature, most fit to take control.
Stronger perhaps, more driven, gifted with resources –
    no matter: able to bind in a firm goal
the enervating local passions native to our kind.
        That force, of course, is

your enemy — whom you cannot choose but love.
     As in yourself,
it's this, it's those so loved, that can grow oppressive
   and steal your hard-bought freedom to choose
that you won't love. Act loving, then. Make no aggressive
   move; make friends. Make, though, for future use,
notes on their debts, beliefs, whom they're most fond of —
     their weaknesses. If

anything, appear more loyal — pretend to feel
     as in yourself
you'd truly want to feel: affectionate and admiring.
   Then hate grows, discovering the way such foes enslave
you worst: if you loved them, you'd *feel* free. Conspiring
   to outwit such subtlety, devise and save
good reasons for your hatred; count wounds. Conceal,
     though, this entire ring

of proofs, excuses, wrongs which you maintain
     as in yourself
might harbor some benign, enfeebling growth.
   As for followers, seek those who'll take your aid:
the weak. In doubt who's weaker, finance both.
   Collect the dawdlers, the brilliant but afraid,
the purchasable losers — those who, merely to gain
     some power they can loathe,

would quite as willingly be out of power
     as in. Yourself?
friend, this is lonely work. Deep cravings will persist
   for true allies, for those you love; you will long
to speak your mind out sometimes, or to assist
   someone who, given that help, might grow strong
and admirable. You've reached your bleakest hour,
     the pitiless test.

But think: why let your own aid diminish you?
     As in yourself,
so in those who take your help, your values or your name,
   you've sought out their best thoughts, their hidden talents
only to buy out, to buy off. Your fixed aim,
   whatever it costs, must still be for a balance
of power in the family, the firm, the whole world through.
     Exactly the same

as a balance of impotence — in any group or nation
    as in yourself.
Suppose some one of them rose up and could succeed
   your foe — he'd *be* your foe. To underlings, dispense
all they can ask, but don't need; give till they need
   your giving. One gift could free them: confidence.
They'd never dare ask. Betray no dedication
    to any creed

or person — talk high ideals; then you'll be known
    as, in yourself,
harmless. Exact no faith from them, no affection;
   suppose they've learned no loyalty to you —
that's one step taken in the right direction.
   Never forbid them. Let no one pay back what's due;
the mere air they breathe should come as a loan
    beyond collection.

Like air, you must be everywhere at once, where-
    as, in your self-
defense, make yourself scarce. Your best disguise
   is to turn gray, spreading yourself so thin
you're one with all unknowns — essential. Vaporize
   into the fog all things that happen, happen in
or fail to happen. In the end, you have to appear
    as unworldly in the eyes

of this whole sanctioned world that your care drained
    as in yours. Self-
sacrifice has borne you, then, through that destruction
   programmed into life; you live on in that loving tension
you leave to those who'll still take your instruction.
   You've built their world; an air of soft suspension
which you survive in, as cradled and sustained
    as in yourself.

W. D. SNODGRASS* *b.* 1926   USA

The Irish Cliffs of Moher

Who is my father in this world, in this house,
At the spirit's base?

My father's father, his father's father, his —
Shadows like winds.

Go back to a parent before thought, before speech,
At the head of the past.

They go to the cliffs of Moher rising out of the mist,
Above the real,

Rising out of present time and place, above
The wet, green grass.

This is not landscape, full of the somnambulations
Of poetry

And the sea. This is my father or, maybe,
It is as he was,

A likeness, one of the race of fathers: earth
And sea and air.

WALLACE STEVENS   1879–1955   USA

To My Father

Peace and her huge invasion to these shores
Puts daily home; innumerable sails
Dawn on the far horizon and draw near;
Innumerable loves, uncounted hopes
To our wild coasts, not darkling now, approach:
Not now obscure, since thou and thine are there,
And bright on the lone isle, the foundered reef,
The long, resounding forelands, Pharos stands.

These are thy works, O father, these thy crown;
Whether on high the air be pure, they shine
Along the yellowing sunset, and all night
Among the unnumbered stars of God they shine;
Or whether fogs arise and far and wide
The low sea-level drown — each finds a tongue
And all night long the tolling bell resounds:
So shine, so toll, till night be overpast,
Till the stars vanish, till the sun return,
And in the haven rides the fleet secure.

In the first hour, the seaman in his skiff
Moves through the unmoving bay, to where the town
Its earliest smoke into the air upbreathes,
And the rough hazels climb along the beach.
To the tugg'd oar the distant echo speaks.
The ship lies resting, where by reef and roost
Thou and thy lights have led her like a child.

This hast thou done, and I — can I be base?
I must arise, O father, and to port
Some lost, complaining seaman pilot home.

ROBERT LOUIS STEVENSON* 1850–1884 Scotland

On My Father's Yortsayt[1]

Snowlight, field-in and field-out — up to my father,
Suntears drip in the snow — up to my father.
Seventy years I walk among snowlight
To reach my father on time.

Is it the silence that cries in the snow, or is it
His red violin accompanying me among snowlight?
What a destiny in snow to feel:
The distance gets close, ever closer.

1 *Yortsayt*: a yearly commemoration of a death, especially of a parent

Shall I tell my father from what place
I bear my breaths in my arms? Can I find
Words to awaken his silence,
To open up his frozen eyes?

Snowlight, field-in and field-out. Mustn't neglect
To tell him: Your son is the same.
For it may be: my father is no more,
Arose long ago for his resurrection.

October 17, 1990

ABRAHAM SUTZKEVER   *b.* 1913, Estonia   Israel
Translated from the Yiddish by Barbara and Benjamin Harshav

Father in America

When father went off to America
he wore a white suit. Later he shaved his head.
Our ancient town burned white throughout the summer
and white flowers blossomed in the cemetery —
the flowers of course remain though he is dead.

It was everybody's most idyllic picture —
white suits against pale brick or amber corn,
and gentlemen and ladies in such posture
with parasols and petticoats in pastoral
benevolence before his head was shorn.

I fear shorn heads — I touch my own skull now
and feel skin pimpling in between the roots,
with father's skull beneath. I feel it grow
progressively more bulbous under mine,
his brain is still developing new shoots.

I feel, but know that feeling isn't knowledge.
The glass distorts in the amusement park,
your skirt blows high, you cross a swaying bridge,
you hear a scream, you stand before the mirror
and face your masters in the gathering dusk.

I wish this train were going elsewhere but
a wish is powerless. The skulls appear,
one on top of another. The doors are shut,
and I'd be lying if the truth were told
on picture postcards, wishing you were here.

GEORGE SZIRTES   *b.* 1948, Hungary   England

The Lost Pilot

for my father, 1922–1944

Your face did not rot
like the others – the co-pilot,
for example, I saw him

yesterday. His face is corn-
mush: his wife and daughter,
the poor ignorant people, stare

as if he will compose soon.
He was more wronged than Job.
But your face did not rot

like the others – it grew dark,
and hard like ebony;
the features progressed in their

distinction. If I could cajole
you to come back for an evening,
down from your compulsive

orbiting, I would touch you,
read your face as Dallas,
your hoodlum gunner, now,

with the blistered eyes, reads
his Braille editions. I would
touch your face as a disinterested

scholar touches an original page.
However frightening, I would
discover you, and I would not

turn you in; I would not make
you face your wife, or Dallas,
or the co-pilot, Jim. You

could return to your crazy
orbiting, and I would not try
to fully understand what

it means to you. All I know
is this: when I see you,
as I have seen you at least

once every year of my life,
spin across the wilds of the sky
like a tiny, African god,

I feel dead. I feel as if I were
the residue of a stranger's life,
that I should pursue you.

My head cocked toward the sky,
I cannot get off the ground,
and, you, passing over again,

fast, perfect, and unwilling
to tell me that you are doing
well, or that it was mistake

that placed you in that world,
and me in this; or that misfortune
placed these worlds in us.

JAMES TATE   *b.* 1943   USA

'Do not go gentle into that good night'

Do not go gentle into that good night,
Old age should burn and rave at close of day;
Rage, rage against the dying of the light.

Though wise men at their end know dark is right,
Because their words had forked no lightning they
Do not go gentle into that good night.

Good men, the last wave by, crying how bright
Their frail deeds might have danced in a green bay,
Rage, rage against the dying of the light.

Wild men who caught and sang the sun in flight,
And learn, too late, they grieved it on its way,
Do not go gentle into that good night.

Grave men, near death, who see with blinding sight
Blind eyes could blaze like meteors and be gay,
Rage, rage against the dying of the light.

And you, my father, there on the sad height,
Curse, bless, me now with your fierce tears, I pray.
Do not go gentle into that good night.
Rage, rage against the dying of the light.

DYLAN THOMAS   1914–1953   Wales

[P. H. T.]

I may come near loving you
When you are dead
And there is nothing to do
And much to be said.

To repent that day will be
Impossible
For you, and vain for me
The truth to tell.

I shall be sorry for
Your impotence:
You can do and undo no more
When you go hence,

Cannot even forgive
The funeral.
But not so long as you live
Can I love you at all.

EDWARD THOMAS   1878–1917   England

Blow, West Wind

I know, I know – though the evidence
Is lost, and the last who might speak are dead.
Blow, west wind, blow, and the evidence, O,

Is lost, and wind shakes the cedar, and O,
I know how the kestrel hung over Wyoming,
Breast reddened in sunset, and O, the cedar

Shakes, and I know how cold
Was the sweat on my father's mouth, dead.
Blow, west wind, blow, shake the cedar, I know

How once I, a boy, crouching at creekside,
Watched, in the sunlight, a handful of water
Drip, drip, from my hand. The drops – they were bright!

But you believe nothing, with the evidence lost.

ROBERT PENN WARREN   1905–1988   USA

Tipping My Chair

I shivered in 1958. I caught a glimpse
of money working and I shut my eyes.
I was a love-sick crammer-candidate, reading
poetry under the desk in History,
wondering how to go about my life.
'Write a novel!' said my father.
'Put everything in! Sell the film rights for a fortune!
Sit up straight!' I sat there, filleting
a chestnut leaf in my lap, not listening.
I wanted to do nothing, urgently.

At his desk, in his dressing-gown,
among compliant womenfolk, he seemed
too masterful, too horrified by me.
He banged the table if I tipped my chair.
He couldn't stand my hair. One day,
struggling with a chestnut leaf, I fell over backwards
or the chair-leg broke. I didn't care any more
if poetry was easier than prose. I lay there
in the ruins of a perfectly good chair
and opened my eyes. I knew what I didn't want to do.

At his desk, in his dressing-room, among
these photographs of my father in costume,
I wonder how to go about his life.
Put everything in? The bankruptcy? The hell?
The little cork-and-leather theatrical
'lifts' he used to wear? The blacking for his hair?
Or again: leave everything out? Do nothing,
tip my chair back and stare at him for once,
my lip trembling at forty?
My father bangs the table: 'Sit up straight!'

HUGO WILLIAMS*   *b.* 1942   England

Two Postures beside a Fire

1

Tonight I watch my father's hair,
As he sits dreaming near his stove.
Knowing my feather of despair,
He sent me an owl's plume for love,
Lest I not know, so I've come home.
Tonight Ohio, where I once
Hounded and cursed my loneliness,
Shows me my father, who broke stones,
Wrestled and mastered great machines,
And rests, shadowing his lovely face.

2

Nobly his hands fold together in his repose.
He is proud of me, believing
I have done strong things among men and become a man
Of place among men of place in the large cities.
I will not waken him.
I have come home alone, without wife or child
To delight him. Awake, solitary and welcome,
I too sit near his stove, the lines
Of an ugly age scarring my face, and my hands
Twitch nervously about.

JAMES WRIGHT   1927–1980   USA

*Son
to
Mother*

Dreaming Up Mother

Understanding is all, my mother would tell me,
and then walk away from the water;

Understanding is nothing I think, as I mumble
embellished phrases of what's left of her story.

Though I keep battering myself against sky,
throwing my body into the open day.

Landscapes are to look at, they told me,
but now the last of the relatives are dead.

Where do these walks by the shore take us
she would say, wanting to clean up,

after the picnic, after the nonsense.
I have been a bother all the years from my birth.

Look out – the river pulls through the day
and Understanding like a flaming cloud, goes by.

ROBERT ADAMSON   *b.* 1943   Australia

'Mother, any distance greater than a single span'

Mother, any distance greater than a single span
requires a second pair of hands.
You come to help me measure windows, pelmets, doors,
the acres of the walls, the prairies of the floors.

You at the zero-end, me with the spool of tape, recording
length, reporting metres, centimetres back to base, then leaving
up the stairs, the line still feeding out, unreeling
years between us. Anchor. Kite.

I space-walk through the empty bedrooms, climb
the ladder to the loft, to breaking point, where something
has to give;
two floors below your fingertips still pinch
the last one-hundredth of an inch . . . I reach
towards a hatch that opens on an endless sky
to fall or fly.

SIMON ARMITAGE   *b.* 1963   England

To My Mother

Most near, most dear, most loved and most far,
Under the window where I often found her
Sitting as huge as Asia, seismic with laughter,
Gin and chicken helpless in her Irish hand,
Irresistible as Rabelais, but most tender for
The lame dogs and hurt birds that surround her, —
She is a procession no one can follow after
But be like a little dog following a brass band.

She will not glance up at the bomber, or condescend
To drop her gin and scuttle to a cellar,
But lean on the mahogany table like a mountain
Whom only faith can move, and so I send
O all my faith and all my love to tell her
That she will move from mourning into morning.

c. 1944

GEORGE BARKER   1913—1991   England

Aspen Tree

Aspen tree, your leaves glance white into the dark.
My mother's hair was never white.

Dandelion, so green is the Ukraine.
My yellow-haired mother did not come home.

Rain cloud, above the well do you hover?
My quiet mother weeps for everyone.

Round star, you wind the golden loop.
My mother's heart was ripped by lead.

Oaken door, who lifted you off your hinges?
My gentle mother cannot return.

PAUL CELAN* 1920–1970   Romania
Translated by Michael Hamburger

On the Receipt of My Mother's Picture out of Norfolk
The Gift of my Cousin Ann Bodham

Oh that those lips had language! Life has pass'd
With me but roughly since I heard thee last.
Those lips are thine! – thy own sweet smiles I see,
The same that oft in childhood solaced me;
Voice only fails, else, how distinct they say,
'Grieve not, my child, chase all thy fears away!'
The meek intelligence of those dear eyes
(Blest be the art that can immortalize,
The art that baffles time's tyrannic claim
To quench it) here shines on me still the same.

Faithful remembrancer of one so dear,
Oh welcome guest, though unexpected, here!
Who bidd'st me honour with an artless song,
Affectionate, a mother lost so long,
I will obey, not willingly alone,
But gladly, as the precept were her own;
And, while that face renews my final grief,
Fancy shall weave a charm for my relief –
Shall steep me in Elysian reverie,
A momentary dream, that thou art she.

My mother! when I learn'd that thou wast dead,
Say, wast thou conscious of the tears I shed?
Hover'd thy spirit o'er thy sorrowing son,
Wretch even then, life's journey just begun?
Perhaps thou gav'st me, though unseen, a kiss;
Perhaps a tear, if souls can weep in bliss –
Ah that maternal smile! it answers – Yes.
I heard the bell toll'd on thy burial day,
I saw the hearse that bore thee slow away,
And, turning from my nursery window, drew
A long, long sigh, and wept a last adieu!
But was it such? – It was. – Where thou art gone
Adieus and farewells are a sound unknown.
May I but meet thee on that peaceful shore,
The parting sound shall pass my lips no more!
Thy maidens griev'd themselves at my concern,
Oft gave me promise of a quick return.
What ardently I wish'd, I long believ'd,
And disappointed still, was still deceiv'd;
By disappointment every day beguil'd,
Dupe of *to-morrow* even from a child.
Thus many a sad to-morrow came and went,
Till, all my stock of infant sorrow spent,
I learn'd at last submission to my lot;
But though I less deplor'd thee, ne'er forgot.

Where once we dwelt our name is heard no more,
Children not thine have trod my nursery floor;
And where the gard'ner Robin, day by day,
Drew me to school along the public way,
Delighted with my bauble coach, and wrapt
In scarlet mantle warm, and velvet capt,

'Tis now become a history little known,
That once we call'd the past'ral house our own.
Short-liv'd possession! but the record fair
That mem'ry keeps of all thy kindness there,
Still outlives many a storm that has effac'd
A thousand other themes less deeply trac'd.
Thy nightly visits to my chamber made,
That thou might'st know me safe and warmly laid;
Thy morning bounties ere I left my home,
The biscuit, or confectionary plum;
The fragrant waters on my cheeks bestow'd
By thy own hand, till fresh they shone and glow'd;
All this, and more enduring still than all,
Thy constant flow of love, that knew no fall,
Ne'er roughen'd by those cataracts and brakes
That humour interpos'd too often makes;
All this still legible in mem'ry's page,
And still to be so, to my latest age,
Adds joy to duty, makes me glad to pay
Such honours to thee as my numbers may;
Perhaps a frail memorial, but sincere,
Not scorn'd in heav'n, though little notic'd here.
   Could time, his flight revers'd, restore the hours,
When, playing with thy vesture's tissued flow'rs,
The violet, the pink, and jessamine,
I prick'd them into paper with a pin,
(And thou wast happier than myself the while,
Would'st softly speak, and stroke my head and smile)
Could those few pleasant hours again appear,
Might one wish bring them, would I wish them here?
I would not trust my heart — the dear delight
Seems so to be desir'd, perhaps I might! —
But no — what here we call our life is such,
So little to be lov'd, and thou so much,
That I should ill requite thee to constrain
Thy unbound spirit into bonds again.
   Thou, as a gallant bark from Albion's coast
(The storms all weather'd and the oceans cross'd)
Shoots into port at some well-haven'd isle,
Where spices breathe and brighter seasons smile,

There sits quiescent on the floods that show
Her beauteous form reflected clear below,
While airs impregnated with incense play
Around her, fanning light her streamers gay;
So thou, with sails how swift! hast reach'd the shore,
'Where tempests never beat nor billows roar,'
And thy lov'd consort on the dang'rous tide
Of life, long since, has anchor'd at thy side.
But me, scarce hoping to attain that rest,
Always from port withheld, always distress'd —
Me howling winds drive devious, tempest toss'd,
Sails ript, seams op'ning wide, and compass lost,
And day by day some current's thwarting force
Sets me more distant from a prosp'rous course.
But oh the thought, that thou art safe, and he!
That thought is joy, arrive what may to me.
My boast is not that I deduce my birth
From loins enthron'd, and rulers of the earth;
But higher far my proud pretensions rise —
The son of parents pass'd into the skies.
And now, farewell — time, unrevok'd, has run
His wonted course, yet what I wish'd is done.
By contemplation's help, not sought in vain,
I seem t'have liv'd my childhood o'er again
To have renew'd the joys that once were mine,
Without the sin of violating thine;
And, while the wings of fancy still are free,
And I can view this mimic shew of thee,
Time has but half succeeded in his theft —
Thyself remov'd, thy power to sooth me left.

WILLIAM COWPER* 1731–1800 England

Opera

Throw all your stagey chandeliers in wheelbarrows and move
    them north
To celebrate my mother's sewing-machine
And her beneath an eighty-watt bulb, pedalling
Iambs on an antique metal footplate
Powering the needle through its regular lines,
Doing her work. To me as a young boy
That was her typewriter. I'd watch
Her hands and feet in unison, or read
Between her calves the wrought-iron letters:
SINGER. Mass-produced polished wood and metal,
It was a powerful instrument. I stared
Hard at its brilliant needle's eye that purred
And shone at night; and then each morning after
I went to work at school, wearing her songs.

ROBERT CRAWFORD   *b.* 1959   Scotland

Buckdancer's Choice

So I would hear out those lungs,
The air split into nine levels,
Some gift of tongues of the whistler

In the invalid's bed: my mother,
Warbling all day to herself
The thousand variations of one song;

It is called Buckdancer's Choice.
For years, they have all been dying
Out, the classic buck-and-wing men

Of traveling minstrel shows;
With them also an old woman
Was dying of breathless angina,

Yet still found breath enough
To whistle up in my head
A sight like a one-man band,

Freed black, with cymbals at heel,
An ex-slave who thrivingly danced
To the ring of his own clashing light

Through the thousand variations of one song
All day to my mother's prone music,
The invalid's warbler's note,

While I crept close to the wall
Sock-footed, to hear the sounds alter,
Her tongue like a mockingbird's break

Through stratum after stratum of a tone
Proclaiming what choices there are
For the last dancers of their kind,

For ill women and for all slaves
Of death, and children enchanted at walls
With a brass-beating glow underfoot,

Not dancing but nearly risen
Through barnlike, theaterlike houses
On the wings of the buck and wing.

JAMES DICKEY   1923–1997   USA

Sanctuary

Once my mother was a wall;
behind my rampart and my keep
in a safe and hungry house
I lay as snug as winter mouse:
till the wall breaks and I weep
for simple reasons first of all.

All the barriers give in,
the world will lance at every point
my unsteady heart, still and still
to subjugate my tired will.
When it's done they will anoint me,
being kinder if they win.

So beyond a desperate fence
I'll cross where I shall not return,
the line between indifference
and my vulnerable mind:
no more then kind or unkind
touch me, no love nor hate burn.

KEITH DOUGLAS*   1920–1944   England

from *Four Songs the Night Nurse Sang*

Madrone Tree that was my mother,
Cast me a cloak as red as your flower.
   My sisters don't know me,
   My father looks for me,
And I am by name the wind's brother.

Madrone Tree, from your thirsty root
feed my soul as if it were your fruit.
   Spread me a table and make it fair.
   Cast down splendor out of the air.
My story has only the wind's truth.

Madrone Tree, red as blood,
that once my mother was, be my rod.
      Death came when I was born.
      And from that earth now you are grown.
My father's a shadow, the wind is my god.

                    *

Let sleep take her, let sleep take her, let sleep
             take her away!
The cold tears of her father
have made a hill of ice.
          Let sleep take her.

Her mother's fear has made a feyrie.
          Let sleep take her.
Now all of the kingdom lies down to die.
          Let sleep take her.

Let dawn wake her, if dawn can find her.
   Let the prince of day take her
from sleep's dominion at the touch of his finger,
   if he can touch her.

The weather will hide her, the spider will bind her

      : so the wind sang.

O, there she lay
in an egg hanging from an invisible thread
spinning out I cannot tell whether

from a grave or a bed, from a grave or a bed.

ROBERT DUNCAN* 1919–1988 USA

from *Kaddish for Naomi Ginsberg*
1894–1956

O mother
what have I left out
O mother
what have I forgotten
O mother
farewell
with a long black shoe
farewell
with Communist Party and a broken stocking
farewell
with six dark hairs on the wen of your breast
farewell
with your old dress and a long black beard around the vagina
farewell
with your sagging belly
with your fear of Hitler
with your mouth of bad short stories
with your fingers of rotten mandolines
with your arms of fat Paterson porches
with your belly of strikes and smokestacks
with your chin of Trotsky and the Spanish War
with your voice singing for the decaying overbroken workers
with your nose of bad lay with your nose of the smell of the
        pickles of Newark
with your eyes
with your eyes of Russia
with your eyes of no money
with your eyes of false China
with your eyes of Aunt Elanor
with your eyes of starving India
with your eyes pissing in the park
with your eyes of America taking a fall
with your eyes of your failure at the piano
with your eyes of your relatives in California

with your eyes of Ma Rainey dying in an ambulance
with your eyes of Czechoslovakia attacked by robots
with your eyes going to painting class at night in the Bronx
with your eyes of the killer Grandma you see on the horizon
     from the Fire-Escape
with your eyes running naked out of the apartment screaming
     into the hall
with your eyes being led away by policemen to an ambulance
with your eyes strapped down on the operating table
with your eyes with the pancreas removed
with your eyes of appendix operation
with your eyes of abortion
with your eyes of ovaries removed
with your eyes of shock
with your eyes of lobotomy
with your eyes of divorce
with your eyes of stroke
with your eyes alone
with your eyes
with your eyes
with your Death full of Flowers

ALLEN GINSBERG 1926–1997 USA

from *Clearances*

When all the others were away at Mass
I was all hers as we peeled potatoes.
They broke the silence, let fall one by one
Like solder weeping off the soldering iron:
Cold comforts set between us, things to share
Gleaming in a bucket of cold water.
And again let fall. Little pleasant splashes
From each other's work would bring us to our senses.

So while the parish priest at her bedside
Went hammer and tongs at the prayers for the dying
And some were responding and some crying
I remembered her head bent towards my head,
Her breath in mine, our fluent dipping knives —
Never closer the whole rest of our lives.

SEAMUS HEANEY *b.* 1939 Ireland

In Memory of My Mother

I do not think of you lying in the wet clay
Of a Monaghan graveyard; I see
You walking down a lane among the poplars
On your way to the station, or happily

Going to second Mass on a summer Sunday —
You meet me and you say:
'Don't forget to see about the cattle —'
Among your earthiest words the angels stray.

And I think of you walking along a headland
Of green oats in June,
So full of purpose, so rich with life —
And I see us meeting at the end of a town

On a fair day by accident, after
The bargains are all made and we can walk
Together through the shops and stalls and markets
Free in the oriental streets of thought.

O you are not lying in the wet clay,
For it is a harvest evening now and we
Are piling up the ricks against the moonlight
And you smile up at us — eternally.

PATRICK KAVANAGH 1904–1976 Ireland

Reference Back

That was a pretty one, I heard you call
From the unsatisfactory hall
To the unsatisfactory room where I
Played record after record, idly,
Wasting my time at home, that you
Looked so much forward to.

Oliver's *Riverside Blues*, it was. And now
I shall, I suppose, always remember how
The flock of notes those antique negroes blew
Out of Chicago air into
A huge remembering pre-electric horn
The year after I was born
Three decades later made this sudden bridge
From your unsatisfactory age
To my unsatisfactory prime.

Truly, though our element is time,
We are not suited to the long perspectives
Open at each instant of our lives.
They link us to our losses: worse,
They show us what we have as it once was,
Blindingly undiminished, just as though
By acting differently we could have kept it so.

PHILIP LARKIN   1922–1985   England

Piano

Softly, in the dusk, a woman is singing to me;
Taking me back down the vista of years, till I see
A child sitting under the piano, in the boom of the tingling
 strings
And pressing the small, poised feet of a mother who smiles as
 she sings.

In spite of myself, the insidious mastery of song
Betrays me back, till the heart of me weeps to belong
To the old Sunday evenings at home, with winter outside
And hymns in the cosy parlour, the tinkling piano our guide.

So now it is vain for the singer to burst into clamour
With the great black piano appassionato. The glamour
Of childish days is upon me, my manhood is cast
Down in the flood of remembrance, I weep like a child for
 the past.

D. H. LAWRENCE   1885–1930   England

The Coals

Before my mother's hysterectomy
she cried, and told me she must never bring
coals in from the cellar outside the house,
someone must do it for her. The thing itself
I knew was nothing, it was the thought
of that dependence. Her tears shocked me
like a blow. As once she had been taught,
I was taught self-reliance, discipline,
which is both good and bad. You get things done,
you feel you keep the waste and darkness back
by acts and acts and acts and acts and acts,

bridling if someone tells you this is vain,
learning at last in pain. Hardest of all
is to forgive yourself for things undone,
guilt that can poison life — away with it,
you say, and it is loath to go away.
I learned both love and joy in a hard school
and treasure them like the fierce salvage of
some wreck that has been built to look like stone
and stand, though it did not, a thousand years.

EDWIN MORGAN   *b.* 1920   Scotland

Prayer to My Mother

It's so hard to say in a son's words
what I'm so little like in my heart.

Only you in all the world know what my
heart always held, before any other love.

So, I must tell you something terrible to know:
From within your kindness my anguish grew.

You're irreplaceable. And because you are,
the life you gave me is condemned to loneliness.

And I don't want to be alone. I have an infinite
hunger for love, love of bodies without souls.

For the soul is inside you, it is you, but
you're my mother and your love's my slavery:

My childhood I lived a slave to this lofty
incurable sense of an immense obligation.

It was the only way to feel life,
the unique form, sole color; now, it's over.

We survive, in the confusion
of a life reborn outside reason.

I pray you, oh, I pray: Don't die.
I'm here, alone, with you, in a future April . . .

PIER PAOLO PASOLINI   1922–1975   Italy
Translated by Norman MacAfee with Luciano Martinengo

Infidelity

The two-toned Olds swinging sideways out of
the drive, the bone-white gravel kicked up in
a shot, my mother in the deathseat half
out the door, the door half shut – she's being
pushed or wants to jump, I don't remember.
The Olds is two kinds of green, hand-painted,
and blows black smoke like a coal-oil fire. I'm
stunned and feel a wind, like a machine, pass
through me, through my heart and mouth; I'm standing
in a field not fifty feet away, the
wheel of the wind closing the distance.
Then suddenly the car stops and my mother
falls with nothing, nothing to break the fall . . .

One of those moments we give too much to,
like the moment of acknowledgement of
betrayal, when the one who's faithless has
nothing more to say and the silence is
terrifying since you must choose between
one or the other emptiness. I know
my mother's face was covered black with blood
and that when she rose she too said nothing.
Language is a darkness pulled out of us.
But I screamed that day she was almost killed,
whether I wept or ran or threw a stone,
or stood stone-still, choosing at last between
parents, one of whom was driving away.

STANLEY PLUMLY   *b.* 1939   USA

From a Childhood

The dark grew ripe like treasure in the room
in which the boy, submerged so deeply, sat.
And as the mother entered like a dream
there trembled, on the silent shelf, a glass.
She sensed it, how the room somehow betrayed her,
and finding, kissed her boy: Are you here? . . .
Slowly his gaze turned hers toward the piano,
for many evenings now she'd played a piece
whose rapture left the child beyond release.

He sat so still. His huge gaze bent
upon her hand which, burdened by the ring,
plowed as if through snowdrifts deepening
and over the white keys went.

RAINER MARIA RILKE   1875—1926   Austria
Translated by Todd Hearon

Seven-year-old Poets

The Mother closed the copybook, and went away
Content, and very proud, and never saw
In the blue eyes, beneath the pimply forehead,
The horror and loathing in her child's soul.

All day he sweat obedience; was very
Bright; still, some black tics, some traits he had
Seemed to foreshadow sour hypocrisies.
In the dark halls, their mildewed paper peeling,
He passed, stuck out his tongue, then pressed two fists
In his crotch, and shut his eyes to see spots.

A door opened: in the evening lamplight
There he was, gasping on the banisters
In a well of light that hung beneath the roof.
Summer especially, stupid, slow, he always tried
To shut himself up in the cool latrine,
There he could think, be calm, and sniff the air.

Washed from the smells of day, the garden, in winter,
Out behind the house, filled with moonlight;
Stretched below a wall, and rolled in dirt,
Squeezing his dazzled eyes to make visions come,
He only heard the scruffy fruit trees grow.
A pity! The friends he had were puny kids,
The ones with runny eyes that streaked their cheeks,
Who hid thin yellow fingers, smeared with mud,
Beneath old cast-off clothes that stank of shit;
They used to talk like gentle idiots.
If she surprised him in these filthy friendships
His mother grew afraid; the child's deep tenderness
Took her astonishment to task. How good . . .
Her wide blue eyes — but they lie.

Seven years old; he made up novels: life
In the desert, Liberty in transports gleaming,
Forests, suns, shores, swamps! Inspiration
In picture magazines: he looked, red-faced,
At Spanish and Italian girls who laughed.
And when, with brown eyes, wild, in calico,
— She was eight — the workers' girl next door
Played rough, jumped right on top of him
In a corner, onto his back, and pulled his hair,
And he was under her, he bit her ass
Because she wore no panties underneath;
Then, beaten by her, hit with fists and heels,
He took the smell of her skin back to his room.

He hated pale December Sunday afternoons:
With plastered hair, on a mahogany couch,
He read the cabbage-colored pages of a Bible;
Dreams oppressed him every night in bed.

He hated God, but loved the men he saw
Returning home in dirty working clothes
Through the wild evening air to the edge of town,
Where criers, rolling drums before the edicts,
Made the crowds around them groan and laugh.
— He dreamed of prairies of love, where shining herds,
Perfumes of life, pubescent stalks of gold
Swirled slowly round, and then rose up and flew.

The darkest things in life could move him most;
When in that empty room, the shutters closed,
High and blue, with its bitter humid smell,
He read his novel — always on his mind —
Full of heavy ocher skies and drowning forests,
Flowers of flesh in starry woods uncurled,
Catastrophe, vertigo, pity and disaster!
— While the noises of the neighborhood swelled
Below — stretched out alone on unbleached
Canvas sheets, a turbulent vision of sails!

ARTHUR RIMBAUD   1854–1891   France
Translated by Paul Schmidt

The Mother

She stands in the dead center like a star;
They form around her like her satellites
Who take her energies, her heat, light
And massive attraction on their paths, however far.

Born of her own flesh; still, she feels them drawn
Into the outer cold by dark forces;
They are in love with suffering and perversion,
With the community of pain. Thinking them gone,

Beyond her reach, she is consoled by evil
In children, neighbors, in the world she cannot change,
That lightless universe where they range
Out of the comforts of her disapproval.

If evil did not exist, she would create it
To die in righteousness, her martyrdom
To that sweet dominion they have bolted from.
At last, she can believe that she is hated

And is content. Things can decay, break,
Spoil themselves; who cares? She'll gather the debris
With loving tenderness to give them; she
Will weave a labyrinth of waste, wreckage,

Of hocus-pocus; leave free no fault
Or cornerhole outside those lines of force
Where she and only she can thread a course.
All else in her grasp grows clogged and halts.

Till one by one, the areas of her brain
Switch off and she has filled all empty spaces;
Then she hallucinates in their right places
Their after-images, reversed and faint,

And the drawn strands of love, spun in her mind,
Turn dark and cluttered, precariously hung
With the black shapes of her mates, her sapless young,
Where she moves by habit, hungering and blind.

W. D. SNODGRASS*   b. 1926   USA

Not Dying

These wrinkles are nothing.
These gray hairs are nothing.
This stomach which sags
with old food, these bruised
and swollen ankles,
my darkening brain,
they are nothing.
I am the same boy
my mother used to kiss.

The years change nothing.
On windless summer nights
I feel those kisses
slide from her dark
lips far away,
and in winter they float
over the frozen pines
and arrive covered with snow.
They keep me young.

My passion for milk
is uncontrollable still.
I am driven by innocence.
From bed to chair I crawl
and back again.
I shall not die.
The grave result
and token of birth, my body
remembers and holds fast.

MARK STRAND   *b.* 1934   USA

[M. E. T.]

No one so much as you
Loves this my clay,
Or would lament as you
Its dying day.

You know me through and through
Though I have not told,
And though with what you know
You are not bold.

None ever was so fair
As I thought you:
Not a word can I bear
Spoken against you.

All that I ever did
For you seemed coarse
Compared with what I hid
Nor put in force.

Scarce my eyes dare meet you
Lest they should prove
I but respond to you
And do not love.

We look and understand,
We cannot speak
Except in trifles and
Words the most weak.

I at the most accept
Your love, regretting
That is all: I have kept
A helpless fretting

That I could not return
All that you gave
And could not ever burn
With the love you have,

Till sometimes it did seem
Better it were
Never to see you more
Than linger here

With only gratitude
Instead of love –
A pine in solitude
Cradling a dove.

EDWARD THOMAS   1878–1917   England

There's a Grandfather's Clock in the Hall

There's a grandfather's clock in the hall, watch it closely. The
    minute hand stands still, then it jumps, and in between
        jumps
there is no-Time,
And you are a child again watching the reflection of early
    morning
    sunlight on the ceiling above your bed,

Or perhaps you are fifteen feet under water and holding your
    breath
    as you struggle with a rock-snagged anchor, or holding your
    breath just long enough for one more long, slow thrust to
    make
    the orgasm really intolerable,
Or you are wondering why you really do not give a damn, as
    they
    trundle you off to the operating room.

Or your mother is standing up to get married and is very pretty,
    and excited and is a virgin, and your heart overflows, and
    you watch her with tears in your eyes, or
She is the one in the hospital room and she is really dying.

They have taken out her false teeth, which are now in a
    tumbler
    on the bedside table, and you know that only the undertaker
    will ever put them back in.
You stand there and wonder if you will ever have to wear false
    teeth.

She is lying on her back, and God, is she ugly, and
With gum-flabby lips and each word a special problem, she is
    asking if it is a new suit that you are wearing.

You say yes, and hate her uremic guts, for she has no right to
    make
    you hurt the way that question hurts.
You do not know why that question makes your heart hurt like a
    kick in the scrotum.

For you do not yet know that the question, in its murderous
    triviality,
  is the last thing she will ever say to you,
Nor know what baptism is occurring in a sod-roofed hut or hole on
  the night-swept steppes of Asia, and a million mouths, like
  ruined stars in darkness, make a rejoicing that howls like
  wind, or wolves,

Nor do you know the truth, which is: *Seize the nettle of*
    innocence
  in both your hands, for this is the only way, and every
Ulcer in love's lazaret may, like a dawn-stung gem, sing – or even
  burst into whoops of, perhaps, holiness.

But, in any case, watch the clock closely. Hold your breath
  and wait.
Nothing happens, nothing happens, then suddenly, quick as a
  wink, and slick as a mink's prick, Time thrusts through
  the time of no-Time.

ROBERT PENN WARREN   1905–1988   USA

My Mother's Lips

Until I asked her to please stop doing it and was astonished to find
  that she not only could
but from the moment I asked her in fact would stop doing it, my
  mother, all through my childhood,
when I was saying something to her, something important, would
  move her lips as I was speaking
so that she seemed to be saying under her breath the very words I
  was saying as I was saying them.

Or, even more disconcertingly – wildly so now that my puberty
  had erupted – *before* I said them.
When I was smaller, I must just have assumed that she was
  omniscient. Why not?

She knew everything else – when I was tired, or lying; she'd know
  I was ill before I did.
I may even have thought – how could it not have come into my
  mind? – that she *caused* what I said.

All she was really doing of course was mouthing my words a split
  second after I said them myself,
but it wasn't until my own children were learning to talk that I
  really understood how,
and understood, too, the edge of anxiety in it, the wanting to
  bring you along out of the silence,
the compulsion to lift you again from those blank caverns of
  namelessness we encase.

That was long afterward, though: where I was now was just
  wanting to get her to stop,
and, considering how I brooded and raged in those days, how
  quickly my teeth went on edge,
the restraint I approached her with seems remarkable, although
  her so unprotestingly,
readily taming a habit by then three children and a dozen years
  old was as much so.

It's endearing to watch us again in that long-ago dusk, facing each
  other, my mother and me.
I've just grown to her height, or just past it: there are our lips
  moving together,
now the unison suddenly breaks, I have to go on by myself, no
  maestro, no score to follow.
I wonder what finally made me take umbrage enough, or heart
  enough, to confront her?

It's not important. My cocoon at that age was already unwind-
  ing: the threads ravel and snarl.
When I find one again, it's that two o'clock in the morning, a grim
  hotel on a square,
the impenetrable maze of an endless city, when, really alone for
  the first time in my life,
I found myself leaning from the window, incanting in a tearing
  whisper what I thought were poems.

I'd love to know what I raved that night to the night, what those
    innocent dithyrambs were,
or to feel what so ecstatically drew me out of myself and beyond
    . . . Nothing is there, though,
only the solemn piazza beneath me, the riot of dim, tiled roofs
    and impassable alleys,
my desolate bed behind me, and my voice, hoarse, and the sweet,
    alien air against me like a kiss.

C. K. WILLIAMS   *b.* 1936   USA

The Horse Show

Constantly near you, I never in my entire
sixty-four years knew you so well as yesterday
or half so well. We talked. You were never
so lucid, so disengaged from all exigencies
of place and time. We talked of ourselves,
intimately, a thing never heard of between us.
How long have we waited? almost a hundred years.

You said, Unless there is some spark, some
spirit we keep within ourselves, life, a
continuing life's impossible – and it is all
we have. There is no other life, only the one.
The world of the spirits that comes afterward
is the same as our own, just like you sitting
there they come and talk to me, just the same.

They come to bother us. Why? I said. I don't
know. Perhaps to find out what we are doing.
Jealous, do you think? I don't know. I
don't know why they should want to come back.
I was reading about some men who had been
buried under a mountain, I said to her, and
one of them came back after two months,

digging himself out. It was in Switzerland,
you remember? Of course I remember. The
villagers tho't it was a ghost coming down
to complain. They were frightened. They
do come, she said, what you call
my 'visions'. I talk to them just as I
am talking to you. I see them plainly.

Oh if I could only read! You don't know
what adjustments I have made. All
I can do is to try to live over again
what I knew when your brother and you
were children — but I can't always succeed.
Tell me about the horse show. I have
been waiting all week to hear about it.

Mother darling, I wasn't able to get away.
Oh that's too bad. It was just a show;
they make the horses walk up and down
to judge them by their form. Oh is that
all? I tho't it was something else. Oh
they jump and run too. I wish you had been
there, I was so interested to hear about it.

WILLIAM CARLOS WILLIAMS 1883–1963 USA

Meanwhile

Meanwhile she comes back to me whenever I sleep, in my
        dream
And I say to her, welcome back, sit down in the meantime,
And she straightens the pillow, as always,
For it is unnatural for a mother not to straighten her son's
        pillow,
And for the son to be the one who straightens his mother's,
Wiping her cold sweat, lightly touching her hair,
Holding her cold hand, saying fear not
From the place you are going you shall not come back

Empty-handed, the way you came back so many times in the
    past
As the place you are going is a place of no hopes,
And no loss, remorse, sorrow, nor motherly pain,
The place you are going is short of nothing. It's a whole place.

NATAN ZACH   *b.* 1930, Germany   Israel
Translated by Amos Oz

Son
to
Parents

Infancy

My father got on his horse and went to the field.
My mother stayed sitting and sewing.
My little brother slept.
A small boy alone under the mango trees,
I read the story of Robinson Crusoe,
the long story that never comes to an end.

At noon, white with light, a voice that had learned
lullabies long ago in the slave-quarters — and never forgot —
called us for coffee.
Coffee blacker than the old black woman
delicious coffee
good coffee.

My mother stayed sitting and sewing
watching me:
Shh — don't wake the boy.
She stopped the cradle when a mosquito had lit
and gave a sigh . . . how deep!
Away off there my father went riding
through the farm's endless wastes.

And I didn't know that my story
was prettier than that of Robinson Crusoe.

CARLOS DRUMMOND DE ANDRADE   1902–1987   Brazil
Translated by Elizabeth Bishop

A Contrast

How broad-minded were Nature and My Parents
in appointing to My Personal City
exactly the sort of *Censor* I would have
   Myself elected.

Who bans from recall any painful image:
foul behaviour, whether by Myself or Others,
days of dejection, breakages, poor cooking,
   are suppressed promptly.

I do wish, though, They had assigned Me a less hostile
Public Prosecutor, Who in the early morning
cross-questions Me with unrelenting venom
   about My future –

'How will You ever pay Your taxes?' 'Where will You
find a cab?' 'Won't Your Speech be a flop?' – and greets My
answers with sarcastic silence. Well, well, I
   must grin and bear it.

W. H. AUDEN   1907–1973   England

A Wedding Portrait

Young man, young woman, gazing out
Straight-backed, straight-eyed, from what would seem
A cloud of sepia and cream,
In your twin pairs of eyes I note
A sense of the ridiculous,
Innocent courage, the strange hope
Things might get better in the lean
Year of the *Lusitania*; gas
Used at the Front; Arras and Ypres
More than place-names. 1915.

My father, Driver Causley, stands
Speckless in 2nd Wessex kit,
A riding-crop in ordered hands,
Lanyard well slicked, and buttons lit
With Brasso; military cap
On the fake pillar for an urn.

Khaki roughens his neck. I see
The mouth half-lifted by a scrap
Of smile. It is a shock to learn
How much, at last, he looks like me.

Serene, my mother wears a white
And Sunday look, and at her throat
The vague smudge of a brooch, a mute
Pale wound of coral. The smooth weight
Of hair curves from her brow; gold chain
Circles a wrist to mark the day,
And on the other is the grey
Twist of a bandage for the flame
That tongued her flesh as if to say,
'I am those days that are to come.'

As I walk by them on the stair
A small surprise of sun, a ruse
Of light, gives each a speaking air,
A sudden thrust, though both refuse
– Silent as fish or water-plants –
To break the narrow stream of glass
Dividing us. I was nowhere
That wedding-day, and the pure glance
They shaft me with acknowledges
Nothing of me. I am not here.

The unregarding look appears
To say, somehow, man is a breath,
And at the end hides in the fire,
In bolting water, or the earth.
I am a child again, and move
Sunwards these images of clay,
Listening for their first birth-cry.
And with the breath my parents gave
I warm the cold words with my day:
Will the dead words to fly. To fly.

CHARLES CAUSLEY *b.* 1917 England

The Two Little Boys at the Back of the Bus

The two little boys at the back of the bus,
You and I.
Where would we have been
Without my mother?
As well as being my mother
She was your mother also.
All you and I were able for
Was playing Rugby Football
Or swooping up and down the touchline
Shrieking at one another
To maim or kill our opponents.

We were Jesuit boys,
Sons of peasants
Who played a burgher's game
Which was called Rugby Union,
The ideology of which was to
Enact in the muck and lawn
Of the playing fields of Ballsbridge
A parody of homosexual aggression:
Scrum, hook, tackle, maul.

We thought it right and fitting,
Manly and amusing,
That our clubs were named
After barbarian tribes.
You played for the Senior Vandals,
I played for the Junior Visigoths.
Our life's ambition was to play
For the Malawians
Against the Springboks
In Johannesburg,
Drinking lager,
Putting the boot in,
Taking the boot out.

After the game
And the whooping-it-up
Of male bodies
In the showers,
The boisterous buttocks,
The coy penis,
The Jesuit priest with a box camera
Lurking outside the cubicles,
The ex-missionary
Father A'bandon with an apostrophe.
You and I always got dressed
Ahead of the rest
To bag the back seat first.
We were always, you and I,
The two little boys at the back of the bus,
Going home to Mother.

Safe in the back of the bus
At seventy-two you share your biscuits with me,
Your packet of digestive biscuits,
As we head back down the Stillorgan Road
To Mother.
Mother will meet us at the bus station
And drive us out to the plane
Which she will pilot herself,
A Fokker 50.
When we are safely ensconced
At an altitude of seventeen thousand feet
Turning left at Liverpool for Preston,
She will come back down from the cockpit
And put us both to sleep
With an injection of Sodium Amytal.
Isn't that what we've always yearned for,
Father and Son,
To be old, wise, male savages in our greatness
Put to sleep by Mother?

PAUL DURCAN   *b.* 1944   Ireland

The Self-Unseeing

Here is the ancient floor,
Footworn and hollowed and thin,
Here was the former door
Where the dead feet walked in.

She sat here in her chair,
Smiling into the fire;
He who played stood there,
Bowing it higher and higher.

Childlike, I danced in a dream;
Blessings emblazoned that day;
Everything glowed with a gleam;
Yet we were looking away!

THOMAS HARDY   1840–1928   England

Child Naming Flowers

When old crones wandered in the woods,
I was the hero on the hill
in clear sunlight.

Death's hounds feared me.

Smell of wild fennel,
high loft of sweet fruit high in the branches
of the flowering plum.

Then I am cast down
into the terror of childhood,
into the mirror and the greasy knives,

the dark
woodpile under the fig trees
in the dark.
                    It is only
the malice of voices, the old horror
that is nothing, parents
quarrelling, somebody
drunk.

I don't know how we survive it.
On this sunny morning
in my life as an adult, I am looking
at one clear pure peach
in a painting by Georgia O'Keefe.
It is all the fullness that there is
in light. A towhee scratches in the leaves
outside my open door.

He always does.

A moment ago I felt so sick
and so cold
I could hardly move.

ROBERT HASS   *b.* 1941   USA

The Portrait

My mother never forgave my father
for killing himself,
especially at such an awkward time
and in a public park,
that spring
when I was waiting to be born.
She locked his name
in her deepest cabinet
and would not let him out,
though I could hear him thumping.

When I came down from the attic
with the pastel portrait in my hand
of a long-lipped stranger
with a brave moustache
and deep brown level eyes,
she ripped it into shreds
without a single word
and slapped me hard.
In my sixty-fourth year
I can feel my cheek
still burning.

STANLEY KUNITZ   *b.* 1905   USA

This Be The Verse

They fuck you up, your mum and dad.
    They may not mean to, but they do.
They fill you with the faults they had
    And add some extra, just for you.

But they were fucked up in their turn
    By fools in old-style hats and coats,
Who half the time were soppy-stern
    And half at one another's throats.

Man hands on misery to man.
    It deepens like a coastal shelf.
Get out as early as you can,
    And don't have any kids yourself.

PHILIP LARKIN   1922–1985   England

For My Brother Jesus

My father had terrible words for you
— whoreson, bastard, *meshumad*;
and my mother loosed Yiddish curses
on your name and the devil's spawn
on their way to church
that scraped the frosted horsebuns
from the wintry Montreal street
to fling clattering into our passageway

Did you ever hear an angered
Jewish woman curse? Never mind the words:
at the intonations alone, Jesus,
the rusted nails would drop out
from your pierced hands and feet
and scatter to the four ends of earth

Luckless man, at least
that much you were spared

In my family you
were a *mamzer*, a *yoshke pondrick*
and main reason for their affliction and pain.
Even now I see the contemptuous curl
on my gentle father's lips;
my mother's never-ending singsong curses
still ring in my ears more loud
than the bells I heard each Sunday morning,
their clappers darkening the outside air

Priests and nuns
were black blots on the snow
    forbidding birds, crows

Up there
up there beside the Good Old Man
we invented and the lyring angels
do you get the picture, my hapless brother:

deserted daily, hourly
by the Philistines you hoped to save
and the murdering heathens,
your own victimized kin hating and despising
you?
      O crucified poet
your agonized face haunts me
as it did when I was a boy;
I follow your strange figure
through all the crooked passageways
of history, the walls reverberating
with ironic whisperings and cries,
the unending sound of cannonfire
and rending groans, the clatter
of bloodsoaked swords falling
on armor and stone
to lose you finally among your excited brethren
haranguing and haloing them
with your words of love,
your voice gentle as my father's

IRVING LAYTON   *b.* 1912   Canada

Because

My father and my mother never quarrelled.
They were united in a kind of love
As daily as the *Sydney Morning Herald*,
Rather than like the eagle or the dove.

I never saw them casually touch,
Or show a moment's joy in one another.
Why should this matter to me now so much?
I think it bore more hardly on my mother,

Who had more generous feeling to express.
My father had damned up his Irish blood
Against all drinking praying fecklessness,
And stiffened into stone and creaking wood.

Her lips would make a switching sound, as though
Spontaneous impulse must be kept at bay.
That it was mainly weakness I see now,
But then my feelings curled back in dismay.

Small things can pit the memory like a cyst:
Having seen other fathers greet their sons,
I put my childish face up to be kissed
After an absence. The rebuke still stuns

My blood. The poor man's curt embarrassment
At such a delicate proffer of affection
Cut like a saw. But home the lesson went:
My tenderness henceforth escaped detection.

My mother sang *Because*, and *Annie Laurie*,
White Wings, and other songs; her voice was sweet.
I never gave enough, and I am sorry;
But we were all closed in the same defeat.

People do what they can; they were good people,
They cared for us and loved us. Once they stood
Tall in my childhood as the school, the steeple.
How can I judge without ingratitude?

Judgment is simply trying to reject
A part of what we are because it hurts.
The living cannot call the dead collect:
They won't accept the charge, and it reverts.

It's my own judgment day that I draw near,
Descending in the past, without a clue,
Down to that central deadness: the despair
Older than any hope I ever knew.

JAMES MCAULEY   1917–1976   Australia

Autobiography

In my childhood trees were green
And there was plenty to be seen.

Come back early or never come.

My father made the walls resound,
He wore his collar the wrong way round.

Come back early or never come.

My mother wore a yellow dress;
Gentle, gently, gentleness.

Come back early or never come.

When I was five the black dreams came;
Nothing after was quite the same.

Come back early or never come.

The dark was talking to the dead;
The lamp was dark beside my bed.

Come back early or never come.

When I woke they did not care;
Nobody, nobody was there.

Come back early or never come.

When my silent terror cried,
Nobody, nobody replied.

Come back early or never come.

I got up; the chilly sun
Saw me walk away alone.

Come back early or never come.

LOUIS MACNEICE*   1907–1963   England

Sun and Rain

Opening the book   at a bright window
above a wide pasture   after five years
I find I am still standing   on a stone bridge
looking down with my mother   at dusk into a river
hearing the current as hers   in her lifetime

now it comes to me   that that was the day
she told me of seeing my father   alive for the last time
and he waved her back from the door   as she was leaving
took her hand   for a while and said
nothing
                at some signal
in a band of sunlight all the black cows   flow down the
    pasture together
to turn uphill and stand   as the dark rain touches them

W. S. MERWIN   *b.* 1927   USA

The Mixed Marriage

My father was a servant-boy.
When he left school at eight or nine
He took up billhook and loy
To win the ground he would never own.

My mother was the school-mistress,
The world of Castor and Pollux.
These were twins in her own class.
She could never tell which was which.

She had read one volume of Proust,
He knew the cure for farcy.
I flitted between a hole in the hedge
And a room in the Latin Quarter.

When she had cleared the supper-table
She opened the *Acts of the Apostles*,
Aesop's Fables, Gulliver's Travels.
Then my mother went on upstairs

And my father further dimmed the light
To get back to hunting with ferrets
Or the factions of the faction-fights,
The Ribbon Boys, the Caravats.

PAUL MULDOON   *b.* 1951   Ireland

The Sick Equation

In school I learned that one and one made two,
It could have been engraved in stone,
An absolute I could not question or refute.
But at home, sweet home, that sum was open to dispute –
In that raw cocoon of parental hate is where
I learned that one and one stayed one and one.
What's more, because all that household's anger and its pain
Stung more than any teacher's cane
I came to believe how it was best
That one remained one,
For by becoming two, one at least would suffer so.

Believing this I threw away so many gifts –
I never let love stay long enough to take root,
But thinking myself of too little worth
I crushed all its messengers.

I grew – or did not grow –
And kept my head down low,
And drifted with the crowd,
One among the many whose dreams of flight
Weighed down the soul,
And kept it down,
Because to the flightless
The dream of flight's an anguish.

I stayed apart, stayed one,
Claiming separateness was out of choice,
And at every wedding ceremony I saw
The shadow of that albatross – divorce –
Fall over groom and bride,
And I took small comfort in believing that, to some degree
They too still harboured dreams of flying free.

I was wrong of course,
Just as those who brought me up were wrong.
It's absurd to believe all others are as damaged as ourselves,
And however late on, I am better off for knowing now
That given love, by taking love all can in time refute
The lesson that our parents taught,
And in their sick equation not stay caught.

BRIAN PATTEN   *b.* 1946   England

The Iron Lung

So this is the dust that passes through porcelain,
so this is the unwashed glass left over from supper,
so this is the air in the attic, in August,
and this the down on the breath of the sleeper . . .

If we could fold our arms, but we can't.
If we could cross our legs, but we can't.
If we could put the mind to rest . . .
But our fathers have set this task before us.

My face moons in the mirror, weightless,
without air, my head propped like a penny.
I'm dressed in a shoe, ready to walk out
of here. I'm wearing my father's body.

I remember my mother standing in the doorway
trying to tell me something. The day is thick
with the heat rising from the road. I am
too far away. She looks like my sister.

And I am dreaming of my mother in a doorway
telling my father to die or go away.
It is the front door, and my drunken father falls
to the porch on his knees like one of his children.

It is precisely at this moment I realize
I have polio and will never walk again.
And I am in the road on my knees, like my father,
but as if I were growing into the ground

I can neither move nor rise.
The neighborhood is gathering, and now
my father is lifting me into the ambulance
among the faces of my family. His face is

a blur or a bruise and he holds me
as if I had just been born. When I wake
I am breathing out of all proportion to myself.
My whole body is a lung; I am floating

above a doorway or a grave. And I know
I am in this breathing room as one
who understands how breath is passed
from father to son and passed back again.

At night, when my father comes to talk,
I tell him we have shared this body long enough.
He nods, like the speaker in a dream.
He knows that I know we're only talking.

Once there was a machine for breathing.
It would embrace the body and make a kind of love.
And when it was finished it would rise
like nothing at all above the earth

to drift through the daylight silence.
But at dark, in deep summer, if you thought you heard
something like your mother's voice calling you home,
you could lie down where you were and listen to the dead.

STANLEY PLUMLY *b.* 1939 USA

Ghosts

1

A large woman in a kimono, her flesh
Already sweating in the poulticing heat
Of afternoon — just from her bath, she stands,
Propping her foot on a chair of faded pink,
Preparing to cut her corns. The sun
Simmers through the pimply glass — as if
Inside a light bulb, the room is lit with heat.
The window is the sun's lens, its dusty slice
Of light falls at the woman's foot. The woman
Is my mother — the clicking of her scissors
Fascinates the little feminine boy
In striped shirt, Tootal tie, thick woollen socks,
His garters down. Memory insists the boy is me.
The house still stands where we stood then.
The inheritance I had, her only child,
Was her party melancholy and a body
Thickening like hers, the wide-pored flesh
Death broke into twenty years ago.

2

The red wind carrying dust on to my Sunday shoes
Reddens also my nostrils and my mouth.
I stand by the school's venerable, fifty-years-old,
Washed cement veranda, waiting for my father.
The Bunya pines along the straggling drive
Drop chunky cones on gravel — windswept bees
Slog across the Master's garden to lemon flowers;
Boys shout, dogs bark, no second is quite silent.
My Father with the Headmaster comes to me.
It is Sunday, Parents' Visiting Day. The drive
Is churned by cars. When we go down town,
Despite milk shakes and a demure tea
In the Canberra Temperance Hotel, I only sulk.

I have kept this priggishness, Father;
The smart world laps you round. Your fear of this
Small child is now my fear – my boarding-school
World of rules rules me – my ghost
Has caught me up to sit and judge
The nightmares that I have, memories of love.

3

My mother married all that there was left
Of an Old Colonial family. The money gone,
The family house remained, surrounded by the dogs
He'd buried, forty years a bachelor –
We came there every Sunday in a silver tram
For tennis, when my mother was alive.
Sometimes I try to find my face in theirs:
My father in the lacrosse team, my Mother
Nursing in the War – they tell no story
In family photographs. Their city is changed;
Coca-Cola bottles bounce upon their lawn,
No one grows flowers, picnics are no fun,
Their aviaries are full of shop-bought birds.
Who goes for weekends down the Bay
In thirty footers to St Helena, Peel and Jumpin' Pin?
No yachts stand off the Old People's Home,
Out past the crab-pot buoys and floating mangrove fruit.
I was born late in a late marriage. Psychiatrists
Say it makes no difference – but now I think
Of what was never said in a tropical house
Of five miscarriages. If the words were said
They'd start the deaths up that I left for dead.

PETER PORTER   *b.* 1929   Australia

Plain Song

There was the chiropodist,
whose wife had a tape-worm
or a fallopian cyst,
and there was my father

reading his tea-leaves.
I was hidden behind the sofa
and could only see a turn-up
and one ox-blood Saxone loafer:

I'd taken all my clothes off
for the lavatory, hours before,
and now Mr Campbell had come.
My mother shut the kitchen door,

firmly, like a good Catholic,
snubbing the two Spiritualists.
I imagined the best china
in my father's massive fists:

a woman in hoops and crinoline,
the dainty rustic handle,
the Typhoo hieroglyphics,
the fate of Mrs Campbell

whom mother felt so sorry for.
My father went into control
and I listened, out of sight,
to the jumbled rigmarole:

someone was passing over
to another world of love.
Why do I only now discover
the woman's thin voice

saying she will be missed,
my father's eyes rolled back
and Mr Campbell's unhappy mouth,
open like a bad ventriloquist?

CRAIG RAINE   *b.* 1944   England

My Father's Leaving

When I came back, he was gone.
My mother was in the bathroom
crying, my sister in her crib
restless but asleep. The sun
was shining in the bay window,
the grass had just been cut.
No one mentioned the other woman,
nights he spent in that stranger's house.

I sat at my desk and wrote him a note.
When my mother saw his name on the sheet
of paper, she asked me to leave the house.
When she spoke, her voice was like a whisper
to someone else, her hand a weight
on my arm I could not feel.

In the evening, though, I opened the door
and saw a thousand houses just like ours.
I thought I was the one who was leaving,
and behind me I heard my mother's voice
asking me to stay. But I was thirteen
and wishing I were a man I listened
to no one, and no words from a woman
I loved were strong enough to make me stop.

IRA SADOFF   *b.* 1945   USA

'My father in the night commanding No'

My father in the night commanding No
Has work to do. Smoke issues from his lips;
    He reads in silence.
The frogs are croaking and the streetlamps glow.

And then my mother winds the gramophone;
The Bride of Lammermoor begins to shriek —
    Or reads a story
About a prince, a castle, and a dragon.

The moon is glittering above the hill.
I stand before the gateposts of the King —
    So runs the story —
Of Thule, at midnight when the mice are still.

And I have been in Thule! It has come true —
The journey and the danger of the world,
    All that there is
To bear and to enjoy, endure and do.

Landscapes, seascapes . . . where have I been led?
The names of cities — Paris, Venice, Rome —
    Held out their arms.
A feathered god, seductive, went ahead.

Here is my house. Under a red rose tree
A child is swinging: another gravely plays.
    They are not surprised
That I am here; they were expecting me.

And yet my father sits and reads in silence.
My mother sheds a tear, the moon is still,
    And the dark wing
Is murmuring that nothing ever happens.

Beyond his jurisdiction as I move
Do I not prove him wrong? And yet it's true
    They will not change
There, on the stage of terror and of love.

The actors in that playhouse always sit
In fixed positions — father, mother, child
    With painted eyes.
How sad it is to be a little puppet!

Their heads are wooden. And you once pretended
To understand them! Shake them as you will,
    They cannot speak.
Do what you will, the comedy is ended.

Father, why did you work? Why did you weep,
Mother? Was the story so important?
    'Listen!' the wind
Said to the children, and they fell asleep.

LOUIS SIMPSON   *b.* 1923   USA

Sorry

Dear parents,
I forgive you my life,
Begotten in a drab town,
The intention was good;
Passing the street now,
I see still the remains of sunlight.

It was not the bone buckled;
You gave me enough food
To renew myself.
It was the mind's weight
Kept me bent, as I grew tall.

It was not your fault.
What should have gone on,
Arrow aimed from a tried bow
At a tried target, has turned back,
Wounding itself
With questions you had not asked.

R. S. THOMAS   *b.* 1913   Wales

The Distant Footsteps

My father is sleeping. His noble face
suggests a mild heart;
he is so sweet now . . .
if anything bitter is in him, I must be the bitterness.

There is loneliness in the parlor; they are praying;
and there is no news of the children today.
My father wakes, he listens
for the flight into Egypt, the good-bye that dresses
     wounds.
Now he is so near;
if anything distant is in him, I must be the distance.

And my mother walks past in the orchard,
savoring a taste already without savor.
Now she is so gentle,
so much wing, so much farewell, so much love.

There is loneliness in the parlor with no sound,
no news, no greenness, no childhood.
And if something is broken this afternoon,
and if something descends or creaks,
it is two old roads, curving and white.
Down them my heart is walking on foot.

CÉSAR VALLEJO 1892–1938 Peru
Translated by James Wright and John Knoepfle

Biographical Notes

ANNA AKHMATOVA

Anna Akhmatova's son Lev (born 1912) spent most of the period between 1934 and 1956 in Soviet concentration camps.

JOHN BERRYMAN

John Berryman's father, a banker, shot himself under his son's bedroom window when Berryman was twelve years old. Born John Smith, Berryman took his stepfather's name when his mother remarried. The poet committed suicide in 1972, after a long struggle with alcoholism and drug addiction.

EDITH BRÜCK

Edith Brück was born to a poor Jewish family on the border between Hungary and the Ukraine. She spent part of her childhood in a concentration camp.

GEORGE GORDON, LORD BYRON

In 1805, when he was seventeen, Byron asked his mother to look after a baby boy, saying that the child was the illegitimate son of a schoolfriend who had died. The child's mother, who died that year, claimed that Byron was the father. A Londoner, William Marshall, was later to identify himself as the boy William, but his claim to relationship with the poet was never officially acknowledged.

PAUL CELAN

[b. Paul Anczel, Czernowitz, Romanian Bukovina, 1920.] Paul Celan's home town was occupied by Russian troops in 1940 and by Germans in 1942, after which he and his parents were placed separately in labour camps. In autumn 1942 Celan's father died of typhus; in the winter of the same year Celan's mother was found unfit for work and shot.

Celan's only son François was born in Paris after the war and died in infancy. Paul Celan committed suicide in 1970.

FRANCES CORNFORD

Frances Cornford's son John, a poet and scholar, was killed in action on his twenty-first birthday, fighting for the Republican cause in the Spanish Civil War.

WILLIAM COWPER

William Cowper was six when his adored mother died in childbirth in 1737. Shortly after this, prolonged bullying at his boarding school precipitated a nervous breakdown. In adulthood Cowper suffered frequently from depression and attempted suicide at the age of thirty-two, following which he was placed for some time in an asylum.

KEITH DOUGLAS

When Keith Douglas was four years old his mother became ill with encephalitis, an illness which persisted throughout the poet's childhood and adolescence. His father moved away from the family when Douglas was six, leaving him effectively responsible for his mother. The poet was killed in action in June 1944.

ROBERT DUNCAN

Robert Duncan's mother died giving birth to him.

KAREN GERSHON

Karen Gershon came to England as a child refugee from Nazi Germany; she lost both parents in the Holocaust.

MICHAEL HOFMANN

Michael Hofmann's father is the German writer Gert Hofmann.

TERESA HOOLEY

Teresa Hooley's brother Basil was killed in the last weeks of the First World War.

VICTOR HUGO

Victor Hugo's beloved eldest daughter Léopoldine and her husband were drowned at the mouth of the Seine in September 1843.

JACKIE KAY

Her adoption by a white Scottish couple is the subject of Jackie Kay's sequence of poems *The Adoption Papers*.

RUDYARD KIPLING

Rudyard Kipling's daughter Josephine died of pneumonia when she was nine. She was the favourite of Kipling's four children and was the 'Best Beloved' of the *Just So Stories*.

WALTER SAVAGE LANDOR

Walter Savage Landor was forced to leave England in 1814 following a quarrel and lived chiefly in Florence for the next seventeen years.

LOUIS MACNEICE

Louis MacNeice's mother suffered a severe depressive illness after having a hysterectomy. She was taken into an asylum when MacNeice was five and he never saw her again. She died of tuberculosis two years later.

GERDA MAYER

Gerda Mayer was born in Karlsbad, Czechoslovakia, in 1927 and came to England as a child refugee one day before the invasion of Czechoslovakia in 1939. Her parents were both victims of the Holocaust.

SYLVIA PLATH

Medusa is both the Gorgon of Greek myth, the mere sight of whose snake-tressed face turned viewers to stone, and the scientific name of the jellyfish *Aurelia*. Sylvia Plath's mother was called Aurelia.

PERCY BYSSHE SHELLEY

Shelley had two children, Eliza Ianthe and Charles, by his first wife Harriet Westbrook, Ianthe being born in June 1813. Despite the affection expressed for Ianthe and her mother in the poem 'To Ianthe', Shelley's marriage was already insecure and he was soon to leave Harriet for Mary Godwin. Mary's and Shelley's son William was born in January 1816.

Following Harriet's suicide her sister Eliza initiated legal proceedings against Shelley, which resulted in his loss of custody of Ianthe and Charles. In 1818 he took Mary and William to live in Italy, where William died of a stomach complaint in 1819.

W. D. SNODGRASS

W. D. Snodgrass's highly critical poems about his parents, 'The Mother' and 'The Diplomat', were first published under the pseudonym S. S. Gardons.

ROBERT LOUIS STEVENSON

Robert Louis Stevenson's father, Thomas Stevenson, was joint engineer to the Board of Northern Lighthouses.

ABRAHAM SUTZKEVER

Abraham Sutzkever's son was born in 1943 in the Vilna Ghetto. Because Jews were forbidden to give birth the baby was immediately poisoned by the Nazis.

Sutzkever himself escaped from the Ghetto, leaving his mother in hiding, and was concealed on a farm by a Christian woman. He later returned to the Ghetto to find his mother, but she had been discovered, taken away and shot. Her death is the subject of Sutzkever's fine poem *The Mother*, which for reasons of length we have not been able to include in this collection.

HUGO WILLIAMS

Hugo Williams's father was the actor Hugh Williams.

WILLIAM WORDSWORTH

The poet's daughter Catherine died at the age of four in 1812.

MEHETABEL WRIGHT

Mehetabel Wright (née Wesley) was the sister of Samuel and John
Wesley and the daughter of the Rev. Samuel Wesley, rector of Epworth.
After she became pregnant at the age of twenty-eight her father forced
her into an unsuitable marriage with William Wright, an uneducated
plumber who was not the child's father. Despite the early death of this
child and of all the other children she bore to Wright, Mehetabel was
never forgiven by her father.

Acknowledgements

The editors and publishers gratefully acknowledge permission to reprint the following copyright poems in this book:

ROBERT ADAMSON: 'Dreaming Up Mother' from *Selected Poems* (Angus & Robertson, 1990), © Robert Adamson, 1989, courtesy ETT Imprint, Watsons Bay; FLEUR ADCOCK: 'On a Son Returned to New Zealand' from *Selected Poems* (1983) and 'The Chiffonier' from *The Incident Book* (1986), by permission of Oxford University Press; ANNA AKHMATOVA: 'Shards' from *The Complete Poems of Anna Akhmatova*, translated by Judith Hemschemeyer (1992, 1997), published by Canongate Books Ltd, 14 High Street, Edinburgh EH1 1TE, reprinted by permission of Canongate Books and Zephyr Press, Massachusetts, USA; DEBRA ALLBERY: 'Assembler' from *Walking Distance* (University of Pittsburgh Press, 1991), © 1991 Debra Allbery, by permission of the publisher; LIZ ALMOND: 'Your Father Will Disown You' from *The Long Pale Corridor*, edited by Judi Benson and Agneta Falk (Bloodaxe Books, 1996), by permission of the author; YEHUDA AMICHAI: 'A Child is Something Else Again' and 'A Song of Lies on Sabbath Eve', translated by Chana Bloch and Stephen Mitchell, from *Selected Poetry of Yehuda Amichai* (Viking Penguin, 1987), translation © Chana Bloch and Stephen Mitchell, 1986; KINGSLEY AMIS: 'In Memoriam W. R. A.' from *Collected Poems 1944–1979* (Hutchinson, 1979), copyright © 1967 Kingsley Amis, reprinted by kind permission of Jonathan Clowes Ltd, London, on behalf of the Literary Estate of Sir Kingsley Amis; CARLOS DRUMMOND DE ANDRADE: 'Infancy', translated by Elizabeth Bishop, from *Elizabeth Bishop: The Complete Poems 1927–1979* (Farrar, Straus & Giroux Inc.), © by Alice Helen Methfessel, 1983; MAYA ANGELOU: 'Amoebaean for Daddy' from *The Complete Collected Poems* (Virago Press), and *Shaker, Why Don't You Sing?* (Random House), copyright © 1983 by Maya Angelou, by permission of Little, Brown & Company (UK); SIMON ARMITAGE: 'My father thought it bloody queer' and 'Mother, any distance further from a single span' from *Book of Matches* (Faber & Faber, 1993), © by Simon Armitage, 1993, by permission of the publisher; W. H. AUDEN: 'A Contrast' from *Thank You, Fog* (Faber & Faber, 1974), © 1973, 1974, by the Estate of W. H. Auden, by permission of the publisher; GEORGE BARKER: 'To My Mother' from *Collected Poems 1930–1955* (Faber & Faber), by permission of the publisher; PATRICIA BEER: 'John Milton and My Father' from *Driving*

West (Victor Gollancz, 1975), © Patricia Beer, 1975 by permission of the publisher. 'The Lost Woman' from *Collected Poems* (1988), © Patricia Beer, 1988, by permission of Carcanet Press Ltd; JAMES BERRY: 'Thoughts on My Father' from *Fractured Circles* (New Beacon Books, 1979), © by James Berry, 1978; JOHN BERRYMAN: 'A Sympathy, A Welcome' from *Collected Poems: 1937–1971*, © 1989 by Kate Donahue Berryman, and 'Dream Song 384' from *The Dream Songs*, copyright © 1969 by John Berryman, by permission of Faber & Faber Ltd and Farrar, Straus & Giroux Inc.; JOHN BETJEMAN: 'On a Portrait of a Deaf Man' from *Collected Poems* (1958), © by John Betjeman, 1940, by permission of John Murray (Publishers) Ltd; D. M. BLACK: 'Kew Gardens' from *Collected Poems 1964–1987* (Polygon, 1991), © by D. M. Black, by permission of the author and publisher; EAVAN BOLAND: 'The Pomegranate' from *In Time of Violence*, © 1994, by Eavan Boland, by permission of Carcanet Press and W. W. Norton & Company Inc.; PHILIP BOOTH: 'First Lesson' from *Relations: New and Selected Poems*, © 1957, by Philip Booth, by permission of Viking Penguin, a division of Penguin Books USA Inc.; JORGE LUIS BORGES: 'Rain', translated by Alastair Reid, from *Weathering: Poems and Translations* (1978), published by Canongate Books Ltd, 14 High Street, Edinburgh EH1 1TE, by permission of the translator and publisher; GWENDOLYN BROOKS: 'The Mother' from *Blacks* (Third World Press, 1991), © Gwendolyn Brooks, 1991, by permission of the author; EDITH BRÜCK: 'Equality, Father', translated by Ruth Feldman from *Against Forgetting: Poems of Witness*, edited by Caroline Forché (originally published in *Il Tatuaggio* by Edith Brück (1975) by Ugo Guanda, Parma), by permission of the author and translator; CHARLES BUKOWSKI: 'The Twins' from *Burning in Water, Drowning in Flame*, © 1974, by Charles Bukowski, by permission of Black Sparrow Press; CHARLES CAUSLEY: 'A Wedding Portrait' from *Collected Poems* (Macmillan, 1975), by permission of David Higham Associates Ltd; PAUL CELAN: 'Aspen Tree' and 'Epitaph for François', from *Poems of Paul Celan*, translated by Michael Hamburger (Anvil Press Poetry, 1995), translation © by Michael Hamburger, 1972, 1980, 1988, by permission of the publisher; MAXINE CHERNOFF: 'How Lies Grow' from *Utopia TV Store* (Yellow Press, 1979); DAVID CITINO: 'The Father and the Son' from *The House of Memory* (Ohio University Press, 1990), by permission of the author and publisher. 'Volare' from *The Gift of Fire*, by permission of the author and University of Arkansas Press, copyright 1986, University of Arkansas Press; STANLEY COOK: 'To My Father' from *Woods Beyond a Cornfield: Collected Poems* (Smith/Doorstop Books, 1995), © by the Estate of Stanley Cook, 1995, by permission of the publisher; FRANCES CORNFORD: 'The Scholar' from *Collected Poems* (Hutchinson), by permission of Dr Hugh Cornford; JENI COUZYN: 'Transformation' and 'The Punishment' from *Life by Drowning* (Bloodaxe Books, 1985), by permission of Andrew

Mann Ltd; ROBERT CRAWFORD: 'Opera' from *A Scottish Assembly* (Chatto & Windus, 1990), © Robert Crawford, 1990, by permission of the author and publisher; VINICIUS DE MORAES: 'Song', translated by Richard Wilbur from *An Anthology of 20th Century Brazilian Poetry* (Wesleyan University Press, 1972), © by Wesleyan University Press, 1972, by permission of the publisher; JAMES DICKEY: 'Buckdancer's Choice' from *Buckdancer's Choice* (Wesleyan University Press), © 1965 by James Dickey, by permission of the publisher. 'The Hospital Window' from *Contemporary American Poetry* (Faber & Faber), © by James Dickey, 1962, 1964, 1965; KEITH DOUGLAS: 'Sanctuary' from *The Complete Poems of Keith Douglas*, edited by Desmond Graham (1978), © by Marie J. Douglas, 1978, by permission of Oxford University Press; RITA DOVE: 'After Reading *Mickey in the Night Kitchen* for the Third Time Before Bed' from *Early Ripening*, edited by Marge Piercy (Pandora), © 1987 by Rita Dove, by permission of the author; CAROL ANN DUFFY: 'Litany' from *Mean Time* (Anvil Press Poetry, 1993), © by Carol Ann Duffy, 1993, by permission of the publisher; ROBERT DUNCAN: from 'Four Songs the Night Nurse Sang' from *Selected Poems* (Carcanet Press, 1993), © 1993 by the Literary Estate of Robert Duncan, by permission of the publisher; STEPHEN DUNN: 'At the Smithville Methodist Church' from *Local Time* (William Morrow & Co. Inc., 1986), © Stephen Dunn, 1986; PAUL DURCAN: 'Margaret, Are You Grieving?' and 'The Two Little Boys at the Back of the Bus' from *Daddy, Daddy* (The Blackstaff Press, 1990), © Paul Durcan, 1990, by permission of The Blackstaff Press and Thistledown Press. 'Poem for My Father' from *O Westport in the Light of Asia Minor* (first published 1975 by Anna Livia Books, Dublin, in the revised edition 1995 by The Harvill Press), © Paul Durcan, 1967, 1975, 1982, 1993, 1995, by permission of The Harvill Press; JEAN EARLE: 'To Father and Mother' from *Selected Poems* (Seren Books, 1990), © Jean Earle, 1990, by permission of the publisher; SUSANNE EHRHARDT: 'I've Worked It Out' from *New Chatto Poets 2* (Chatto & Windus, 1989), © by Susanne Ehrhardt, 1989; PIERRE EMMANUEL: 'The Father's Death', translated by Francis Scarfe from *Modern Poetry in Translation, No.1 New Series* (1992), by permission of Greta Scarfe; D. J. ENRIGHT: 'A Grand Night' from *The Terrible Shears* (Chatto & Windus, 1973); RUTH FAINLIGHT: 'Handbag' from *Selected Poems* (Sinclair-Stevenson, 1995), by permission of the author; U. A. FANTHORPE: 'Fanfare' from *Standing To* (1982), © U. A. Fanthorpe, by permission of Peterloo Poets; EDWARD FIELD: 'A Bill to My Father' from *Counting Myself Lucky: Selected Poems 1963–1992*, © 1992 by Edward Field, by permission of the author and Black Sparrow Press; DONALD FINKEL: 'Letter to My Daughter at the End of Her Second Year' from *Simeon* (Atheneum Publishers, 1964), © by Donald Finkel, 1964, by permission of the author; ROY FULLER: 'Fathers' from *From the Joke Shop* (André Deutsch, 1975), by permission of John Fuller; ROBERT

GARIOCH: 'My Faither Sees Me' from *Complete Poetical Works* (Macdonald Publishers, 1983), © by Ian G. Sutherland, by permission of the Saltire Society; KAREN GERSHON: 'I Was Not There' from *Selected Poems* (Victor Gollancz), © C. V. M. Tripp, by permission; ALLEN GINSBERG: from 'Kaddish' from *Collected Poems 1947–1980* (Harper Collins Inc.), © by Allen Ginsberg, 1959, by permission of Penguin Books Ltd; LOUISE GLÜCK: 'The Apple Trees' from *The House on the Marshland*, © 1971–5 by Louise Glück, by permission of The Ecco Press and Carcanet Press. 'Mirror Image' from *First Five Books of Poems* (Carcanet Press, 1997), by permission of the publisher; CAROLINE GRIFFIN: 'I can remember' from *One Foot on the Mountain: British Feminist Poetry 1969–1979*, edited by Lilian Mohin (Onlywomen Press, 1979), by permission of the publisher; MARILYN HACKER: 'Iva's Pantoum' from *Taking Notice* (Knopf, 1980), © 1979 by Marilyn Hacker, by permission of Frances Collin Literary Agent; DONALD HALL: 'My Son My Executioner' from *The One Day: Poems 1947–1990* (Carcanet Press, 1991), © by Donald Hall, 1988, 1990, by permission of the author and publisher; THOMAS HARDY: 'The Self-Unseeing' from *The Complete Poems*, edited by James Gibson (Papermac), by permission of Macmillan General Books; MICHAEL S. HARPER: 'Nightmare Begins Responsibility' from *Nightmare Begins Responsibility* (University of Illinois Press, 1975), © Michael S. Harper, 1974, by permission of the author and publisher; TONY HARRISON: 'Marked With D' from *Selected Poems* (Penguin Books, 1984), © by Tony Harrison, 1984, by permission of the author; GWEN HARWOOD: 'Dialogue' and 'Father and Child, I & II' from *Selected Poems* (Angus & Robertson, 1974), © 1974 by Gwen Harwood, courtesy ETT Imprint, Watsons Bay; ROBERT HASS: 'Child Naming Flowers' from *Praise*, © 1974–9 by Robert Hass, by permission of The Ecco Press; ROBERT HAYDEN: 'Those Winter Sundays' from *Angle of Ascent: New and Selected Poems* (Liveright), © by Robert Hayden, 1966, by permission of Liveright Publishing Corporation; SEAMUS HEANEY: from 'Clearances' from *The Haw Lantern* (Faber & Faber, 1987), © Seamus Heaney, 1987. 'Man and Boy' from *Seeing Things* (Faber & Faber, 1991), © Seamus Heaney, 1991. 'A Hazel Stick for Catherine Ann' from *Station Island* (Faber & Faber, 1984), © Seamus Heaney, 1984, by permission of the publisher; ANTHONY HECHT: 'It Out-Herods Herod. Pray You, Avoid It' from *The Hard Hours* (1967), © by Anthony E. Hecht, by permission of Oxford University Press; MIGUEL HERNANDEZ: 'To My Son' from *The Unending Light*, translated by Edward Honig, reprinted with permission, The Sheep Meadow Press, NY; SELIMA HILL: 'Mother Stone' from *My Darling Camel* (Chatto & Windus, 1988), © Selima Hill, 1988, 'The Fowlers of the Marshes' from *Saying Hello at the Station* (Chatto & Windus, 1984), © Selima Hill, 1984, by permission of the author; HITTAAN BIN AL-MU'ALLAA: 'The Children in Our Midst', translated by

David Pryce-Jones from *Jellyfish Cupfull: Writings in Honour of John Fuller*, edited by Barney Cokeliss and James Fenton (Ulysses Books, 1997), by permission of The Peters Fraser & Dunlop Group Ltd; MICHAEL HOFMANN: 'The Means of Production' from *Acrimony* (Faber & Faber, 1986), © by Michael Hofmann, by permission of the publisher; TERESA HOOLEY: 'A War Film' from *An Anthology of Poetry by Women*, edited by Linda Hall (Cassell, 1994); ROBERT HUFF: 'The Course' and 'Getting Drunk With Daughter' from *The Course* (Wayne State University Press, 1966), © 1966 by Robert Huff; TED HUGHES: 'Full Moon and Little Frieda' from *Selected Poems 1957–1967* (Faber & Faber, 1972), © Ted Hughes, 1972, by permission of the publisher; VICTOR HUGO: 'My Thoughts' and 'She formed the habit', translated by Harry Guest from *Victor Hugo: the Distance, the Shadows* (Anvil Press, 1981), © Harry Guest, 1981, by permission of the publisher; EMYR HUMPHREYS: 'From Father to Son' from *Ancestor Worship* (Gee & Son), © Emyr Humphreys, 1970, by permission of Richard Scott Simon Ltd; KATHLEEN JAMIE: 'The Tay Moses' from *Penguin Modern Poets 9* (Penguin Books, 1996), © by Kathleen Jamie, 1996; ELIZABETH JENNINGS: 'One Flesh' from *Collected Poems* (Macmillan, 1967), by permission of David Higham Associates Ltd; SHIRLEY KAUFMAN: 'Mothers, Daughters' from *Selected Poems* (Copper Canyon Press, 1996), by permission of the author; PATRICK KAVANAGH: 'In Memory of My Mother' from *Collected Poems* (1972), © by Patrick Kavanagh, 1972, by kind permission of the Trustees of the Estate of Patrick Kavanagh, c/o Peter Fallon, Literary Agent, Loughcrew, Oldcastle, Co. Meath, Ireland; JACKIE KAY: 'The Red Graveyard' from *Other Lovers* (Bloodaxe Books, 1993), © Jackie Kay, 1993; RUDYARD KIPLING: 'Of all the Tribe of Tegumai' from *Just So Stories*, by permission of A. P. Watt Ltd on behalf of The National Trust; CAROLYN KIZER: 'Thrall' from *The Nearness of You* (Copper Canyon Press) and 'The Intruder' from *Mermaids in the Basement* (Copper Canyon Press), by permission of the author; MAXINE KUMIN: 'Changing the Children' from *Selected Poems 1960–1990*, © 1978 by Maxine Kumin, by permission of the author and W. W. Norton & Company Inc.; STANLEY KUNITZ: 'The Portrait' from *Passing Through: the Later Poems New and Selected*, © 1971 by Stanley Kunitz, and 'Father and Son' from *The Poems of Stanley Kunitz 1928–1978*, © 1944 by Stanley Kunitz, by permission of W. W. Norton & Company Inc.; PHILIP LARKIN: 'Reference Back' from *The Whitsun Weddings* (Faber & Faber, 1964), © Philip Larkin 1964. 'This be the Verse' from *High Windows* (Faber & Faber, 1974), © Philip Larkin, 1974, by permission of the publisher; D. H. LAWRENCE: 'Piano' from *The Complete Poems of D. H. Lawrence*, by permission of Laurence Pollinger Ltd and the Estate of Frieda Lawrence Ravagli; IRVING LAYTON: 'Song for Naomi' and 'For My Brother Jesus' from *A Wild Peculiar Joy: Selected Poems 1945–81*, © 1982 by Irving Layton, used by permission, McClelland & Stewart Inc., The Canadian Publishers; GEOFFREY LEHMANN: 'Parenthood' from *Collected Poems* (Random House Australia), by permission of the publisher; DENISE LEVERTOV: 'The 90th Year' from *Selected Poems* (Bloodaxe Books, 1975), © Denise Levertov, 1975; PHILIP LEVINE: 'Night Thoughts Over a Sick Child' from *On the Edge and Over: Poems by Philip Levine* (Cloud Marauder Press, 1976), © by Philip Levine, 1976, by permission of the author; LEWIS GLYN COTHI: 'Lament for Siôn y Glyn', translated by Joseph P. Clancy from *Medieval Welsh Lyrics* (Macmillan, 1965); C DAY LEWIS: 'Walking Away' from *The Complete Poems* (Sinclair-Stevenson, 1992), © 1992 in this edition, The Estate of C Day Lewis, by permission of Random House UK Ltd; TONY LINTERMANS: 'The Escape from Youth' from *The Shed Manifesto* (1989), by permission of Scribe Publications Pty Ltd, PO Box 287, Carlton North, Victoria 3054, Australia; AUDRE LORDE: 'Outside' from *The Black Unicorn*, © 1978 by Audre Lorde, by permission of W. W. Norton & Company Inc.; ROBERT LOWELL: 'Commander Lowell' from *Selected Poems* (Faber & Faber, 1965), by permission of the publisher; EDWARD LUCIE-SMITH: 'The Lesson' from *A Tropical Childhood and Other Poems* (Oxford University Press), © Edward Lucie-Smith, 1961, by permission of the author, c/o Rogers, Coleridge & White Ltd, 20 Powis Mews, London W11 1JN; GEORGE MACBETH: 'A Celebration' from *Trespassing: Poems from Ireland* (Hutchinson, 1991), © George MacBeth, 1991, by permission of Sheil Land Associates. 'The Shell' from *The Colour of Blood* (Macmillan, 1967), © George MacBeth, 1967; HUGH MACDIARMID: 'At My Father's Grave' from *First Hymn to Lenin, and Other Poems* (Unicorn Press), by permission of Carcanet Press; KENNETH MACKENZIE: 'Two Trinities' from *Selected Poems*, courtesy ETT Imprint, Watsons Bay; LOUIS MACNEICE: 'Autobiography' from *Selected Poems* (Faber & Faber, 1964), by permission of David Higham Associates Ltd; JAMES MCAULEY: 'Because' from *Collected Poems 1936–1970* (Angus & Robertson, 1971), by permission of Harper Collins Publishers Australia; PATRICIA MCCARTHY: 'Pregnancy After Forty' from *The Virago Book of Birth Poetry* (1993), by permission of the author; ROGER MCGOUGH: 'Cinders' from *Defying Gravity* (Penguin Books, 1993), © Roger McGough, 1991, 1992, by permission of The Peters Fraser & Dunlop Group Ltd on behalf of Roger McGough; MEDBH MCGUCKIAN: 'Elegy for an Irish Speaker' from *Captain Lavender* (1994), by kind permission of the author and The Gallery Press; AIDAN CARL MATHEWS: 'Mongol' from *Minding Ruth* (1983), © by Aidan Carl Mathews, 1983, by kind permission of the author and The Gallery Press; GERDA MAYER: 'Their Bones are Silver' from *Monkey on the Analyst's Couch* (Ceolfrith Press, 1980), © by Gerda Mayer; PAULA MEEHAN: 'Child Burial' from *The Man Who Was Marked by Winter* (1991), © by Paula Meehan, 1991, by kind permission of the author and The Gallery Press; PETER MEINKE:

'This is a poem to my son Peter' from *Liquid Paper: New and Selected Poems* (University of Pittsburgh Press, 1991), © by Peter Meinke, 1991, by permission of the publisher; W. S. MERWIN: 'Sun and Rain' and 'Yesterday' from *Opening the Hand* (Atheneum Publishers, 1983), © by W. S. Merwin, 1983, by permission of David Higham Associates Ltd; MARIANNE MOORE: 'Silence' from *Selected Poems* (Faber & Faber, 1969), © by Marianne Moore, by permission of the publisher; EDWIN MORGAN: 'The Coals' from *Collected Poems 1949–1987* (Carcanet Press, 1990), © by Edwin Morgan, 1990, by permission of the publisher; BLAKE MORRISON: 'A Child in Winter' from *Dark Glasses* (Chatto & Windus), by permission of The Peters Fraser & Dunlop Group Ltd; STANLEY MOSS: 'Fishermen 2' from *Asleep in the Garden*, reprinted with permission, Anvil Press, UK c 1997, and The Sheep Meadow Press; ANDREW MOTION: 'A Dying Race' from *Dangerous Play* (Penguin Books, 1985), by permission of The Peters Fraser & Dunlop Group Ltd; PAUL MULDOON: 'The Mixed Marriage' from *Mules* (Faber & Faber, 1977), © by Paul Muldoon, 1977, by permission of the publisher; LES MURRAY: 'It Allows a Portrait in Line Scan at Fifteen' and 'The Last Hellos' from *Suburban Redneck Poems*, copyright © 1997 by Les Murray, by permission of Carcanet Press and Farrar, Straus & Giroux Inc.; PABLO NERUDA: 'The Father' from *Isla Negra: A Notebook*, translated by Alastair Reid, by permission Alastair Reid; ALDEN NOWLAN: 'Subway Psalm' from *I Might Not Tell Everybody This* (Clarke, Irwin & Co., 1982), by permission of Stoddart Publishing Co. Ltd; NAOMI SHIHAB NYE: 'Blood' from *A New Geography of Poets* (University of Arkansas Press, 1992), by permission of the author; FRANK O'HARA: 'To My Dead Father' from *Collected Poems*, edited by Donald Allen (Alfred A. Knopf, 1971), © 1971 by Maureen Granville-Smith, Administratrix of the Estate of Frank O'Hara, by permission of the publisher; SHARON OLDS: 'Bestiary', 'I Go Back to May 1937', 'After 37 Years My Mother Apologizes for My Childhood', 'The Moment the Two Worlds Meet', 'The Month of June 13½' from *Sign of Saturn* (Martin Secker & Warburg, 1991), and 'My Father Speaks to Me from the Dead' from *The Father* (Martin Secker & Warburg, 1993), by permission of the author and Random House UK Ltd; CAROLE SIMMONS OLES: 'To a Daughter at Fourteen Forsaking the Violin' from *The Deed* (Baton Rouge and London: Louisiana State University Press, 1991); first publication *TriQuarterly*, reprinted in *Bread Loaf Anthology* (Hanover and London: University Press of New England, 1985), by permission of the author; GORONWY OWEN: 'Elegy for his Daughter Ellen', translated by Kenneth Hurlstone Jackson from *A Celtic Miscellany* (Routledge, 1951), by permission of the publisher; ROBERT PACK: 'The Boat' from *Selected Poems* (Chatto & Windus, 1964), © by Robert Pack, 1964, and 'Departing Words to a Son' from *Fathering the Map: New and Selected Later Poems* (University of Chicago Press, 1993), © by Robert Pack, 1993, by permission of the author; RUTH PADEL: 'Darwin's Great-great-great-granddaughter Smiles' from *Summer Snow* (Hutchinson, 1990), © by Ruth Padel, 1990, by permission of the publisher. 'Ptarmigans' (previously unpublished), by permission of the author; PIER PAOLO PASOLINI: 'Prayer To My Mother', translated by Norman MacAfee with Luciano Martengo from *Selected Poems* (John Calder Publications, 1984), translation © by Norman MacAfee, 1982, by permission of The Calder Educational Trust; LINDA PASTAN: 'Shadows' from *A Fraction of Darkness*, © 1985 by Linda Pastan, by permission of the author and W. W. Norton & Company Inc.; BRIAN PATTEN: 'The Sick Equation' from *Armada* (Flamingo, 1996), © by Brian Patten, 1996, by permission of the author, c/o Rogers, Coleridge & White Ltd, 20 Powis Mews, London W11 1JN; ROBERT PETERSON: 'The Young Conquistador, 15' from *Under Sealed Orders*, © by Robert Peterson, 1976, by permission of the author; SYLVIA PLATH: 'Medusa', 'For a Fatherless Son' and 'The Colossus' from *Collected Poems* (Faber & Faber, 1981), © Ted Hughes, 1965, 1971, 1981, by permission of the publisher; STANLEY PLUMLY: 'The Iron Lung' from *Out-of-the-Body Travel* (The Ecco Press, 1977), by permission of the author. 'With Stephen in Maine' and 'Infidelity' from *Boy on the Step*, copyright © 1989 by Stanley Plumly, reprinted by permission of The Ecco Press; PO CHU-I: 'Remembering Golden Bells' and 'Rising Late and Playing with A-ts'ui, Aged Two', translated by Arthur Waley from *170 Chinese Poems* (Constable & Co., 1918), by permission of the publisher; PETER PORTER: 'Ghosts' from *Collected Poems* (1983), by permission of Oxford University Press; SÉAN RAFFERTY: 'You grow like a beanstalk' from *Collected Poems* (Carcanet Press, 1995), © by the Estate of Séan Rafferty, 1995, by permission of the publisher; CRAIG RAINE: 'In Modern Dress' and 'Plain Song' from *Rich* (Faber & Faber, 1984), © Craig Raine, 1984, by permission of the publisher; KATHLEEN RAINE: 'Heirloom' from *The Lost Country* (Dolmen Press, 1971), © 1971, Kathleen Raine, by permission of the author; DACHINE RAINER: 'Double Ritual' from *The Faber Book of Modern American Verse*, edited by W. H. Auden (Faber & Faber, 1956); JOHN CROWE RANSOM: 'Janet Walking' from *Selected Poems* (Carcanet Press, 1991), © by Alfred A. Knopf Inc., 1962, 1963, 1969, by permission of Carcanet Press; ALASTAIR REID: 'Daedalus' from *Weathering: Poems and Translations* (1978), published by Canongate Books Ltd, 14 High Street, Edinburgh EH1 1TE, by permission of the author and publisher; JAMES REISS: 'The Green Tree' from *The Breathers*, © 1966, 1968–74, by James Reiss, reprinted by permission of The Ecco Press; ADRIENNE RICH: 'After Dark' from *Collected Early Poems: 1950–1970*, © 1966 by W. W. Norton & Company Inc., by permission of the publisher; LAURA RIDING: 'Mortal' from *The Poems of Laura Riding* by Laura (Riding) Jackson, © 1938, 1980, by Laura (Riding) Jackson, reprinted by permission of Carcanet Press and the author's Board of

Literary Management. In conformity with the late author's wish, her Board of Literary Management asks us to record that, in 1941, Laura (Riding) Jackson renounced, on grounds of linguistic principle, the writing of poetry: she had come to hold that 'poetry obstructs general attainment to something better in our linguistic way-of-life than we have'; ANNE RIDLER: 'Sick Boy' and from 'For a Christening' from *Collected Poems* (Carcanet Press), by permission of the publisher; RAINER MARIA RILKE: 'From a Childhood', translated by Todd Hearon from *The Formalist*, Vol. 7, Issue 1, 1996, by permission of the publisher; ARTHUR RIMBAUD: 'Seven-Year-Old Poets', translated by Paul Schmidt from *Arthur Rimbaud: Complete Works*, © 1967, 1970, 1971, 1972, 1975, by Paul Schmidt, by permission of HarperCollins Publishers Inc.; CAROLYN M. RODGERS: 'Mama's God' from *How I Got Ovah*, © 1968, 1969, 1970, 1971, 1972, 1973, 1975, by Carolyn M. Rodgers, by permission of Doubleday, a division of Bantam Doubleday Dell Publishing Group Inc.; JUDITH RODRIGUEZ: 'Rebeca in a Mirror' from *The House by Water: New and Selected Poems* (University of Queensland Press, 1988), © by Judith Rodriguez, 1976, by permission of the publisher; THEODORE ROETHKE: 'My Papa's Waltz' from *Selected Poems* (Faber & Faber, 1969), © Beatrice Roethke, 1969, by permission of the publisher; IRA SADOFF: 'My Father's Leaving' from *Palm Reading in Winter* (Houghton Mifflin Poets, 1978), © by Ira Sadoff, 1978, by permission of the author; REG SANER: 'Passing It On' from *Climbing into the Roots* (Harper & Row, 1976), © by Reg Saner, 1976, by permission of the author; MAY SARTON: 'A Child's Japan' from *Collected Poems 1930–1993*, © 1966 by May Sarton, reprinted by permission of W. W. Norton & Company Inc.; CAROLE SATYAMURTI: 'Passed On' and 'Where Are You?' from *Striking Distance* (1994) and 'Broken Moon' from *Broken Moon* (1987), by permission of Oxford University Press; VERNON SCANNELL: 'My Father's Face' from *New and Collected Poems 1950–1993* (Robson Books, 1993), © by Vernon Scannell, 1993, by permission of the publisher; E. J. SCOVELL: 'Child Waking' from *Collected Poems* (Carcanet Press, 1988), by permission of the publisher; ANNE SEXTON: 'Christmas Eve' and 'Pain for a Daughter' from *The Selected Poems of Anne Sexton* (Virago Press), by permission of The Peters Fraser & Dunlop Group Ltd; IZUMI SHIKIBU: 'After the Death of her Daughter in Childbirth, Looking at the Child', translated by Edwin A. Cranston from *The Izumi Shikibu Diary: A Romance of the Heian Court* (Harvard University Press), © 1969 the Harvard-Yenching Institute; SHEILA SHULMAN: 'for years I slept in the same room' from *One Foot on the Mountain: British Feminist Poetry 1969– 1979*, edited by Lilian Mohin (Onlywomen Press, 1979), by permission of the publisher; JON SILKIN: 'Death of a Son' from *Selected Poems* (Sinclair-Stevenson, 1980), © by Jon Silkin, 1980, 1988, 1993, by permission of the author and Random House UK Ltd; LOUIS SIMPSON: 'My

Father in the Night Commanding No' from *At the End of the Open Road* (Wesleyan University Press, 1963), © Louis Simpson, 1963, by permission of the publisher; STEVIE SMITH: 'Papa Love Baby' from *The Collected Poems of Stevie Smith* (Penguin Twentieth Century Classics), by permission of James MacGibbon; W. D. SNODGRASS: 'Diplomacy: The Father', 'The Mother' and 'Reconstructions' from *Selected Poems 1957–1987* (Soho Press), © by W. D. Snodgrass, 1985, by permission of the author; GARY SNYDER: 'Axe Handles' from *Axe Handles* (North Point Press, 1983), © by Gary Snyder, 1983, by permission of the author and Farrar, Straus & Giroux Inc.; STEPHEN SPENDER: 'To My Daughter' from *Selected Poems* (Faber & Faber, 1965), by permission of the publisher; JON STALLWORTHY: 'At Bedtime' from *Hand in Hand* (Hogarth Press, 1974), © Jon Stallworthy, 1974, by permission of the publisher; WALLACE STEVENS: 'The Irish Cliffs of Moher' from *The Collected Poems of Wallace Stevens* (Faber & Faber, 1955), by permission of the publisher; ANNE STEVENSON: 'The Victory' and 'The Spirit is too Blunt an Instrument' from *The Collected Poems of Anne Stevenson 1955–1995* (1996), by permission of Oxford University Press; MARK STRAND: 'Not Dying' from *Selected Poems*, © 1979, 1980, by Mark Strand, by permission of Alfred A. Knopf Inc.; ABRAHAM SUTZKEVER: 'The Painter', translated by Ruth Whitman from *The Fiddle Rose: Poems 1970–1972* (Wayne State University Press, 1990), © by Wayne State University Press 1990, by permission of the publisher. 'For My Child', translated by Seymour Mayne from *Burnt Pearls – Ghetto Poems* (Mosaic Press/Valley Editions), © 1981 by Seymour Mayne. 'On My Father's *Yortsayt*', translated by Barbara and Benjamin Harshav (1991); GEORGE SZIRTES: 'Father in America' from *Metro* (1988), © George Szirtes, 1988, by permission of Oxford University Press; JAMES TATE: 'The Lost Pilot' from *Selected Poems* (Carcanet Press, 1997), © by James Tate, 1991, by permission of the publisher; DYLAN THOMAS: 'Do not go gentle into that good night' from *The Poems* (J. M. Dent & Sons), by permission of David Higham Associates Ltd; R. S. THOMAS: 'The Son' and 'Sorry' from *Collected Poems 1945–1990* (Phoenix Giants, 1995), © by R. S. Thomas, 1993, by permission of the author; ANTHONY THWAITE: 'Looking On' from *Poems 1953–1988* (Hutchinson, 1989), © by Anthony Thwaite, 1989, by permission of the author; CÉSAR VALLEJO: 'The Distant Footsteps', translated by James Wright and John Knoepfle from *20 Poems of César Vallejo*, edited by Robert Bly (Sixties Press, 1962), © by the Sixties Press, 1962, by permission of John Knoepfle; ROBERT PENN WARREN: 'Blow, West Wind' and 'Ways of Day' from *Selected Poems: New and Old 1923–1966* (Random House Inc.), © by Robert Penn Warren, by permission of William Morris Agency Inc., on behalf of the author's estate. 'There's a Grandfather's Clock in the Hall' from *Or Else: Poem/Poems 1968–1974* (Random House Inc.), © 1966, 1968, 1970, 1971, 1972, 1973, 1974, by

Robert Penn Warren, by permission of the publisher and William Morris Agency Inc., on behalf of the author's estate; VERNON WATKINS: 'Before A Birth' from *Cypress and Acacia* (Faber & Faber), © Mrs Gwen Watkins, Executor of the Estate of Vernon Watkins 1993, by permission of Mrs Gwen Watkins; SUSAN WICKS: 'Flames' from *The Clever Daughter* (Faber & Faber, 1996), © by Susan Wicks, 1996, by permission of the publisher; RICHARD WILBUR: 'The Writer' from *The Mind Reader* (Harcourt Brace & Company), © by Richard Wilbur, 1971; C. K. WILLIAMS: 'My Mother's Lips' from *Poems 1963–1983* (Bloodaxe Books, 1988), © C. K. Williams, 1969, 1971, 1977, 1983, 1988, by permission of Richard Scott Simon Ltd; HUGO WILLIAMS: 'Sugar Daddy' and 'Tipping My Chair' from *Selected Poems* (1989), by permission of Oxford University Press; WILLIAM CARLOS WILLIAMS: 'The Horse Show' from *Collected Later Poems* (Carcanet Press, 1963), by permission of the publisher; JAMES WRIGHT: 'Two Postures Beside a Fire' from *Collected Poems* (Wesleyan University Press), © 1971 by James Wright, by permission of the publisher; MEHETABEL WRIGHT: 'To Her Father', reprinted with kind permission of the Board of Trustees of the Victoria and Albert Museum. Forster MSS XVI, 14/3 (F48.E.10); W. B. YEATS: 'A Prayer for My Daughter' from *The Collected Poems of W. B. Yeats* (Macmillan, 1933), by permission of A. P. Watt Ltd on behalf of Michael Yeats; PATRICIA YOUNG: 'Photograph, 1958' from *Those were the Mermaid Years* (Ragweed Press, 1991), © by Patricia Young, 1991; NATAN ZACH: 'Meanwhile', translated by Amos Oz from *Seven Ages*, edited by David Owen (Penguin Books), © by David Owen, 1992.

Index of Titles and First Lines

Index of Poets and Translators

INDEX OF TRANSLATORS